MySQL Connector/Python Revealed

SQL and NoSQL Data Storage Using MySQL for Python Programmers

Jesper Wisborg Krogh

Apress®

MySQL Connector/Python Revealed

Jesper Wisborg Krogh
Hornsby, New South Wales, Australia

ISBN-13 (pbk): 978-1-4842-3693-2   ISBN-13 (electronic): 978-1-4842-3694-9
https://doi.org/10.1007/978-1-4842-3694-9

Library of Congress Control Number: 2018952522

Managing Director, Apress Media LLC: Welmoed Spahr
Acquisitions Editor: Jonathan Gennick
Development Editor: Laura Berendson
Coordinating Editor: Jill Balzano

Cover designed by eStudioCalamar

Cover image designed by Freepik (www.freepik.com)

Distributed to the book trade worldwide by Springer Science+Business Media New York, 233 Spring Street, 6th Floor, New York, NY 10013. Phone 1-800-SPRINGER, fax (201) 348-4505, e-mail orders-ny@springer-sbm.com, or visit www.springeronline.com. Apress Media, LLC is a California LLC and the sole member (owner) is Springer Science + Business Media Finance Inc (SSBM Finance Inc). SSBM Finance Inc is a **Delaware** corporation.

For information on translations, please e-mail rights@apress.com, or visit www.apress.com/rights-permissions.

Apress titles may be purchased in bulk for academic, corporate, or promotional use. eBook versions and licenses are also available for most titles. For more information, reference our Print and eBook Bulk Sales web page at www.apress.com/bulk-sales.

Any source code or other supplementary material referenced by the author in this book is available to readers on GitHub via the book's product page, located at www.apress.com/9781484236932. For more detailed information, please visit www.apress.com/source-code.

Printed on acid-free paper

To my wife, Ann-Margrete, and my parents.

Table of Contents

About the Author

 **Jesper Wisborg Krogh** is a member of the Oracle MySQL Support team and has spoken on several occasions at Oracle OpenWorld. He has a Ph.D. in Computational Chemistry but he switched to working with MySQL and other software development in 2006. His areas of expertise include MySQL Cluster, MySQL Enterprise Backup, and the Performance and sys schemas. He is an active author in the Oracle Knowledge Base and regularly blogs on MySQL topics.

Jesper lives in Sydney, Australia, and enjoys spending time outdoors, walking, traveling, and reading.

About the Technical Reviewer

 **Charles Bell** conducts research in emerging technologies. He is a member of the Oracle MySQL Development team and works on various teams including Replication, Utilities, and MySQL Enterprise Backup. He received his Ph.D. in Engineering from Virginia Commonwealth University in 2005.

Charles is an expert in the database field and has extensive knowledge and experience in software development and systems engineering. His research interests include 3D printers, microcontrollers, 3D printing, database systems, software engineering, and sensor networks.

Charles lives in a small town in rural Virginia with his loving wife. He spends his limited free time as a practicing Maker, focusing on microcontroller projects and the refinement of 3D printers.

Acknowledgments

I would like to thank all of the people who made this book possible. The Apress team has again been a great help, and I would in particular like to thank Jonathan Gennick, Jill Balzano, and Laura Berendson, the three editors I worked with while getting this book ready for production.

Several people have been invaluable sparring partners in technical discussions. Thanks to Charles Bell for providing a thorough and speedy technical review; his comments were, as always, very useful. The discussions with Nuno Mariz, Israel Gomez Delgado, and Philip Olson have also been invaluable.

Last but not least, thanks to my wife Ann-Margrete for her patience and support while I wrote this book.

Introduction

MySQL Connector/Python is the official driver used by Python programs to communicate with MySQL. It is maintained by Oracle and is part of the MySQL suite of products. It allows you to connect to a MySQL database from your Python program and execute queries. You have a choice of several APIs including the option of using SQL statements or a NoSQL interface.

This book goes through the high-level usage as well as the low-level details. When you have read all ten chapters of this book, you will be able to decide which API is the best for your project and you'll be able to use it to execute your MySQL queries, handle errors, and troubleshoot when things go wrong.

Book Audience

The book was written for developers who need to use MySQL as a backend data store or are otherwise interested in learning about the capabilities of MySQL Connector/Python and how to use it. No prior knowledge of MySQL Connector/Python is required. It is, however, an advantage to be familiar with databases in general and with SQL and Python.

Book Structure

The chapters are divided into four parts. The journey starts out with some general background information, the installation of MySQL Connector/Python and MySQL Server, and the preparation for the example programs that are included throughout the book. The next two parts are dedicated to each of the main APIs included in MySQL Connector/Python: the legacy (classic) API and the new X DevAPI. The final part discusses how to handle errors and how to troubleshoot.

Part I - Getting Ready

The first part consists of just one chapter:

1. Introduction and Installation - This chapter starts out with an introduction to MySQL Connector/ Python. It then goes through the process of downloading and installing it. The chapter finishes off with instructions for getting a MySQL Server instance set up for the example programs that are included throughout the rest of the book.

Part II - The Legacy APIs

The second part goes through the details of the MySQL Connector/Python APIs based on the Python Database API specification (PEP 249), which is the API traditionally used when connecting from Python to MySQL. The four chapters are as follows:

2. Connecting to MySQL – The first task when using MySQL Connector/Python is to connect to the database instance. This chapter covers how to create and configure the connection. This chapter also includes a discussion of character sets and collations.

3. Basic Query Execution – In this chapter, you start executing queries. The discussion is split over two chapters; this chapter covers the basic parts including simple queries returning a single result set, using cursors, and the important topic of handling user input.

4. Advanced Query Execution – This chapter continues where the previous one ended. It goes through more advanced concepts of executing queries such as handling multiple result sets and loading data from a CSV file. The topic of connection properties is also revisited with a focus on the options that affect how transactions work, the behavior of queries, etc. Then there is a discussion of utilities, for example to test whether the connection is still alive. Finally, there is a discussion of the C Extension.

5. Connection Pooling and Failover – MySQL Connector/Python has built-in support for connection pooling and failover. This chapter discusses how to set up and use a connection pool as well as how to fail over to a different MySQL instance should the current become unavailable.

Part III - The X DevAPI

The third part switches the focus to the new API called the X DevAPI. This API has reached general available status with MySQL 8.0 and provides uniform access from several programming languages. It includes support for both NoSQL and SQL access as well as native support for working with JSON documents in the MySQL Document Store. The three chapters are as follows:

6. The X DevAPI – This chapter introduces the X DevAPI, including details of the parts that are shared between using MySQL as a document store and using SQL tables. It covers how to create connections and how to work with schemas, statements, and results.

7. The MySQL Document Store – While MySQL traditionally has been a relational SQL database, the MySQL Document Store allows you to use it to store JSON documents. This chapter goes through the details of how to use the X DevAPI to work with collections and documents.

8. SQL Tables – The X DevAPI also supports using MySQL with SQL tables, both using a NoSQL interface and to execute SQL statements. This chapter explains how to use the X DevAPI with SQL tables.

Part IV - Error Handling and Troubleshooting

The fourth and final part covers two important topics: error handling and troubleshooting. The two chapters are as follows:

9. Error Handling – An important part of writing a program is knowing how to handle errors appropriately. This chapter covers errors from a MySQL Server and MySQL Connector/Python perspective including MySQL error numbers, SQL states, lock issues, and what to do when an error occurs.

10. Troubleshooting – When writing a program, something inevitably goes wrong. An error may occur or a query may not return the expected result. This chapter discusses how to find information that can help determine what the issue is and offers several examples of problems and their solution.

Downloading the Code

The code for the examples shown in this book is available on the Apress web site, www.apress.com. A link can be found on the book's information page at https://www.apress.com/gp/book/9781484236932.

PART I

Getting Ready

CHAPTER 1

Introduction and Installation

You are about to embark on a journey through the world of MySQL Connector/Python. Welcome aboard! This is the first chapter out of a ten-step guide that will take you through everything from installation to troubleshooting. Along the way you will become acquainted with the features and workings of the connector and its APIs.

This chapter will introduce MySQL Connector/Python by going through the versions, editions, and the APIs. The middle part of this chapter will discuss how to download and install the connector, and the final part will talk about MySQL Server, how to set up the server for the examples in this book, and a word on the examples themselves.

Introduction

MySQL Connector/Python is the glue that is used between a Python program and a MySQL Server database. It can be used to manipulate the database objects using data definition language (DDL) statements as well as to change or query the data through data manipulation language (DML) statements.

You can also call MySQL Connector/Python a database driver. It is the official MySQL connector for Python, developed and maintained by Oracle Corporation by the MySQL development team. It effectively supports three different APIs, although only two are commonly used directly.

© Jesper Wisborg Krogh 2018
J. W. Krogh, *MySQL Connector/Python Revealed*,
https://doi.org/10.1007/978-1-4842-3694-9_1

This section introduces the MySQL Connector/Python versions, editions, and the three APIs.

Versions

Before 2012, there was no Python connector maintained by Oracle. There were other third-party connectors, such as the MySQL-python (MySQLdb) interface; however, it was getting aged and only officially supported up to MySQL 5.5 and Python 2.7.

MySQL decided to develop its own connector: MySQL Connector/Python. It was written to be compatible with the MySQL-python interface and to be up to date with the latest MySQL Server and Python versions. The initial general availability (GA) release was version 1.0.7, which was released in September 2012. A major update occurred with version 2.1; it introduced the C Extension, which allows better performance. The latest GA release as of April 2018 is version 8.0.11, which additionally introduces the X DevAPI. This is the version that is the primary focus of this book.

Note   If you look at the change history of MySQL Connector/Python, you may be a little puzzled. The version series before 8.0 was 2.1 with a few pre-GA releases of version 2.2. The list of 8.0 releases is no less puzzling: the latest pre-GA release is 8.0.6 with the first GA release being 8.0.11. Why the jumps? The version numbers of most MySQL products were aligned, which required some irregularity in release numbers, but it now means that MySQL Server 8.0.11 and MySQL Connector/Python 8.0.11 are released together.

It is recommended to use the latest patch release of the latest series of GA quality. Only the latest GA series receives all improvements and bug fixes. That means that, at the time of writing, it is recommended to use the latest MySQL Connector/Python 8.0 release. While the MySQL

Connector/Python 8.0 releases are coupled together with the release of MySQL Server and other MySQL products,[1] they are backward compatible with older MySQL Server versions. So, even if you are still using, for example, MySQL Server 5.7, you should still use MySQL Connector/Python 8.0.

Tip   Use the latest release of the latest release series of GA quality to ensure you have access not only to all the latest features but also the latest available bug fixes. The latest MySQL Connector/Python version can be used with older MySQL Server versions. On the other hand, an older version of MySQL Connector/Python may not be compatible with the latest MySQL Server version. For example, MySQL Server 8.0 uses the `caching_sha2_password` authentication plugin by default, which is not supported until recently in MySQL Connector/Python.

As with any product under active development, new features are regularly added and bugs are fixed. You can follow the changes in the release notes, which are available from `https://dev.mysql.com/doc/relnotes/connector-python/en/`.

In addition to the various versions of MySQL Connector/Python, there are (as with other MySQL products) two different editions to choose from. Let's take a look at them.

Community and Enterprise Editions

MySQL products are available in two different editions: Community and Enterprise. The Enterprise Edition is a commercial offering from Oracle. The difference between the two editions varies among the products. For example, for MySQL Server, several additional plugins are available for

---

[1]`https://mysqlrelease.com/2018/03/mysql-8-0-it-goes-to-11/`

the Enterprise Edition. For MySQL Connector/Python, the difference
is subtler.

A common difference for all products is the license. The Community
Edition is released under the GNU General Public License, version 2.0,
whereas the Enterprise Edition uses a proprietary license. Additionally, the
Enterprise Edition includes technical support through MySQL Technical
Support Services. These are presently the only differences between the two
editions for MySQL Connector/Python itself.

This book will work with either of the two editions and, except when
briefly discussing download locations and install methods later in this
chapter, there will be no mention of the edition. All examples have been
written and tested with the Community Edition.

In contrast, when it comes to APIs, it makes a big difference which API
you use.

APIs

There are effectively three different APIs that can be used in MySQL
Connector/Python. How to use the APIs is the main purpose of
Chapters 2-9. Before you get started for real, it is worth taking a brief view
of the differences.

Table 1-1 shows the three APIs, which MySQL Connector/Python
module they are available in, the first GA version including support for the
API, and the chapters where they are discussed.

Table 1-1. *MySQL Connector/Python APIs*

API	Module	First Version	Chapters
Connector/Python API	mysql.connector	1.0.7	2, 3, 4, 5, 9, 10
C Extension API	_mysql_connector	2.1.3	4
X DevAPI	mysqlx	8.0.11	6, 7, 8, 9, 10

Additionally, the Connector/Python API and X DevAPI exist both in a pure Python implementation and one using C Extension under the hood. These two implementations are meant to be interchangeable. Some differences between the two implementations will be mentioned when encountered throughout the book.

As you can see, the main focus is on the Connector/Python API and X DevAPI. The Connector/Python API and the C Extension API exclusively use SQL statements to execute queries. The X DevAPI, on the other hand, supports NoSQL methods to handle JSON documents and SQL tables as well as support for SQL statements. The X DevAPI is a common API available for other programming languages as well, including JavaScript (Node.js), PHP, Java, DotNet, and C++.

So which API should you choose? From the description thus far, it sounds like it is a no-brainer to choose the X DevAPI. However, there is a little more to it than that.

If you are exclusively using SQL statements to execute queries, the C Extension and C Extension API are more mature. For example, they offer much better support for features such as parameter binding and prepared statements. If you need a connection pool, they are also the APIs to choose. If you have existing Python programs, they are also most likely using the Connector/Python API (with or without the C Extension implementation enabled).

On the other hand, the X DevAPI is a new API that has been designed from the ground up to fit modern requirements. The API also exists for other programming languages, making it easier to switch between languages when several languages are required for the applications. The NoSQL parts of the API makes simple queries against SQL tables and working with JSON documents simpler. The new command-line client, MySQL Shell, also supports using the X DevAPI via either Python or JavaScript. So, the X DevAPI there is a lot talking for new projects.

Since the X DevAPI is essentially in its version 1.0 (MySQL 8.0 is the first GA version for the X DevAPI), new features are more likely to become available in relatively short succession. If you are missing a feature, keep an eye on the release notes to see if the feature has become available, or register your interest at `https://bugs.mysql.com/`.

Whether to use the C Extension or not is to a large degree a question of performance compared to "convenience." The C Extension implementation provides better performance particularly when working with large result sets and prepared statements. However, the pure Python implementation is available on more platforms, is easier to work with when building MySQL Connector/Python yourself, and is easier to modify (as the name suggest, the pure Python implementation is written entirely in Python).

This concludes the introduction to MySQL Connector/Python. It is time to get started with the installation process. The first step is to download MySQL Connector/Python.

Downloading

It is straightforward to download MySQL Connector/Python; however, there are still a few considerations. These considerations and the steps to perform the download are the topics of this section.

The first thing to ask is whether you need the Community or Enterprise Edition of the connector. This decides both the download and the install options. The Community Edition is available from several locations and both in the form of source code and as binary distributions. The Enterprise Edition is only available as the binary distribution from Oracle.

Tip   The recommended way to install the Community Edition of MySQL Connector/Python is to use packages from the Python Packaging Authority (PyPa)/Python Package Index (PyPi). This is done using the `pip` tool and does not require predownloading any files. One downside of using PyPi is there can be a small lag from when the release is made to when it becomes available in PyPi.

Table 1-2 shows an overview of the delivery methods available for MySQL Connector/Python and whether the method is available for the Community and Enterprise Editions.

Table 1-2. *MySQL Connector/Python Download Options*

Distribution	Community Edition	Enterprise Edition
Python Packages (`pip`)	Available; see installation	
Windows Installer	Available	Available
MSI Installer	Available	Available
APT repository	Available	
SUSE repository	Available	
Yum repository	Available	
RPM downloads	Available	Available
DEB packages	Available	Available
Solaris package	Available	Available
macOS	Available	Available
Platform-independent tar or zip files	Available	Available

As you can see, MySQL Connector/Python is available for a large range of platforms and in different distributions. The Community Edition is available directly using the `pip` command-line tool; using the MySQL Yum repository for Red Hat Enterprise Linux, Oracle Linux, and Fedora Linux; the MySQL APT repository for Debian and Ubuntu; and using the MySQL SUSE repository for SLES. The `pip` and package repository options are only available for the Community Edition.

Tip   Both a MySQL Installer and a MSI Installer for MySQL Connector/Python are available for Microsoft Windows. If you want to use one of these installers, MySQL Installer is recommended because it also supports most of the other MySQL products.

Table 1-3 shows the URLs for the download locations for the various sources and installers. The MySQL repositories count as installers in this context even though they are more like definition files used with an installer.

Table 1-3. *Download Sources*

Source/Installer	URL
Community:	
MySQL Installer for Microsoft Windows	`https://dev.mysql.com/downloads/installer/`
APT repository	`https://dev.mysql.com/downloads/repo/apt/`
SUSE repository	`https://dev.mysql.com/downloads/repo/suse/`
Yum repository	`https://dev.mysql.com/downloads/repo/yum/`
MySQL downloads	`https://dev.mysql.com/downloads/connector/python/`
GitHub	`https://github.com/mysql/mysql-connector-python`
Enterprise:	
My Oracle Support	`https://support.oracle.com/`
Oracle Software Delivery Cloud	`https://edelivery.oracle.com/`

The Community Edition-related downloads are available from pages under `https://dev.mysql.com/downloads`. If you need the source code, it is available from the MySQL Downloads site and MySQL's GitHub repository.[2]

The Enterprise Edition is available either from the *Patches & Updates* tab in My Oracle Support (MOS) or from the Oracle Software Delivery Cloud (requires creating an account and signing in). MySQL customers are

---

[2]If you are familiar with git, it is recommended to use GitHub to get the source code because it allows you to easily switch branches, which includes older releases. However, as with PyPi, there can be a lag of the newest changes to be uploaded.

recommended to use My Oracle Support because it contains more releases and is updated more often than the Oracle Software Delivery Cloud. On the other hand, a 30-day trial version of the Enterprise Edition of the MySQL products is available from Oracle Software Delivery Cloud. MySQL Installer for Microsoft Windows is also available in an Enterprise Edition; this can be downloaded from either My Oracle Support or Oracle Software Delivery Cloud.

The downloads are pretty straightforward. Figure 1-1 shows the download screen to download the MySQL Installer for Microsoft Windows.

Figure 1-1. *Downloading the MySQL Installer for Microsoft Windows*

Once you click *Download*, you will be taken to the page in Figure 1-2 if you are not logged in. Here you can choose to log into an existing Oracle Web account, sign up for a new Oracle Web account, or download without using an account by clicking *No thanks, just start my download*. Choose the option that suits you best. The Oracle Web account is also used for My Oracle Support and Oracle Software Delivery Cloud, so if you are an Oracle customer you can use your existing account.

Begin Your Download

mysql-installer-community-8.0.11.0.msi

Login Now or Sign Up for a free account.

An Oracle Web Account provides you with the following advantages:

- Fast access to MySQL software downloads
- Download technical White Papers and Presentations
- Post messages in the MySQL Discussion Forums
- Report and track bugs in the MySQL bug system
- Comment in the MySQL Documentation

MySQL.com is using Oracle SSO for authentication. If you already have an Oracle Web account, click the Login link. Otherwise, you can signup for a free account by clicking the Sign Up link and following the instructions.

No thanks, just start my download.

Figure 1-2. *Ready to download*

Downloading other MySQL Products including MySQL Connector/ Python from the community download page follows the same pattern. The main difference is that you will need to choose the operating system and optionally the operating system version you are using. The default operating system chosen will be the one you are browsing from. Figure 1-3 shows how the operating system can be chosen when downloading MySQL Connector/Python.

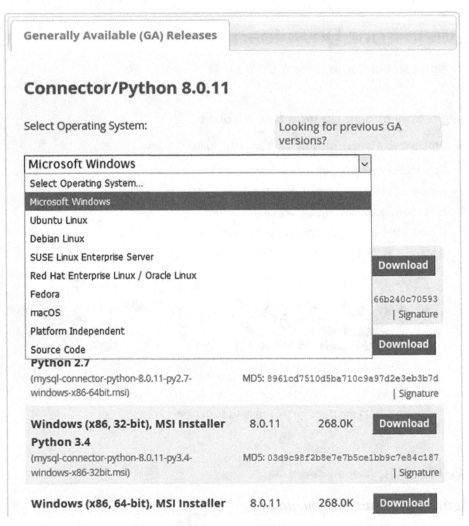

Figure 1-3. *Choosing a platform for MySQL Connector/Python*

Once you have chosen the platform, you can choose the specific file to download. The differences may be which Python version to use MySQL Connector/Python with and whether it is the pure Python or the C Extension implementation.

One word about the C Extension and downloads. Depending on the platform, the C Extension implementation may be bundled with the rest of the download and automatically installed, or there may be a separate file to download. On Microsoft Windows, the C Extension is always included if it available for the Python version. In general, the latest couple of supported Python versions will include the C Extension; for older Python versions, it is not included. For RPM and DEB packages, there are two packages for each MySQL Connector/Python release and supported Python version: one file with the pure Python implementation and one with the C Extension implementation.

The web sites where the Enterprise Edition of MySQL Installer and MySQL Connector/Python can be downloaded are designed differently, but the idea is the same. How downloads work from My Oracle Support and the Oracle Software Delivery Cloud will not be discussed further in this book. Instead, let's look at the installation process itself.

Installation

MySQL Connector/Python supports several ways to install the connector. The available methods depend on the operating system. The steps should give few surprises if you are used to installing software.

If your installation method includes the option of whether to install the C Extension or not (for example, RPM or DEB packages), it is recommended to include the C Extension package. Even if you do not plan on using the _mysql_connector module directly, using the C Extension implementation of the other APIs can provide better performance.

The type of installation that will be required closely follows the choice of how to download the installation file. The most unique way of installing MySQL Connector/Python is to use MySQL Installer. This section will go through installation using the pip command, using MySQL Installer, and using the MySQL Yum repository.

pip – All Platforms

The recommended way to install MySQL Connector/Python if you use the Community Edition is to use the pip command to install the package from the Python Packaging Authority (PyPa). This ensures that any potential dependencies are resolved automatically, and the same installation method can be used across all platforms where you need MySQL Connector/Python.

The pip command is available as part of the normal Python installation for Python version 2.7.9 and later if you downloaded Python from https://www.python.org/. Noticeable exceptions are some Linux distributions such as RedHat Enterprise Linux, Oracle Linux, and CentOS Linux., which still use relatively old versions of Python. General installation instructions can be found at https://pip.pypa.io/en/stable/installing/ and https://packaging.python.org/guides/installing-using-linux-tools/. The sidebar "Installing pip On the RedHat Family of Linux" includes an example of how to install pip on RedHat Enterprise Linux, Oracle Linux, and CentOS.

When pip is available, it is simple to install the latest available MySQL Connector/Python release using the install command. The exact output of the installation varies, for example, depending on whether dependencies such as protobuf have already been installed. An example output is

```
PS: Python> pip install mysql-connector-python
Collecting mysql-connector-python
```

```
Downloading https://files.pythonhosted.org/.../mysql_
connector_python-8.0.11-cp36-cp36m-win_amd64.whl
(3.0MB)
    100% |████████████████████████████████| 3.0MB 3.5MB/s
Collecting protobuf>=3.0.0 (from mysql-connector-python)
  Using cached https://files.pythonhosted.org/.../protobuf-
  3.5.2.post1-cp36-cp36m-win_amd64.whl
Requirement already satisfied: six>=1.9 in c:\users\jesper\
appdata\local\programs\python\python36\lib\site-packages (from
protobuf>=3.0.0->mysql-connector-python)
 (1.11.0)
Requirement already satisfied: setuptools in c:\users\jesper
\appdata\local\programs\python\python36\lib\site-packages (from
protobuf>=3.0.0->mysql-connector-python)
 (28.8.0)
Installing collected packages: protobuf, mysql-connector-python
Successfully installed mysql-connector-python-8.0.11 protobuf-
3.5.2.post1
```

The example is from Microsoft Windows executing the `pip` command in PowerShell. The command assumes that the `pip` command is in the search path for executables (this can be enabled when installing Python on Windows and will in general be the case on Linux). If the `pip` command is not in the search path, you must use the full path. When the installation is performed on other platforms, the command is the same and the output very similar.

If you want to uninstall the package, the command is very similar; just use the `uninstall` command instead.

So

```
PS: Python> pip uninstall mysql-connector-python
Uninstalling mysql-connector-python-8.0.11:
```

```
Would remove:
  c:\users\jesper\appdata\local\programs\python\python36\lib\
  site-packages\_mysql_connector.cp36-win_amd64.pyd
  c:\users\jesper\appdata\local\programs\python\python36\lib\
  site-packages\_mysqlxpb.cp36-win_amd64.pyd
  c:\users\jesper\appdata\local\programs\python\python36\lib\
  site-packages\libeay32.dll
  c:\users\jesper\appdata\local\programs\python\python36\lib\
  site-packages\libmysql.dll
  c:\users\jesper\appdata\local\programs\python\python36\lib\
  site-packages\mysql\*
  c:\users\jesper\appdata\local\programs\python\python36\lib\
  site-packages\mysql_connector_python-8.0.11.dist-info\*
  c:\users\jesper\appdata\local\programs\python\python36\lib\
  site-packages\mysqlx\*
  c:\users\jesper\appdata\local\programs\python\python36\lib\
  site-packages\ssleay32.dll
Proceed (y/n)? y
  Successfully uninstalled mysql-connector-python-8.0.11
```

INSTALLING PIP ON THE REDHAT FAMILY OF LINUX

The best way to install the pip command on Oracle Linux, RedHat Enterprise Linux, and CentOS is to use the EPEL Yum repository. The following steps assume you are using version 7 of the respectively Linux distribution. Older versions will require slightly different instructions. The steps are as follows:

1. Download the EPEL repository definition from https://dl.fedoraproject.org/pub/epel/epel-release-latest-7.noarch.rpm.

2. Install the downloaded EPEL RPM.

3. Install the python-pip and python-wheel packages.

4. Optionally, let `pip` upgrade itself using the `pip install –upgrade pip` command.

The python-wheel package provides support for the wheel built-package format used for Python packages. See also `https://pypi.org/project/wheel/`.

The combined steps executed in the Linux shell are as follows:

shell$ wget https://dl.fedoraproject.org/pub/epel/epel-release-latest-7.noarch.rpm

...

```
2018-03-10 20:26:28 (55.3 KB/s) - 'epel-release-latest-7.noarch.
rpm' saved [15080/15080]
```

shell$ sudo yum localinstall epel-release-latest-7.noarch.rpm

```
...
Downloading packages:
Running transaction check
Running transaction test
Transaction test succeeded
Running transaction
   Installing : epel-release-7-11.noarch                         1/1
   Verifying  : epel-release-7-11.noarch                         1/1

Installed:
   epel-release.noarch 0:7-11

Complete!
```

shell$ sudo yum install python-pip python-wheel

```
...
Running transaction check
Running transaction test
Transaction test succeeded
Running transaction
```

```
Installing : python-wheel-0.24.0-2.el7.noarch              1/2
Installing : python2-pip-8.1.2-5.el7.noarch                2/2
Verifying  : python2-pip-8.1.2-5.el7.noarch                1/2
Verifying  : python-wheel-0.24.0-2.el7.noarch              2/2

Installed:
  python-wheel.noarch 0:0.24.0-2.el7
  python2-pip.noarch 0:8.1.2-5.el7

Complete!
```

shell$ sudo pip install --upgrade pip
```
Collecting pip
  Downloading pip-9.0.1-py2.py3-none-any.whl (1.3MB)
    100% |████████████████████████████████| 1.3MB 296kB/s
Installing collected packages: pip
  Found existing installation: pip 8.1.2
    Uninstalling pip-8.1.2:
      Successfully uninstalled pip-8.1.2
Successfully installed pip-9.0.1
```

At this point, the pip command has been installed as /usr/bin/pip. In most
cases, commands in /usr/bin can be executed without specifying the
full path.

Microsoft Windows – MySQL Installer

For installations on Microsoft Windows where you for one reason or
another do not wish to use the pip command, the preferred installation
method is MySQL Installer. One advantage is that it can be used to install
both the Community and Enterprise Editions of MySQL Connector/
Python. Which version will be installed depends on the edition of MySQL
Installer.

The following instructions assume you have MySQL Installer on your computer already. If that is not the case, please see the "MySQL Installer for Microsoft Windows" sidebar for instructions. The first step is to launch MySQL Installer. The first time you use the installer, you will be asked to accept the license terms. Then you will be taken to a screen where you can choose which MySQL products you want to install. We will pick up at that point again after the discussion of Figure 1-4.

If you have already used MySQL Installer to install products, you will be shown the screen in Figure 1-4; it's an overview of the MySQL products already installed and the available actions.

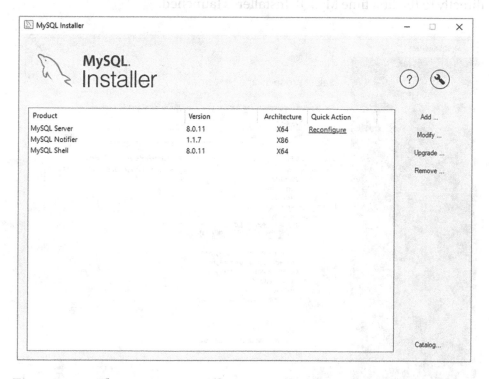

Figure 1-4. *The MySQL Installer screen showing already installed MySQL products*

If you installed MySQL Installer some time ago and have not recently updated the catalog, it is recommended first to click the *Catalog* action in the lower right corner to ensure you can choose from all the latest releases. This will take you to a screen where you can execute a catalog update. The update does not change any of the products installed; it only updates the list of products that MySQL Installer uses to notify of upgrades and you choose from when installing new products.

Once the catalog is up to date, you can add a new product using the *Add* action to the right of the list of installed products. This brings you to the screen shown in Figure 1-5, which is also the screen you are taken directly to the first time MySQL Installer is launched.

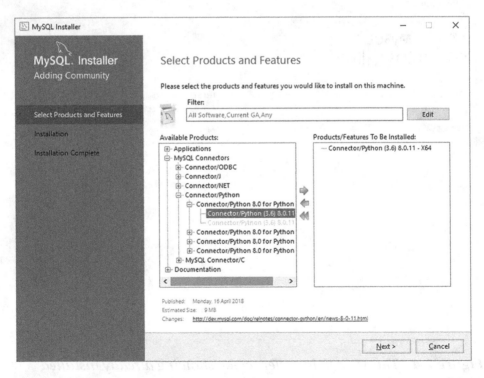

Figure 1-5. *Choosing what to install*

The filter at the top can be used to narrow down or expand which products and releases should be included. By default, the latest GA releases are included for all software in both the 32-bit and 64-bit architectures. If you want to try out a development milestone release or release candidate, you need to include pre-releases by editing the filter. An example of filtering to search for GA releases of Connector/Python under The MySQL Connectors category and requiring it to be 64-bit can be seen in Figure 1-6.

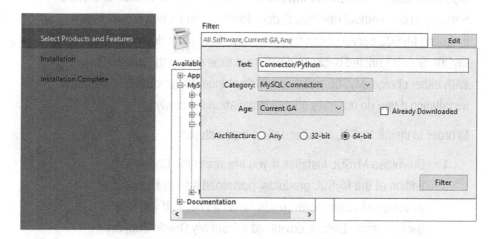

Figure 1-6. *Filtering the list of products*

MySQL Connector/Python can be found under *Available Products* by expanding the *MySQL Connectors* group. There is one product listed for each supported Python version. MySQL Installer will check whether the correct Python version is installed. When you have found the right release, add it to the list of products and features to be installed by clicking the arrow pointing to the right and then clicking *Next*.

The next screen shows an overview of the products to install. Once you have confirmed everything is correct, click *Execute* to start the installation. The execution may take a little time because it includes downloading the connector. Once the installation has completed, click *Next*. This will allow you to copy the log to the clipboard and finish.

MYSQL INSTALLER FOR MICROSOFT WINDOWS

The MySQL Installer for Microsoft Windows is the entry point to manage the various MySQL products (MySQL NDB Cluster is an exception). It allows you to install, upgrade, and remove the products and features from one interface. There is also limited support for configuring MySQL Server.

MySQL Installer comes in two flavors: one that includes a version of MySQL Server and one without (the "web" download). If you know you will be installing MySQL Server, it can be convenient to use the download that has MySQL Server bundled because it will save time during the installation. With either choice, MySQL Installer will download the product as part of the installation if you do not have a local installation file ready.

In order to install MySQL Installer, follow these steps:

1. Download MySQL Installer. If you are using the Community Edition of the MySQL products, download it from `https://dev.mysql.com/downloads/installer/`. If you use the Enterprise Edition, download it from My Oracle Support (`https://support.oracle.com/`) or Oracle Software Delivery Cloud (`https://edelivery.oracle.com/`). Both locations for the Enterprise Edition require using an existing Oracle account or creating a new one. My Oracle Support is recommended if you are an existing customer.

2. The downloaded file is an MSI Installer but will for the Enterprise Edition be inside a zip file, which you can unzip and then execute the MSI Installer and follow the instructions.

3. If you have not downloaded the latest release of MySQL Installer, you will be offered the opportunity to upgrade it. It is recommended to do this.

4. When the installation has completed, MySQL Installer automatically launches.

The installer also can be launched later, for example through the Start menu.

Linux – MySQL Yum Repository

The easiest way to install MySQL products in the Community Edition on Linux distributions is to use the MySQL repository. For RedHat Enterprise Linux, Oracle Linux, CentOS, and Fedora, this means the MySQL Yum repository. This way the packages can be found by the yum command and Yum will be able to resolve dependencies automatically. Except for using the pip command to install MySQL Connector/Python, this is the recommended way to install MySQL software if you want the install to be managed.

That the installation is managed means the installer (pip or yum) handles dependencies for you, and it is possible to request an upgrade using the installer. For both installs and upgrades, the software is automatically downloaded from the repository.

The MySQL Yum repository is installed using the RPM that can be downloaded from https://dev.mysql.com/downloads/repo/yum/. Choose the RPM that corresponds to your Linux distribution. The RPM can, for example, be installed using the yum localinstall command:

```
shell$ sudo yum localinstall \
            mysql57-community-release-el7-11.noarch.rpm
...
Running transaction
  Installing : mysql57-community-release-el7-11.noarch      1/1
  Verifying  : mysql57-community-release-el7-11.noarch      1/1
Installed:
  mysql57-community-release.noarch 0:el7-11

Complete!
```

The MySQL RPMs are signed with GnuPG. To make the `rpm` command (invoked by yum) check the signatures and not complain about missing keys, you need to install the public key used by MySQL. There are several ways to do this as described in `https://dev.mysql.com/doc/refman/en/checking-gpg-signature.html`. One option is to get the public key from this page and save it in a file. You need the part starting with `-----BEGIN PGP PUBLIC KEY BLOCK-----` and finishing with `-----END PGP PUBLIC KEY BLOCK-----` (everything included). Save the key into a file, for example named `mysql_pubkey.asc`. Then you import the key into RPM's keyring:

```
shell$ sudo rpm --import mysql_pubkey.asc
```

Once the repository and the public key have been installed, MySQL Connector/Python can be installed as shown in Listing 1-1.

Listing 1-1. Installing MySQL Connector/Python Using Yum on Linux

```
shell$ sudo yum install mysql-connector-python \
                        mysql-connector-python-cext
...
Downloading packages:
(1/2): mysql-connector-python-8.0.11-1.el7.x86_64.rpm | 418 kB
00:00
(2/2): mysql-connector-python-cext-8.0.11-1.el7.x86_6 | 4.8 MB
00:01
-------------------------------------------------------------------
Total                                   3.3 MB/s | 5.2 MB 00:01
Running transaction check
Running transaction test
Transaction test succeeded
Running transaction
  Installing : mysql-connector-python-8.0.11-1.el7.x86_64    1/2
  Installing : mysql-connector-python-cext-8.0.11-1.el7.
  x86_64    2/2
```

```
Verifying   : mysql-connector-python-8.0.11-1.el7.
x86_64          1/2
Verifying   : mysql-connector-python-cext-8.0.11-1.el7.
x86_64     2/2
```

```
Installed:
  mysql-connector-python.x86_64 0:8.0.11-1.el7
  mysql-connector-python-cext.x86_64 0:8.0.11-1.el7
```

```
Complete!
```

This code installed both the pure Python and the C Extension (with *cext* in the name) implementations of MySQL Connector/Python. Before moving on, let's verify the MySQL Connector/Python installation.

Verifying the Installation

A simple way to verify that the installation of MySQL Connector/Python works is to create a small test program to print a few properties from the `mysql.connector` module. If the program executes without errors, the installation was successful.

Listing 1-2 shows an example of retrieving the MySQL Connector/Python version as well as a few other properties.

Listing 1-2. Verifying That the MySQL Connector/Python Installation Works

```
import mysql.connector

print(
  "MySQL Connector/Python version: {0}"
  .format(mysql.connector.__version__)
)
```

```
print("Version as tuple:")
print(mysql.connector.__version_info__)

print("")
print("API level: {0}"
  .format(mysql.connector.apilevel))

print("Parameter style: {0}"
  .format(mysql.connector.paramstyle))

print("Thread safe: {0}"
  .format(mysql.connector.threadsafety))
```

The version is printed in two different ways, as a string and as a tuple. The tuple can be useful if you need an application to be compatible with two different versions of MySQL Connector/Python and need different code paths depending on the version.

The API level, parameter style, and thread safety properties do not, in general, change. They are related to the Python Database API specification (https://www.python.org/dev/peps/pep-0249/) that the mysql. connector module implements. These three properties are required global properties of the module.

The output when using MySQL Connector/Python 8.0.11 is

```
PS: Chapter 1> python listing_1_1.py
MySQL Connector/Python version: 8.0.11
Version as tuple:
(8, 0, 11, '', 1)

API Level: 2.0
Parameter style: pyformat
Thread safe: 1
```

MySQL Server

MySQL Connector/Python is not worth much on its own. Unless you have a MySQL Server instance to connect to, you will be limited to doing things such as checking the version, as in the example in the previous section. So, if you do not already have access to an installation of MySQL Server, you will also need to install it. This section will give a brief overview of installing and configuring MySQL Server.

Installation

The installation process of MySQL Server is similar to the steps described for MySQL Connector/Python if you use the MySQL Installer or the MySQL Yum repository. In both of these cases, the installer will set up MySQL for you. Additionally, there is an option to install using a zip archive on Microsoft Windows or a tar archive on Linux, macOS, Oracle Solaris, and FreeBSD.

Note   This discussion assumes a new installation. If you already have MySQL installed, you can also choose to upgrade. However, if your current MySQL installation is not from the MySQL repository, it is best to remove the existing installation first to avoid conflicts, and then do a clean install.

Since the installation steps are so similar for MySQL Server compared to MySQL Connector/Python when using an installer, this discussion will focus on installing using a zip or tar archive. The discussion about retrieving the password that is set for the administrator account (root@ localhost) is also relevant when using installers on Linux. Since MySQL Installer is an interactive installer, it will ask you what the password should be and set it for you.

Tip   The discussion about the installation of MySQL Server in
this book only covers some of the basics. For the full installation
instructions, see `https://dev.mysql.com/doc/refman/`
`en/installing.html` and `https://dev.mysql.com/doc/`
`refman/en/data-directory-initialization-mysqld.html`.

Using a zip or tar archive can be particularly useful if you need multiple
different versions installed on the same computer because it allows you
to locate the installation where you like. If you choose this approach, you
need to initialize the data directory manually. An example of doing this on
Microsoft Windows can be seen in the following example:

```
PS: Python> D:\MySQL\mysql-8.0.11-winx64\bin\mysqld
            --basedir=D:\MySQL\mysql-8.0.11-winx64
            --datadir=D:\MySQL\Data_8.0.11
            --log_error=D:\MySQL\Data_8.0.11\error.log
            --initialize
```

The command is split over several lines to improve readability. Make
sure you combine all of the parts into one line when you execute it.
The command may take a little time to complete, particularly if you are
installing on a non-memory-based (i.e. a spinning) disk drive.

The command in Linux and other Unix-like systems is very similar
except that the `--user` option has been added:

```
shell$ /MySQL/base/8.0.11/bin/mysqld \
          --basedir=/MySQL/base/8.0.11/ \
          --datadir=/MySQL/Data_8.0.11 \
          --log_error=/MySQL/Data_8.0.11/error.log \
          --user=mysql \
          --initialize
```

The two commands use several arguments. They are

- **--basedir**: This option tells where MySQL Server binaries, libraries, etc. are installed. This directory includes a bin, lib, share, and more subdirectories with the files required by MySQL Server.

- **--datadir**: This option tells where to store the data. This is the directory that is initialized by the command. This directory must either not exist or be empty. If it does not exist, the **--log_error** option cannot point to a file inside the data directory.

- **--log_error**: This option tells where to write the log messages to.

- **--user**: On Linux and Unix, this option is used to tell which user MySQL will be executed as. This is only required (but is allowed in general) if you initialize the data directory as the root user. In that case, MySQL will ensure that the newly created files are owned by the user specified by the **--user** argument. The user traditionally used is the **mysql** user, but for personal test instances, you can also use your normal login user.

- **--initialize**: This option tells MySQL to initialize the data directory.

The initialization includes setting the password for the **root@localhost** account. The password is random and can be found in the error log; this also applies when MySQL has been installed using, for example, RPMs. However, MySQL Installer will ask for the password during the installation and set it. If you are using macOS, the password will also be shown in the notifications. An example of the error log that includes the temporary password is

```
2018-03-11T05:01:08.871014Z 0 [System] [MY-010116] D:\MySQL\
mysql-8.0.4-rc-winx64\bin\mysqld.exe (mysqld 8.0.4-rc) starting
as process 3964 ...
2018-03-11T05:01:20.240818Z 0 [Warning] [MY-010068] CA
certificate ca.pem is self signed.
```
2018-03-11T05:01:20.259178Z 5 [Note] [MY-010454] A temporary
password is generated for root@localhost: fj3dJih6Ao*T

You need this password the first time you connect. Once you have connected, you must change the password before you can execute general queries because the random one generated during the installation is marked as expired. You change the password using the ALTER USER statement, as shown in Listing 1-3.

Listing 1-3. Changing the Password of the root@localhost Account

```
PS: Python> D:\MySQL\mysql-8.0.11-winx64\bin\mysql --user=root
--password
Enter password: ************
Welcome to the MySQL monitor.  Commands end with ; org.
Your MySQL connection id is 7
Server version: 8.0.11 MySQL Community Server - GPL

Copyright (c) 2000, 2018, Oracle and/or its affiliates. All
rights reserved. Oracle is a registered trademark of

Oracle Corporation and/or its affiliates. Other names may be
trademarks of their respective owners. Type 'help;' or '\h' for
help. Type '\c' to clear the current input statement.
```
mysql> ALTER USER 'root'@'localhost' IDENTIFIED BY
'&lknjJ2lAc1)#';
```
Query OK, 0 rows affected (0.15 sec)
```

Ensure that you choose a password that is hard for others to guess. You can also use the command to change other settings for the user such as the SSL requirements, the authentication plugin, and so on.

Tip   The default authentication plugin in MySQL 8.0 is the `caching_sha2_password` plugin. It provides good security because it is based on sha256 salted hashes. At the same time, the caching makes it perform well. However, since it is a new authentication plugin, older connectors and clients including MySQL Connector/Python 2.1.7 and earlier, the MySQL command-line client from MySQL Server 5.7, and third-party connectors such as those for PHP and Perl do not at the time of writing support the `caching_sha2_password` plugin. If you need to connect using one of these connectors or clients, you can use the older (and less secure because it is sha1-based and not salted) `mysql_native_password` plugin instead. See `https://dev.mysql.com/doc/refman/en/create-user.html` and `https://dev.mysql.com/doc/refman/en/alter-user.html` for more information about the syntax of the `CREATE USER` and `ALTER USER` statements.

The instance will, unless you used MySQL Installer, use the default configuration. The final thing to consider is how to change the configuration.

Configuration

In some cases, it is necessary to change the configuration of the newly installed MySQL Server instance. In general, the default values are a great starting point. Obviously, for a production server, there are some changes that are required, but often it is a case of few changes are better than many changes. For the purpose of the examples in this book, the default configuration works well.

That said, you already saw some non-default settings in the examples where the data directory was initialized manually. Additionally, if you are developing an application that will be deployed to production, it is recommended to use a configuration that is as close to the production configuration as possible to avoid gotchas due to differences. While this, of course, does not mean the desktop you are developing on should be able to allocate half a terabyte of memory to the InnoDB buffer pool just because the production server is using that, you can use a configuration that is similar but scaled down.

Tip   You can read more about configuring MySQL in the Reference Manual, including the complete list of options, at `https://dev.mysql.com/doc/refman/en/server-system-variables.html` and `https://dev.mysql.com/doc/refman/en/option-files.html`.

In general, it is also best to use a MySQL configuration file to set any required options. This avoids missing some options when starting MySQL. You can then start the MySQL daemon (`mysqld` on Linux/Unix and `mysqld.exe` on Microsoft Windows) with the `--defaults-file` option with the path to the configuration file. By convention, the MySQL configuration file is named `my.ini` on Microsoft Windows and `my.cnf` on other platforms.

If you are using Microsoft Windows and chose to install MySQL as a service, you will be starting and stopping the MySQL service through the control panel application (or letting Microsoft Windows do it automatically). In this case, a configuration file is even more useful because you can specify to use it in the service definition, which avoids modifying the service if you later want to change the MySQL configuration.

The configuration file follows the INI file format. The following is an example with the options from the initialization on Microsoft Windows from earlier in the section as well as the TCP port number:

```
[mysqld]
basedir   = D:\MySQL\mysql-8.0.11-winx64
datadir   = D:\MySQL\Data_8.0.11
log_error = D:\MySQL\Data_8.0.11\error.log
port      = 3306
```

This concludes the discussion about installing and configuring MySQL Server. A related topic is how to create the database user that the application will use to connect to MySQL.

Creating the Application User

When an application connects to MySQL, it is necessary to specify the username to use for the connection. Additionally, MySQL takes the hostname where the connection comes from into account, so the account name for the user is formed as username@hostname. The user's privileges determine what the user is allowed to do in the database.

MySQL Server has one standard user available for logins, the root@localhost user. This user has all privileges; that is, it is an administrator account. Applications should not use this user for several reasons, which will be explained in the following discussion.

The application should, in general, not have permission to do everything. For example, the application should not be allowed to access tables it does not need, and there is rarely a requirement for an application to manage users. Additionally, MySQL has a limit on the number of concurrent connections allowed (the max_connections configuration option). However, there is one extra connection reserved for a user with the CONNECTION_ADMIN (SUPER) privilege. So, if the application user has all privileges, it can block out the database administrator from investigating why all connections are in use.

It is beyond the scope of this book to go into the details of the MySQL privilege system. The main takeaway is that you should assign the minimum required privileges to your users, including during the development phase, because it is much easier to add new privileges as required than remove unnecessary privileges when you are ready to deploy the application.

Tip   It is worth getting familiar with MySQL security features including the access privilege system and user account management. The Security chapter in the MySQL Reference Manual is an excellent source: `https://dev.mysql.com/doc/refman/en/security.html`.

The following SQL statements can be used to create a test user who has the required privileges for the examples in this book:

```
mysql> CREATE USER 'pyuser'@'localhost'
              IDENTIFIED BY 'Py@pp4Demo';

mysql> GRANT ALL PRIVILEGES
              ON world.*
              TO 'pyuser'@'localhost';

mysql> GRANT ALL PRIVILEGES
              ON py_test_db.*
              TO 'pyuser'@'localhost';
```

It is assumed that the test programs will be executed on the same host as where MySQL is installed. If this is not the case, replace `localhost` with the hostname where the test programs are executed. `ALL PRIVILEGES` in the `GRANT` statements gives all available privileges on the schema (database) level, but the administrative privileges are not included. This will still be more than the typical application needs, but it is used here for simplicity and to allow demonstrating queries that are not typically executed from within an application.

The password has been chosen as Py@pp4Demo. This is not a very strong password, and it is strongly recommended to use a different password that is more difficult to guess.

If you want to play with the world_x sample database that is briefly mentioned in Chapter 7, you will also need the following privileges:

```
mysql> GRANT ALL PRIVILEGES
          ON world_x.*
          TO 'pyuser'@'localhost';
```

However, none of the examples discussed in this book use the world_x sample database. The installation instructions for the world_x sample database are very similar to those in the next step, which is to install some sample data for the code examples in Chapters 3, 4, and 5.

Installing the world Sample Database

Throughout the book, the *world sample database* is used for several of the examples. The example databases are considered part of the "other MySQL documentation" and can be accessed from https://dev.mysql.com/doc/index-other.html. The world database can be downloaded either as a gzip file or zip file; either way, after decompression, there is a single file: world.sql.

Note   There is the world database and the world_x database. Chapters 3, 4, and 5 use the world database. The world_x database is not required but can optionally be installed using similar steps as shown here if you would like to have it for your own testing.

The world.sql file is self-contained. It will drop the world schema if it exists and recreate it with three tables: country, countrylanguage, and city, including some sample data. The easiest way to apply the world.sql file is to use the `mysql` command-line client (https://dev.mysql.com/ doc/refman/en/mysql.html) from the same directory as where the world.sql file is located:

```
shell$ mysql --user=pyuser --password \
             --host=127.0.0.1 --port=3306 \
             --execute="SOURCE world.sql"
Enter password:
```

This assumes that the `mysql` binary is in the execution search path; otherwise, the full path must be used. On Microsoft Windows, keep the whole command on the same line and remove the backslashes. The resulting tables are outlined in Listing 1-4.

Listing 1-4. The Tables of the world Sample Database

```
mysql> SHOW TABLES FROM world;
+-----------------+
| Tables_in_world |
+-----------------+
| city            |
| country         |
| countrylanguage |
+-----------------+
3 rows in set (0.00 sec)

mysql> SHOW CREATE TABLE world.city\G
*************************** 1. row ***************************
       Table: city
Create Table: CREATE TABLE `city` (
  `ID` int(11) NOT NULL AUTO_INCREMENT,
  `Name` char(35) NOT NULL DEFAULT '',
  `CountryCode` char(3) NOT NULL DEFAULT '',
  `District` char(20) NOT NULL DEFAULT '',
  `Population` int(11) NOT NULL DEFAULT '0',
```

```
  PRIMARY KEY (`ID`),
  KEY `CountryCode` (`CountryCode`),
  CONSTRAINT `city_ibfk_1` FOREIGN KEY (`CountryCode`)
REFERENCES `country` (`code`)
) ENGINE=InnoDB AUTO_INCREMENT=4080 DEFAULT CHARSET=latin1
1 row in set (0.00 sec)

mysql> SELECT COUNT(*) FROM world.city;
+----------+
| COUNT(*) |
+----------+
|     4079 |
+----------+
1 row in set (0.00 sec)

mysql> SHOW CREATE TABLE world.country\G
*************************** 1. row ***************************
       Table: country
Create Table: CREATE TABLE `country` (
  `Code` char(3) NOT NULL DEFAULT '',
  `Name` char(52) NOT NULL DEFAULT '',
  `Continent` enum('Asia','Europe','North America','Africa',
   'Oceania','Antarctica','South America') NOT NULL DEFAULT
   'Asia',
  `Region` char(26) NOT NULL DEFAULT '',
  `SurfaceArea` float(10,2) NOT NULL DEFAULT '0.00',
  `IndepYear` smallint(6) DEFAULT NULL,
  `Population` int(11) NOT NULL DEFAULT '0',
  `LifeExpectancy` float(3,1) DEFAULT NULL,
  `GNP` float(10,2) DEFAULT NULL,
  `GNPOld` float(10,2) DEFAULT NULL,
  `LocalName` char(45) NOT NULL DEFAULT '',
  `GovernmentForm` char(45) NOT NULL DEFAULT '',
```

```
  `HeadOfState` char(60) DEFAULT NULL,
  `Capital` int(11) DEFAULT NULL,
  `Code2` char(2) NOT NULL DEFAULT '',
  PRIMARY KEY (`Code`)
) ENGINE=InnoDB DEFAULT CHARSET=latin1
1 row in set (0.00 sec)

mysql> SELECT COUNT(*) FROM world.country;
+----------+
| COUNT(*) |
+----------+
|      239 |
+----------+
1 row in set (0.00 sec)

mysql> SHOW CREATE TABLE world.countrylanguage\G
*************************** 1. row ***************************
       Table: countrylanguage
Create Table: CREATE TABLE `countrylanguage` (
  `CountryCode` char(3) NOT NULL DEFAULT '',
  `Language` char(30) NOT NULL DEFAULT '',
  `IsOfficial` enum('T','F') NOT NULL DEFAULT 'F',
  `Percentage` float(4,1) NOT NULL DEFAULT '0.0',
  PRIMARY KEY (`CountryCode`,`Language`),
  KEY `CountryCode` (`CountryCode`),
  CONSTRAINT `countryLanguage_ibfk_1` FOREIGN KEY
(`CountryCode`) REFERENCES `country` (`code`)
) ENGINE=InnoDB DEFAULT CHARSET=latin1
1 row in set (0.00 sec)
```

```
mysql> SELECT COUNT(*) FROM world.countrylanguage;
+----------+
| COUNT(*) |
+----------+
|      984 |
+----------+
1 row in set (0.00 sec)
```

Tip   For more information about the world sample database including installation instructions, see `https://dev.mysql.com/doc/world-setup/en/world-setup-installation.html`.

Before concluding this chapter, a word regarding the code examples is required.

Code Examples

There are a number of example programs in this book. The programs have been tested with Python 3.6. For other Python versions, including Python 2.7 from Oracle Linux 7/Red Hat Enterprise Linux (RHEL) 7/CentOS 7, the examples will work with minor modifications. No changes are required for the MySQL Connector/Python-specific parts.

In Python 2, it is recommended to load the print function from__ future__:

```
from __future__ import print_function
```

Additionally the UTF-8 string handling is different in Python 2, so it may be necessary to use the `encode()` method to print strings. For example:

```
print(
  "{0:15s}   {1:^7s}   {2:4.1f}".format(
    city['Name'].encode('utf8'),
    city['CountryCode'].encode('utf8'),
    city['Population']/1000000
  )
)
```

The examples using the `mysql.connector` module assume that a file named `my.ini` is present in the directory where Python is executed with the connection options required to connect to MySQL Server. An example configuration file is

```
[connector_python]
user     = pyuser
host     = 127.0.0.1
port     = 3306
password = Py@pp4Demo
```

The examples using the `mysqlx` module store the configuration in a file named `config.py`, which is also located in the same directory where Python is executed. The example configuration is

```
connect_args = {
  'host': '127.0.0.1',
  'port': 33060,
  'user': 'pyuser',
  'password': 'Py@pp4Demo',
};
```

The coding style in the examples is optimized for print and in particular eBook readers such as Kindle. Since this leaves very little real estate to work with, the lines have in general been kept below 40 characters with "long" lines up to 50 characters to minimize the amount of wrapping.

The downside is that this means it has not really been possible to follow a standard coding style such as the one specified in PEP 8 (https://www.python.org/dev/peps/pep-0008/). It is recommended to follow PEP 8 or another well-established coding standard in your own projects.

All example programs that appear in a listing are available for download. The file name reflects the listing number; for example, the code in Listing 1-2 can be found in the file listing_1_2.py. See the book's homepage for instructions on how to download the source.

This concludes the installation and preparations. The next step is to create connections from MySQL Connector/Python to MySQL Server, which is the topic of the next chapter.

Summary

This chapter got you up and running. First, MySQL Connector/Python was introduced. The latest GA release series is version 8.0, the same as for most other MySQL products. MySQL products are available as a Community Edition and a commercial Enterprise Edition. For MySQL Connector/Python, the main difference is the license and support, and either edition can be used with this book.

MySQL Connector/Python has three APIs: two legacy APIs that only work with SQL statements and a new API called the X DevAPI that supports both NoSQL and SQL queries. How to use the three APIs is the topic of the rest of the book.

In order to get started, you downloaded and installed both MySQL Connector/Python and MySQL Server. There was a brief discussion about configuring MySQL Server, instructions on how to create a user that can be used for this book, how to install the test data, and a word on the code examples.

You are ready to use MySQL Connector/Python. The next chapter will show you how to connect using the API in the Connector/Python API (the mysql.connector module).

PART II

The Legacy APIs

PART II

The Legacy APIs

CHAPTER 2

Connecting to MySQL

In the previous chapter, you installed MySQL Connector/Python and made
sure that the module worked. However, printing the version string for the
connector is hardly very exciting, so this chapter will begin the journey
through the features of the two legacy APIs.

The mysql.connector module includes the implementation of the
Python Database API, which is defined in PEP249 (https://www.python.
org/dev/peps/pep-0249/). This includes the option to use the C Extension
while using the same API. This API is the main focus of Chapters 2-5.
Additionally, the _mysql_connector module with the implementation of
the C Extension API is briefly discussed in Chapter 4.

This chapter goes through the ins and outs of creating and configuring
connections to MySQL. Creating a connection is simple and is the first
thing you will learn. There is a little more to the connection than just
creating it, though. The rest of the chapter will discuss how to configure the
connection, including tips to avoid hardcoding the username and password
into the application. The chapter finishes with a discussion of other
connection-related options, with a particular focus on the character set.

Creating the Connection from Python

It has taken some work to get to this point, but now you are ready to connect
to MySQL from Python for the first time. This section will go through the
syntax of creating the connection, the most common connection options,

© Jesper Wisborg Krogh 2018
J. W. Krogh, *MySQL Connector/Python Revealed*,
https://doi.org/10.1007/978-1-4842-3694-9_2

examples of creating a connection, reconfiguring a connection, and some best practices for connections.

Syntax

There are several ways to create the connection. Four of them are

- The `mysql.connector.connect()` function: This is the most flexible connection method. It provides a uniform way of creating connections using the C Extension or enabling the connection pooling and the failover-related options. This function works as a wrapper that returns an object of the appropriate class depending on the settings.

- The `MySQLConnection()` constructor

- The `MySQLConnection.connect()` method: It requires first instantiating the `MySQLConnection` class without arguments and then creating the connection.

- The same as before using the `MySQLConnection.connect()` method, but with the difference that the `MySQLConnection.config()` method is called explicitly to configure the connection.

The `MySQLConnection` class is the pure Python implementation. Alternatively, the `CMySQLConnection` class can be used, which provides implementation of the C Extension backend to the Python Database API.

All of the methods end up with the same connection object, and they all take the connections options as keyword arguments. This means that you can choose whatever way to create the connection that works best for the program. However, since the `mysql.connector.connect()` function is the most powerful, it is the preferred way to connect because it makes it easier to switch between the pure Python and C Extension implementations or to enable connection pooling or failover.

Tip   Creating a connection using the mysql.connector.
connect() function gives access to all connection-related features.

Figure 2-1 shows the basic flow of using the four ways to create a connection. The red (dark grey) boxes are called directly from the application code, and the yellow (light grey) boxes are called by the last method called indirectly. The figure uses the MySQLConnection class; however, the same applies if the CMySQLConnection class is used.

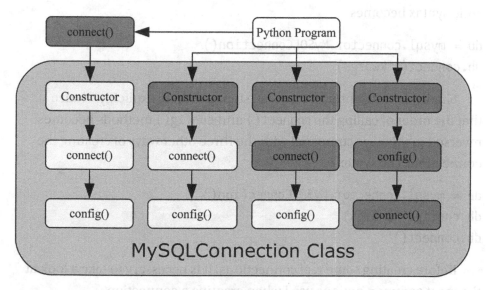

Figure 2-1. *The flow of creating a connection*

The leftmost route is the one using the mysql.connector.connect() function. The Python program calls the function with the connection arguments, and the function then handles the rest. The figure assumes a MySQLConnection connection (using the pure Python implementation) is created, but the function can also return a CMySQLConnection object if the C Extension is used. The basic syntax for the mysql.connector.connect() function is

```
db = mysql.connector.connect(**kwargs)
```

The route second from the left has the Python program send the connections arguments to the constructor when instantiating the MySQLConnection class. This triggers the constructor to call the connect() method, which in turn calls the config() method. The syntax when using the MySQLConnection class is

```
db = mysql.connector.MySQLConnection(**kwargs)
```

In the third route from the left, the MySQLConnection class is first instantiated and then the connect() method is explicitly invoked. The code syntax becomes

```
db = mysql.connector.MySQLConnection()
db.connect(**kwargs)
```

Finally, in the rightmost route, all steps are done explicitly. Notice that the order of calling the connect() and config() methods becomes reversed in this case compared with the three other ways of creating the connection. The syntax is

```
db = mysql.connector.MySQLConnection()
db.config(**kwargs)
db.connect()
```

Before creating some real connections, it is necessary to take a look at the most common options used when creating a connection.

Common Connection Options

The most commonly used options for specifying how to connect to MySQL, whom to authenticate as, and which password to use are summarized in Table 2-1.

Table 2-1. *Common Connection-Related Options*

Argument	Default Value	Description
host	127.0.0.1	The hostname of the host, where the MySQL instance you want to connect to is installed. The default is to connect to the loopback (that is the local host).
port	3306	The port on which MySQL is listening. Port 3306 is the standard MySQL port.
unix_socket		On Linux and Unix, it is possible to connect to a MySQL instance on the local host by using a Unix socket. Specify the path to the socket file.
user		The username of the application user. Do not include the @ and the following hostname; that is for the test user created in Chapter 1. Just specify pyuser.
password		The password with which to authenticate. For the test user, this would be Py@pp4Demo.
ssl_ca		The path to the file containing the SSL certificate authority (CA).
ssl_cert		The path to the file containing the public SSL certificate.
ssl_cipher		The SSL cipher to use for the connection. You can get a list of valid ciphers by connecting to MySQL using SSL and executing the query SHOW GLOBAL STATUS LIKE 'Ssl_cipher_list'; The current cipher in use can be determined through the Ssl_cipher session status variable.

(continued)

Table 2-1. (*continued*)

Argument	Default Value	Description
ssl_disabled		Force a non-SSL connection.
ssl_key		The path to the file containing the private SSL key.
ssl_verify_cert	False	Whether MySQL Connector/Python should verify the certificate used by MySQL Server against the CA specified with the ssl_ca option.

The option names may seem familiar if you have, for example, used the MySQL command-line client. That is not a coincidence. Using these options, it is possible to demonstrate how to create connections.

Tip   There are a number of example programs in this chapter. All example programs that appear in a listing are available for download. See the discussion of example programs in Chapter 1 for more information about using the example programs.

Connection Examples

It is time to combine the four ways of creating a connection as well as the most common connection option to create source code examples for creating MySQL Connector/Python connections. Listing 2-1 shows how to connect using the four ways of creating the connection. The examples are in the same order as when they were discussed earlier in the section.

Listing 2-1. Examples of Connecting to MySQL

```
import mysql.connector

connect_args = {
  "host": "127.0.0.1",
  "port": 3306,
```

```
  "user": "pyuser",
  "password": "Py@pp4Demo",
};
# ---- connect() function ----
db1 = mysql.connector.connect(
  **connect_args
)
print(
  "MySQL connection ID for db1: {0}"
  .format(db1.connection_id)
)
db1.close()
# ---- Explicit MySQLConnection ----
db2 = mysql.connector.MySQLConnection(
  **connect_args
)
print(
  "MySQL connection ID for db2: {0}"
  .format(db2.connection_id)
)
db2.close()
# ---- Two steps manually ----
db3 = mysql.connector.MySQLConnection()
db3.connect(**connect_args)
print(
  "MySQL connection ID for db3: {0}"
  .format(db3.connection_id)
)
```

```
db3.close()
# ---- All three steps manually ----
db4 = mysql.connector.MySQLConnection()
db4.config(**connect_args)
db4.connect()
print(
  "MySQL connection ID for db4: {0}"
  .format(db4.connection_id)
)
db4.close()
```

The four connections use the same connection options. Once the connection is created, the connection ID (from the MySQL Server side) of the connection is printed using the connection_id property of the connection. Finally, the connection is closed using the close() method. It is best practice to always explicitly close the connection when the application is done with it.

Tip   Always close the connection when you are done with it. Closing the connection ensures a clean disconnect from MySQL Server. It may also take some time before the server kills the connection; in the meantime, it occupies one of the available connections.

The output is similar to the following sample except the connection IDs will be different:

```
MySQL connection ID for db1: 13
MySQL connection ID for db2: 14
MySQL connection ID for db3: 15
MySQL connection ID for db4: 16
```

The config() method can also be invoked for an existing connection. Let's discuss how to reconfigure the connection and reconnect next.

Reconfiguration and Reconnect

It is not commonly done, but it is possible to reconfigure an existing connection and reconnect. In this context, reconfiguring means potentially changing all options including the MySQL Server instance that the application is connected to. When such changes are made, it is necessary to explicitly tell MySQL Connector/Python to reconnect.

To reconfigure a connection, use the config() method in the same way as you did before the initial connection was made. Once the new, desired configuration has been created, call the reconnect() method if any of the configuration changes require a new connection. Calling reconnect() closes the old connection and creates a new one with the new configuration. Listing 2-2 shows an example of reconfiguring a connection.

Listing 2-2. Reconfiguring a Connection

```
import mysql.connector

initial_args = {
  "host": "127.0.0.1",
  "port": 3306,
  "user": "pyuser",
  "password": "Py@pp4Demo",
};

# Create initial connection
db = mysql.connector.connect(
  **initial_args
)

print(
  "Initial MySQL connection ID ...: {0}"
  .format(db.connection_id)
)
```

55

```
new_args = {
  "host": "<your_IP_goes_here_in_quotes>",
};
db.config(**new_args)
db.reconnect()
print(
  "New MySQL connection ID .......: {0}"
  .format(db.connection_id)
)

db.close()
```

This example requires that there is a second user account on the same MySQL instance. The user is identical to the existing pyuser@localhost connection, but is defined to connect from the public IP address (replace with the IP address of your computer or if the IP address resolves with the hostname):

```
mysql> CREATE USER pyuser@'<your_IP_goes_here_in_quotes>'
                 IDENTIFIED BY 'Py@pp4Demo';
Query OK, 0 rows affected (0.84 sec)
```

It is also necessary that any firewall allows the connection.

As you can see from the example, it is not necessary to change all of the configuration options. Those that are not explicitly set in the new set of options keep their old value. The output of the program is (except for the IDs)

```
Initial MySQL connection ID ...: 21
New MySQL connection ID .......: 22
```

The last topic of the section is a few best practices regarding connections.

Connection Best Practices

There are a few best practices that are good to follow when it comes to connections. It is always difficult with best practices because all applications have unique requirements. So, the suggestions will focus on the technical side of MySQL Connector/Python.

The main best practices are

- Always close the connection when you are done with it. This has already been discussed.

- Use SSL (TLS) to encrypt the connections. This is particularly important if you are connecting to a remote host and even more so if the connection is over an insecure network. An exception is when you use a Unix socket for the connection as that is always considered a secure connection even without using SSL.

- Do not hardcode the configuration into the source code. This particularly applies to the password.

Note While MySQL uses `ssl_` as the prefix for the options related to encrypting the connection, in reality TLS is used.

In MySQL 8.0 and in some builds of MySQL 5.7, SSL is enabled by default using a self-signed certificate, and MySQL Connector/Python will use an encrypted connection by default.

The examples thus far have had a major flaw: they hardcoded not only where to connect to, but also the username and particularly the password. This makes the code harder to maintain, and it is also a security concern because the password is visible to anyone with access to the source code. Hardcoding the connection options also means that either the development and production system must share connection options or the deployment procedure needs to change the source code to update the configuration parameters.

Caution   Never store the password in the source code.

Neither is a good option, so an alternative solution must be found. The next section will discuss an alternative: using configuration files.

Configuration Files

The method of specifying the connection options directly in with the call to create the connection to MySQL can be very useful for doing quick tests, but it is neither practical nor secure (for the password) to do in real applications. This section will start out discussing some alternatives and then will go into details of using MySQL configuration files.

Alternatives to Hardcoding the Configuration

There are several ways to avoid hardcoding the connection configuration into the source code. There are pros and cons for each method, so it is not a matter of one size fits all. Four methods will be discussed:

- Asking for the information interactively

- Using environment variables

- Reading the information from the application's own configuration file or as a command-line argument

- Using a MySQL configuration file.

The interactive approach is great if you are writing a program that can be used by different users, so it is not known who the program will connect as. It is also the safest way to pass the password to the program. It is, however, not very convenient for more daemon-like processes to require starting the process manually each time it is necessary to restart it.

Environment variables can be used to specify options for the session. Child processes will inherit the environment of the parent, so the environment variables can be used to pass settings to a child process, such as from a shell to the application. It can be a great way to configure applications without requiring files or parsing the options on the command line. For example, it is a common way to configure applications running inside containers such as Docker.[1]

There are some downsides to using environment variables. When automatically starting processes, it will be necessary to store the environment variables in a file, which means it ends up being an alternative format for a configuration file. The environment is also in general long-lived; for example, if the application starts new processes on its own, it will by default pass on its environment, including potential secret information such as the password. The environment variables may also be readable by users with high privileges. So, care should be taken when using environment variables.

Using the application's own configuration file or providing the options as command-line arguments means that all of the configuration is done in one place. In this case, the MySQL options are treated the same way as other options, and all that is required when writing the code is to pass the options and their values to the MySQL connection.

Caution   Be very careful with passwords as command-line options. It may be possible for other users on the host to see the arguments passed to the program, such as by using the ps command on Linux. So, it is recommended not to specify the password as a command-line argument.

---

[1]See https://docs.docker.com/engine/reference/commandline/run/#set-environment-variables--e---env---env-file for the Docker documentation on setting environment variables.

There is another way, however. MySQL Connector/Python has native support for reading MySQL configuration files. Some of the reasons for using this approach over the application's own configuration file are that the application may not need a configuration file except for the MySQL-related options, or there may be different owners of the application configuration and the MySQL configuration. The latter can happen if the developer is responsible for defining the behavior of the application itself but the database administrator is in charge of the MySQL-specific options.

Since this book is about using the MySQL Connector/Python features rather than general Python programming, the only one of the four options to be discussed in more detail is the one using a MySQL configuration file.

Using MySQL Configuration Files

MySQL uses the INI file format for its configuration files. The following is a simple example for use with MySQL Connector/Python using the same configuration as previously in this chapter:

```
[connector_python]
user     = pyuser
host     = 127.0.0.1
port     = 3306
password = Py@pp4Demo
```

There are two connection options that control the use MySQL configuration files:

- `option_files`: This option specifies the path to one or more configuration files to read. The value can either be a string or a list of strings. There is no default value.

- `option_groups`: This option specifies which option groups to read from. The option group is specified as a name between square brackets; in the example

configuration, the option group is `connector_python`.
The value is a list of strings with the names of the group.
The default is to read from the `client` and `connector_`
`python` groups.

By convention, MySQL configuration files are called `my.ini` on Microsoft
Windows and `my.cnf` on other platforms. There are no requirements for the
file name or file extension from a functional point of view.

An important feature to be aware of is that the `option_groups` option
does not treat all groups equally. Specifically, the `connector_python` group
is special because all options in this group must be valid or a `ValueError`
exception will be raised. For other groups, unknown options are ignored.
The reason to ignore unknown options is that several programs may read
the same option groups. For example, the client group is also read by the
`mysql` command-line client and other MySQL client programs.

Listing 2-3 shows an example of connecting to MySQL with the
connection options read from the `my.ini` file located in the same directory
as the program.

Listing 2-3. Using a MySQL Configuration File

```
import mysql.connector

db = mysql.connector.connect(
  option_files="my.ini")

print(__file__ + " - single config file:")
print(
  "MySQL connection ID for db: {0}"
  .format(db.connection_id)
)

db.close()
```

The output is similar to the previous examples printing the ID for the connection, for example:

```
listing_2_3.py - single config file:
MySQL connection ID for db: 35
```

In some cases, you may want to split the MySQL configuration into several files. For example, say several applications need to connect to the same MySQL backend, so they share the host and port information, but each application uses different credentials for the connection. Continuing the example, the two files, my_shared.ini and my_app_specific.ini, can be created with the following content:

my_shared.ini:

```
[client]
host      = 127.0.0.1
port      = 3306
```

my_app_specific.ini:

```
[connector_python]
user      = pyuser
password = Py@pp4Demo
```

The only change required to the test program is to change the value of option_files into a list. To demonstrate how the option_groups option can be set, it is also added to the program. The resulting source code can be seen in Listing 2-4.

Listing 2-4. Using Multiple Configuration Files

```
import mysql.connector

db = mysql.connector.connect(
```

```
  option_files = [
    "my_shared.ini",
    "my_app_specific.ini"
  ],
  option_groups = [
    "client",
    "connector_python"
  ]
)

print(__file__ + " - two config files:")
print(
  "MySQL connection ID for db: {0}"
  .format(db.connection_id)
)

db.close()
```

The output is (except for the ID, which will change from execution to execution) the following:

```
listing_2_4.py - two config files:
MySQL connection ID for db: 42
```

One final consideration is path names. If a relative path is specified, it is the directory where Python is executed that is used as the base directory. Take, for example, the following command to execute a program (the ID will in general be different):

```
PS C:\MySQL> python Source/test.py
MySQL connection ID for db: 56
```

This is executed while C:\MySQL is the current working directory. If test.py has option_files="my.ini", then the my.ini file must be located in C:\MySQL.

Another observation is that for Microsoft Windows it is optional whether backslashes (\) or forward slashes (/) are used to separate the path components (directories).

This concludes the discussion of configuration files. The final topic of the chapter is the remaining options that MySQL Connector/Python supports for the connection.

General Configuration

Thus far the only configuration options that have been discussed are the ones required to specify where to connect to, whom to connect as, and whether to use SSL. There are several other options that are more related to the behavior of the application. These options are the topic of this section.

The options that were not included in the list of connection options earlier in the chapter are summarized in Table 2-2 through Table 2-5 with one table for each of the following option types: connection, character set, query behavior, and warnings. The rest of the book will include examples of using several of these options.

Connection

There are more connection options than were discussed in the "Creating the Connection" section. They are not as commonly used but can be required for some use cases. The options are summarized in Table 2-2. Some of the options will be discussed in more detail after the table.

Table 2-2. *Less Common Connection-Related Options*

Name	Default Value	Description
auth_plugin		Which authentication plugin to use. This is, for example, required when using MySQL Connector/Python 2.1 to connect to MySQL Server 8.0 because the server's default authentication plugin is not supported by old MySQL Connector/Python versions.
client_flags		An alternative way to configure several options through flags.
compress	False	When enabled, the network traffic is compressed.
connection_timeout		How long to wait before timing out when creating the connection.
converter_class		Specifies a custom converter class for converting the raw row data to Python types.
failover		Tuple of dictionaries specifying alternative MySQL Server instances to fail over to if the primary connection fails. This is only supported using the `mysql.connector.connect()` function.
force_ipv6	False	When True, IPv6 is always used when possible.

(continued)

65

Table 2-2. (*continued*)

Name	Default Value	Description
pool_name	Auto generated	The name of a connection pool. By default, the name is generated by joining the values of the host, port, user, and database connection options. The name can be at most pooling. CNX_POOL_MAXNAMESIZE (defaults to 64) characters long and is allowed to use alphanumeric characters as well as the following characters: ., _, :, -, *, $, and #. This is only supported using the mysql.connector.connect() function or by instantiating the pooling. MySQLConnectionPool constructor class directly.
pool_reset_session	True	When True, the session variables are reset when the connection is returned to the pool. This is only supported using the mysql.connector.connect() function or by instantiating the pooling. MySQLConnectionPool constructor class directly.

(*continued*)

Table 2-2. (*continued*)

Name	Default Value	Description
pool_size	5	The number of connections to hold in the pool. The value must be at least 1 and at most pooling.CNX_POOL_MAXSIZE (defaulting to 32). This is only supported using the mysql.connector.connect() function or by instantiating the pooling.MySQLConnectionPool constructor class directly.
use_pure	False	When True, the pure Python implementation of the connector is used. When False, the C Extension is used. If the option is not specified, the default is to use the C Extension if it is installed; otherwise it falls back on the pure Python implementation. This is only supported using the mysql.connector.connect() function. In most cases, it is recommended to use the C Extension.

The compress option can be used to reduce the amount of network traffic by compressing the data transferred between the application and MySQL Server (and vice versa) at the cost of additional computational resources. This can be particularly useful if large SQL statements are sent to the server or large query results are returned to the application and the application is installed on a remote host.

Four options that deserve a little more attention are the failover and pool options. The failover option can be used to define one or more MySQL Server instances that MySQL Connector/Python will fail over to if the connection to the primary instance fails. Each alternative

MySQL Server instance is specified as a dictionary in a tuple or list. The pool options set up a connection pool that the application can request connections from. These options are discussed in more detail in Chapter 5.

The client_flags option can be used to set several options. The list of options that is available can be determined using the get_full_info() method of the ClientFlag constants:

```
from mysql.connector.constants import ClientFlag

print("\n".join(
  sorted(ClientFlag.get_full_info())
))
```

The output from Connector/Python 8.0.11 can be seen in Listing 2-5. The name of the client flag is first listed, followed by a description of what the flag controls. Most of the flags also have dedicated options, but there are a few additional flags such as INTERACTIVE that can only be set through the client_flags option.

Listing 2-5. List of Client Flags

```
CAN_HANDLE_EXPIRED_PASSWORDS : Don't close the connection for a
connection with expired password
COMPRESS : Can use compression protocol
CONNECT_ARGS : Client supports connection attributes
CONNECT_WITH_DB : One can specify db on connect
DEPRECATE_EOF : Client no longer needs EOF packet
FOUND_ROWS : Found instead of affected rows
IGNORE_SIGPIPE : IGNORE sigpipes
IGNORE_SPACE : Ignore spaces before ''
INTERACTIVE : This is an interactive client
LOCAL_FILES : Can use LOAD DATA LOCAL
LONG_FLAG : Get all column flags
LONG_PASSWD : New more secure passwords
```

MULTI_RESULTS : Enable/disable multi-results

MULTI_STATEMENTS : Enable/disable multi-stmt support

NO_SCHEMA : Don't allow database.table.column

ODBC : ODBC client

PLUGIN_AUTH : Client supports plugin authentication

PLUGIN_AUTH_LENENC_CLIENT_DATA : Enable authentication response packet to be larger than 255 bytes

PROTOCOL_41 : New 4.1 protocol

PS_MULTI_RESULTS : Multi-results in PS-protocol

REMEMBER_OPTIONS :

RESERVED : Old flag for 4.1 protocol

SECURE_CONNECTION : New 4.1 authentication

SESION_TRACK : Capable of handling server state change information

SSL : Switch to SSL after handshake

SSL_VERIFY_SERVER_CERT :

TRANSACTIONS : Client knows about transactions

In order to configure client_flags, specify a list of the flags that should be enabled or disabled. To enable the flag, just specify the name of the flag; to disable the flag, prepend a minus sign. Listing 2-6 shows an example to tell the connection it is an interactive connection, but it cannot handle expired passwords.

Listing 2-6. Using Client Flags in the Connection

```
import mysql.connector
from mysql.connector.constants import ClientFlag

connect_args = {
    "host": "127.0.0.1",
    "port": 3306,
    "user": "pyuser",
    "password": "Py@pp4Demo",
```

```
  "client_flags": [
    ClientFlag.INTERACTIVE,
    -ClientFlag.CAN_HANDLE_EXPIRED_PASSWORDS
  ]
};
db = mysql.connector.connect(
  **connect_args
)

print(__file__ + " - Client flags:")
print(
  "MySQL connection ID for db: {0}"
  .format(db.connection_id)
)

db.close()
```

This gives the following output (again except for the values of the ID):

```
listing_2_6.py - Client flags:
MySQL connection ID for db: 60
```

The use_pure option can be used to specify whether the C Extension or the pure Python implementation of the connector will be used. The C Extension provides better performance than the pure implementation, particularly when working with large result sets and prepared statements. On the other hand, the pure Python implementation is supported on more platforms, has a few more features, and it is easier to modify the source code. The C Extension is the default in versions 8.0.11 and later when it is installed, whereas earlier versions used the pure Python implementation by default.

The C Extension can also be used by importing the _mysql_connector module instead of the usual mysql.connector module. An example of using the C Extension is included in Chapter 4.

The other connection options will not be discussed in any more detail. Instead, focus will be moved to the character set options.

Character Set

The character set defines how characters are encoded. In the early days of the Internet, the ASCII character set was often used. ASCII uses seven bits for each character, which is space efficient but it means there are only 128 different characters available. This works reasonably well for plain text in English, but it is missing characters for other languages. Over the years, various other character sets have been used, such as the Latin character sets.

The locale-specific character sets help support all languages, but with the downside that different encodings are required for different languages. One response to that is the Unicode Transformation Format (UTF) encodings; UTF-8 in particular has become popular. UTF-8 uses a variable number of bytes to store characters. The original 128 ASCII characters have the same encoding in UTF-8; other characters use two to four bytes.

Until and including MySQL Server 5.7, the default character set for the server side was Latin1, but this changed in MySQL 8.0 when utf8mb4 became the default. The mb4 suffix indicates that up to four bytes are used for each character (mb = multi-byte). The reason this is required is that utf8 in MySQL previously has meant up to three bytes per character is supported per character. However, a three-byte UTF-8 implementation misses out on several emojis and it has been deprecated, so it is better to use the four-byte variant. The default character set for Connector/Python until version 8.0.12 is utf8, which is a three-byte implementation of UTF-8 (called utf8 or utf8mb3 in MySQL Server). Starting from version 8.0.12 the default is utf8mb4 as in MySQL Server.

There is also the concept of collation to consider. The collation defines how to compare two characters or character sequences with each other, such as whether ä and a should be considered the same character in comparisons and whether ss is considered equal to ß (German sharp s). The collation also defines the sorting order of characters and whether the comparison is case sensitive or not. Each character set has a default collation, but it is also possible to explicitly request a collation.

Tip   Unless you have specific country requirements, the default collation in MySQL Server is often a good choice when choosing utf8 or utf8mb4 as the character set.

The character sets and collations that are available in MySQL do not, in general, change much between versions. However, one of the major changes for MySQL Server 8.0 is the addition of a range of UCA 9.0.0 collations. Information about the available character sets and their default collation can be found using the CHARACTER_SETS table in the Information Schema, as shown in Listing 2-7.

Listing 2-7. Character Set Collations in MySQL 8.0.11

```
mysql> SELECT CHARACTER_SET_NAME AS Name,
              DEFAULT_COLLATE_NAME
         FROM information_schema.CHARACTER_SETS
        ORDER BY CHARACTER_SET_NAME;
+----------+-----------------------+
| Name     | DEFAULT_COLLATE_NAME  |
+----------+-----------------------+
| armscii8 | armscii8_general_ci   |
| ascii    | ascii_general_ci      |
| big5     | big5_chinese_ci       |
| binary   | binary                |
...
```

```
| ujis      | ujis_japanese_ci     |
| utf16     | utf16_general_ci     |
| utf16le   | utf16le_general_ci   |
| utf32     | utf32_general_ci     |
| utf8      | utf8_general_ci      |
| utf8mb4   | utf8mb4_0900_ai_ci   |
+-----------+----------------------+
41 rows in set (0.00 sec)
```

Similarly, the collations available for a specific character set can be determined using the COLLATIONS table. Listing 2-8 shows the output for the utf8mb4 character set.

Listing 2-8. The Collations Available for the utf8mb4 Character Set

```
mysql> SELECT COLLATION_NAME, IS_DEFAULT
        FROM information_schema.COLLATIONS
        WHERE CHARACTER_SET_NAME = 'utf8mb4';
+-----------------------------+------------+
| COLLATION_NAME              | IS_DEFAULT |
+-----------------------------+------------+
| utf8mb4_general_ci          |            |
| utf8mb4_bin                 |            |
| utf8mb4_unicode_ci          |            |
...
| utf8mb4_0900_ai_ci          | Yes        |
| utf8mb4_de_pb_0900_ai_ci    |            |
| utf8mb4_is_0900_ai_ci       |            |
| utf8mb4_lv_0900_ai_ci       |            |
...
```

```
| utf8mb4_vi_0900_as_cs    |            |
| utf8mb4_ja_0900_as_cs    |            |
| utf8mb4_ja_0900_as_cs_ks |            |
| utf8mb4_0900_as_ci       |            |
| utf8mb4_ru_0900_ai_ci    |            |
| utf8mb4_ru_0900_as_cs    |            |
+--------------------------+------------+
73 rows in set (0.00 sec)
```

The output shows the 73 collations that are available for utf8mb4 in MySQL Server 8.0.11. The collation names consist of several parts:

- The character set name

- Which country the collation is for (for example ja for Japan) or whether it is of a more general nature

- Modifiers (accents): These are not present for all collations. Examples are ai for accent insensitive, as for accent sensitive, ci for case insensitive, and cs for case sensitive.

Tip   The topic of character sets and collations in MySQL is large. For a deeper discussion, see https://dev.mysql.com/doc/refman/en/charset.html and references therein.

There are three options related to characters sets and collations for MySQL Connector/Python. These are summarized in Table 2-3.

Table 2-3. *Character Set-Related Options*

Name	Default Value	Description
charset	utf8mb4	The character set used for the connection. In MySQL Connector/Python 8.0.11 and earlier, the default is utf8. In most cases, it is recommended to use utf8mb4.
collation	utf8mb4_general_ci	The collation to use for comparisons and ordering of strings. In many cases, the default can be used. The default value for MySQL Connector/Python 8.0.11 and earlier is utf8_general_ci. In MySQL Server 8.0, the default collation for the utf8mb4 character set is utf8mb4_0900_ai_ci which is often a good choice unless specific requirements exist.
use_unicode	True	Whether to return strings in query results as Python Unicode literals. The default is True, and this is usually also the best value to use.

Listing 2-9 shows an example of configuring the character set-related options.

Listing 2-9. Specifying the Character Set and Collation

```
import mysql.connector

connect_args = {
  "host": "127.0.0.1",
  "port": 3306,
  "user": "pyuser",
  "password": "Py@pp4Demo",
```

```
  "charset": "utf8mb4",
  "collation": "utf8mb4_unicode_ci",
  "use_unicode": True
};

db = mysql.connector.connect(
  **connect_args)

print(__file__ + " - Setting character set:")
print(
  "MySQL connection ID for db: {0}"
  .format(db.connection_id)
)

db.close()
```

The available character sets and collations are coded into the MySQL Connector/Python source code. This means that when you upgrade MySQL Server, if there are new character sets or collations included, you can only use them in your Python program if you update MySQL Connector/Python to a version that includes support for the new character sets and collations.

Tip   If you upgrade MySQL Server, you may also need to upgrade MySQL Connector/Python to get support for all of the new features.

It is possible to change the character set and collation used by the connection after the initial connection to MySQL Server has been made. The best way to do this is to change the charset and collation properties of the connection using the set_charset_collation() method as demonstrated in Listing 2-10. Notice that unlike the rest of the examples, this example first instantiates the MySQLConnection class to be able to print the initial character set and collation before creating the connection.

Listing 2-10. Changing the Character Set of a Connection

```python
import mysql.connector

db = mysql.connector.MySQLConnection()

# Print banner and initial settings
print(
  "{0:<9s}   {1:<7s}   {2:<18s}".format(
    "Stage", "charset", "collation"
  )
)
print("-" * 40)
print(
  "{0:<9s}   {1:<7s}   {2:<18s}".format(
    "Initial", db.charset, db.collation
  )
)

# Create the connection
connect_args = {
  "host": "127.0.0.1",
  "port": 3306,
  "user": "pyuser",
  "password": "Py@pp4Demo"
};

db.connect(**connect_args)

# The connection does not change the
# settings
print(
  "{0:<9s}   {1:<7s}   {2:<18s}".format(
    "Connected",
```

```
      db.charset, db.collation
   )
)

# Change only the character set
db.set_charset_collation(
   charset = "utf8mb4"
)
print(
   "{0:<9s}   {1:<7s}   {2:<18s}".format(
      "Charset", db.charset, db.collation
   )
)

# Change only the collation
db.set_charset_collation(
   collation = "utf8mb4_unicode_ci"
)
print(
   "{0:<9s}   {1:<7s}   {2:<18s}".format(
      "Collation",
      db.charset, db.collation
   )
)

# Change both the character set and
# collation
db.set_charset_collation(
   charset   = "latin1",
   collation = "latin1_general_ci"
)
```

```
print(
  "{0:<9s}   {1:<7s}   {2:<18s}".format(
    "Both", db.charset, db.collation
  )
)
```

```
db.close()
```

As you can see from the example, the character set and collation properties can be used even before the connection has been established. However, it is not possible to use the set_charset_collation() method to change the character set or collation until the connection has been established.

Note   Always use the set_charset_collation() method to change the character set and/or collation for a connection. Compared with executing SET NAMES as an SQL statement directly, it ensures that Connector/Python knows which settings are used for converting bytearrays into Python strings (see the next chapter), the character set and collation choice are validated against those known by Connector/Python, and the C Extension settings are kept in sync.

Establishing the connection will not change the value of the charset and collation properties. The character set can be changed on its own, in which case the collation is set to the default for the character set. In this case, the character set is set to utf8mb4, so the default character set is utf8mb4_general_ci.

The collation can also be set separately, and finally both the character set and collation are set. The output of executing the program in Listing 2-10 using version 8.0.11 is

```
Stage       charset    collation
----------------------------------------
Initial     utf8       utf8_general_ci
Connected   utf8       utf8_general_ci
Charset     utf8mb4    utf8mb4_general_ci
Collation   utf8mb4    utf8mb4_unicode_ci
Both        latin1     latin1_general_ci
```

If you are using MySQL Connector/Python 8.0.12 or later, the character set and collation for Initial and Connected are utf8mb4 and utf8mb4_general_ci.

Query Behavior

There are several options that control how queries behave. These range from defining whether features are allowed over transaction configuration to defining how MySQL Connector/Python will handle the results. The options are listed in Table 2-4.

Table 2-4. *Query-Related Options*

Name	Default Value	Description
allow_local_ infile	True	Whether the LOAD DATA LOCAL INFILE statement is allowed.
autocommit	False	When True, an implicit COMMIT is executed after each query.
buffered	False	When True, the result set is fetched immediately and buffered in the application.
consume_ results	False	When True, query results are fetched automatically if there are unfetched rows and a new query is executed.

(continued)

Table 2-4. (*continued*)

Name	Default Value	Description
database		Which database (schema) to use as the default for queries where the database name is not explicitly given for a table.
raw	False	By default, result values are converted to Python types when cursors are used. When setting this option to True, the results are returned without conversion.
sql_mode	(Server default)	The SQL mode used when executing queries. See https://dev.mysql.com/doc/refman/en/sql-mode.html.
time_zone		When set, timestamps are converted to that time zone instead of using the server-side time zone.

Chapters 3 and 4 offer discussions on several of these options, including code examples where these options are used.

Warnings

It is very important that warnings and errors are handled in the correct way. Failure to do so can result in corrupted or lost data. There are two options that control how MySQL Connector/Python handles warnings when you use a cursor (cursors are discussed in the next chapter). The options are shown in Table 2-5.

Table 2-5. *Warning-Related Options for Cursors*

Name	Default Value	Description
get_warnings	False	When set to True, warnings are automatically fetched after each query.
raise_on_warnings	False	When set to True, warnings cause an exception to be raised.

Since it so important that warnings and errors are handled correct, Chapter 9 is dedicated to discussing this topic.

Summary

This chapter went through how to create and configure a connection from a Python program to a MySQL Server database. The following topics were discussed:

- Four different ways to establish the connection including the initial configuration. The mysql. connector.connect() function is the most flexible of the four methods.

- The configuration options.

- Best practices for connections: Close connections, use SSL/TLS to encrypt the traffic, do not hardcode connection options (particularly the password) in the source code.

- MySQL configuration files.

- Character sets.

It is all well and good to be able to create the connection to the database, but it is not very useful unless you can execute queries. The next two chapters will go into query execution, starting with the more basic use cases.

## CHAPTER 3

Basic Query Execution

The previous chapter discussed how to connect to MySQL from the Python program. However, there is not much point in creating a connection just to get a connection ID or do nothing. The whole point of MySQL Connector/Python, after all, is to execute queries. This chapter will look at the basics of query execution.

First, you will learn how to execute queries using the cmd_query() method of the connection object. Then you will explore the more advanced concept of cursors. Lastly, you'll see how to handle user input.

Tip   There are a number of example programs in this chapter. All example programs that appear in a listing are available for download. See the discussion of example programs in Chapter 1 for more information about using the example programs.

Simple Execution

There are a few different methods to execute queries through MySQL Connector/Python. The simplest, but also least powerful, is the cmd_query() method of the connection object. I will also discuss the get_rows() and get_row() methods to fetch the result of a SELECT statement.

© Jesper Wisborg Krogh 2018
J. W. Krogh, *MySQL Connector/Python Revealed*,
https://doi.org/10.1007/978-1-4842-3694-9_3

Before diving into the three methods for querying and fetching results, it is useful to consider the relationship between them so take a look at Figure 3-1.

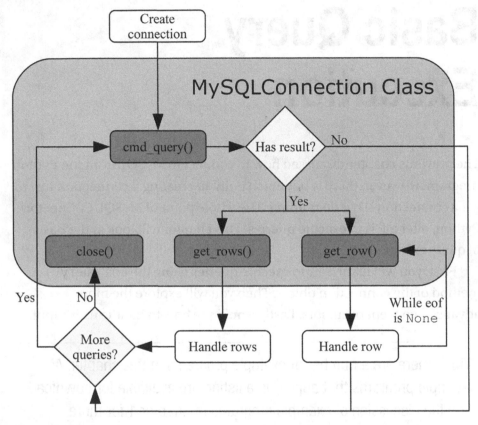

Figure 3-1. *The flow of executing queries through the connection object*

Figure 3-1 shows that once the connection has been created, a query can be executed using the cmd_query() method. If there is a result (rows are returned), either the get_rows() or get_row() method can be used to read the rows. The connection can be reused for more queries. At the end, when there are no more queries, the connection is closed using the close() method. This is a little simplified compared to real-world programs; for example, there is no consideration about transactions. However, it serves as a useful high-level overview.

The cmd_query(), get_rows(), and get_row() methods, as well as how to handle the results, are the main topics of this section. For more general usage, it is necessary to use a cursor; this will be the topic of the next section as well as the next chapter.

Note   In most cases, it is best to use cursors as described in the next section. However, this section is important because it explains how cursors work under the hood.

Executing the Query: cmd_query( )

The cmd_query() method is very simple. It takes one argument, which is the query to execute, and it returns a dictionary with information about the executed query. The exact content of the returned dictionary depends on the query. For example, for a SELECT query, the dictionary will include information about the selected columns. For all queries, the status of the query is also included. The examples in this section will include the content of the result dictionary.

A simple example of using cmd_query() to execute a SELECT query that returns a single row is shown in Listing 3-1.

Listing 3-1. Executing a Simple SELECT Using cmd_query()

```
import mysql.connector
import pprint

printer = pprint.PrettyPrinter(indent=1)

# Create connection to MySQL
db = mysql.connector.connect(
  option_files="my.ini")

# Execute a query
result = db.cmd_query(
  """SELECT *
      FROM world.city
    WHERE ID = 130"""
)

# Print the result dictionary
print("Result Dictionary\n" + "="*17)
printer.pprint(result)

db.close()
```

Caution   This example (and several of the other examples in this chapter) has the query parameter (130 for the value of ID in this example). This is acceptable since it is a fixed query. However, never inline user-submitted data into the queries. The "Handling User Input" section later in the chapter will show you how to safely handle user-submitted values.

The program creates a connection, as you saw in Chapter 2. After the connection has been established, the query is executed using the cmd_query() method and the returned dictionary is stored in the result variable, which is printed using the pretty printing module (pprint):

```
Result Dictionary
==================
{'columns': [('ID', 3, None, None, None, None, 0, 49667),
             ('Name', 254, None, None, None, None, 0, 1),
             ('CountryCode', 254, None, None, None, None, 0,
                16393),
             ('District', 254, None, None, None, None, 0, 1),
             ('Population', 3, None, None, None, None, 0,
                32769)],
 'eof': {'status_flag': 16385, 'warning_count': 0}}
```

The columns part of the result dictionary will be discussed in detail in the next chapter; for now, just know that the first element of the tuple for a column is the column name. The second part of the result dictionary, the eof element, includes some details for the query; the fields included depend on the query. The values you get for the last integer in the column tuples and for the status_flag may be different from the example output because they depend, for example, on whether the C Extension is used or not.

Common fields in the eof element are the status_flag and warning_count fields. The status flag is not nearly as useful as it sounds; in fact, the value is undocumented, and no significance should be taken from its value. The warning count, on the other hand, shows the number of warnings that occurred during the query. Chapter 9 covers how to check for warnings.

For queries without a result set (i.e. not returning rows), the eof information is an "OK package," which includes information about the query. For example, the following information is the result of an UPDATE statement that updates 14 rows using the pure Python implementation:

```
Result Dictionary
==================
{'affected_rows': 14,
 'field_count': 0,
 'info_msg': 'Rows matched: 14  Changed: 14  Warnings: 0',
 'insert_id': 0,
 'status_flag': 1,
 'warning_count': 0}
```

The two most important parameters are

- affected_rows: This shows the number of affected rows. In this case, 14 rows were updated.

- insert_id: For INSERT and REPLACE statements inserting data into a table with an auto-increment column, the insert_id is the ID of the first row inserted by the statement.

When use_pure = False, the info_msg parameter is not present and the status_flag is replaced with server_status.

A sibling to cmd_query() is the cmd_query_iter() method, which can be used to send multiple queries to MySQL. Executing multiple queries in one call and handling multiple result sets are topics of the next chapter.

It is all well and good to execute queries like in the example just discussed, but without retrieving the results, queries like the SELECT statement in Listing 3-1 are not very interesting. To fetch the rows found, the get_rows() and get_row() methods are used.

Retrieving Rows – get_rows( )

Some queries, such as CREATE TABLE, ALTER TABLE, INSERT, UPDATE, and DELETE statements, do not return any result and checking whether the query succeeded is all that needs to be done. However, in general, the majority of queries in a program are SELECT queries that return a result set. For queries that return a result set, the rows must be fetched. When the query is executed with cmd_query(), the corresponding method for fetching the rows is get_rows(), which returns all rows found by the query.

The usage of get_rows() is simple. All that is required is to call it, and the rows are returned as a list of tuples, as illustrated in Listing 3-2.

Listing 3-2. Fetching Rows with get_rows()

```
import mysql.connector
import pprint

printer = pprint.PrettyPrinter(indent=1)

# Create connection to MySQL
db = mysql.connector.connect(
  option_files="my.ini", use_pure=True)

# Execute a query
result = db.cmd_query(
  """SELECT Name, CountryCode,
            Population
      FROM world.city
      WHERE Population > 9000000
      ORDER BY Population DESC"""
)
```

```
# Fetch the rows
result_set = db.get_rows()

# Print the result dictionary
print("Result Dictionary\n" + "="*17)
printer.pprint(result)

# Print the rows
print("\nResult Set\n" + "="*10)
printer.pprint(result_set)

db.close()
```

The program in Listing 3-2 is similar to the one in Listing 3-1, except in this case, it forces the use of the pure Python implementation by using use_pure = True. The query this time looks for the cities with a population greater than nine million and asks for the resulting rows to be sorted by the population in descending order. The output looks like Listing 3-3. The output is generated with MySQL Connector/Python version 8.0.11.

Note   An important change in MySQL Connector 8.0.12 is to align the behavior of get_rows() and get_row() between the pure Python and the C Extenstion implementation. This means that in MySQL Connector/Python 8.0.12 and later, the pure Python implementation of get_rows() and get_row() no longer return the result as byte arrays. The following discussion is never the less useful to illustrate what happens with the result.

Listing 3-3. The Output of Executing the Program in Listing 3-2

```
Result Dictionary
==================
{'columns': [('Name', 254, None, None, None, None, 0, 1),
             ('CountryCode', 254, None, None, None, None, 0,
               16393),
             ('Population', 3, None, None, None, None, 0, 1)],
 'eof': {'status_flag': 33, 'warning_count': 0}}

Result Set
==========
([[(bytearray(b'Mumbai (Bombay)'), bytearray(b'IND'),
bytearray(b'10500000')),
  (bytearray(b'Seoul'), bytearray(b'KOR'),
bytearray(b'9981619')),
  (bytearray(b'S\xc3\xa3o Paulo'), bytearray(b'BRA'),
bytearray(b'9968485')),
  (bytearray(b'Shanghai'), bytearray(b'CHN'),
bytearray(b'9696300')),
  (bytearray(b'Jakarta'), bytearray(b'IDN'),
bytearray(b'9604900')),
  (bytearray(b'Karachi'), bytearray(b'PAK'),
bytearray(b'9269265'))],
 {'status_flag': 33, 'warning_count': 0})
```

The result dictionary is similar to the previous example with the column information and the eof information. More interesting is the result set returned by get_rows(). The values are returned as strings represented by an array of their binary data (bytearray). While this is technically a correct representation of the result, it is not very useful. For example, the population is an integer, so it's better to have the data as an integer rather than a string. Another issue is a city like São Paulo where the byte sequence is "S\xc3\xa3o Paulo"; note that the ã is represented as \xc3\xa3.

Note   If you use the C Extension or version 8.0.12 and later, the values are not returned as byte arrays but as Unicode string. This is an example where the two implementations were not identical in earlier versions.

In order for the data to be really useful in the program, it is necessary to convert the byte arrays to native Python data types. The exact way to convert depends on the data, and it is beyond the scope of this book to implement explicit conversion for each data type. However, it is also not required because MySQL Connector/Python already includes the code for it; more about this shortly. For now, see Listing 3-4 for an example of converting the strings and integer in the result of Listing 3-2.

Note   This example and the following examples where the output includes non-ASCII characters show how the difference in Unicode handling between Python 2 and Python 3 makes a difference. The examples assume Python 3 and MySQL Connector/Python 8.0.11. The examples will not work in version 8.0.12 and later.

Listing 3-4. Converting the Result to Native Python Types

```
import mysql.connector

# Create connection to MySQL
db = mysql.connector.connect(
  option_files="my.ini", use_pure=True)
```

```python
# Execute a query
result = db.cmd_query(
  """SELECT Name, CountryCode,
            Population
       FROM world.city
      WHERE Population > 9000000
      ORDER BY Population DESC"""
)

# Fetch the rows
(cities, eof) = db.get_rows()

# Print the rows found
print(__file__ + " - Using decode:")
print("")
print(
  "{0:15s}  {1:7s}  {2:3s}".format(
    "City", "Country", "Pop"
  )
)
for city in cities:
  print(
    "{0:15s}   {1:^7s}   {2:4.1f}".format(
      city[0].decode(db.python_charset),
      city[1].decode(db.python_charset),
      int(
        city[2].decode(db.python_charset)
      )/1000000.0
    )
  )

# Print the eof package
print("\nEnd-of-file:");
```

```
for key in eof:
  print("{0:15s} = {1:2d}".format(
    key, eof[key]
  ))
```

```
db.close()
```

The main difference between Listing 3-2 and Listing 3-4 is in the handling of the result set. First, the result set is split into the returned rows (cities) and the end-of-file (eof) package. The cities are then printed while converting the values to native Python types.

String values are converted using the decode() method of the bytearray type. This requires parsing the character set of the connection. In this case, the character set is utf8 (using the default); however, to ensure that any character set can be handled, the python_charset property of the connection is used to set the character set to use in the conversion. Since utf8mb4 is a MySQL invention, it is necessary to catch that and use utf8 instead; this is the difference between the charset and python_charset properties. The population can be converted using the int() function and then divided by one million to get the population in millions.

Finally, the end-of-file part of the result set is printed. This is the same information as is available in the eof part of the results returned by cmd_query(). The output of the program is

```
listing_3_4.py - Using decode
```

```
City              Country  Pop
Mumbai (Bombay)     IND    10.5
Seoul               KOR    10.0
São Paulo           BRA    10.0
Shanghai            CHN     9.7
Jakarta             IDN     9.6
Karachi             PAK     9.3
```

```
End-of-file:
status_flag    = 33
warning_count  = 0
```

Manually converting the arrays of bytes is not feasible in general and it is not necessary, as it will be shown next, when automatic conversion of rows is discussed.

Automatic Conversion into Native Python Types

In the previous examples, the rows returned by the query were handled manually. This can be a great way to understand what is going on, but in more real-world cases, it is usually preferred to get the result returned as native Python types.

Note   As with the previous example, this discussion is only required for MySQL Connector/Python 8.0.11 and earlier including version 2.1. In later versions, the conversion happens automatically; however, it is safe to call `row_to_python()` as it will just be a null-operation if the conversion has already happened.

MySQL Connector/Python includes the conversion module that provides tools for doing conversions of the results returned by MySQL Server. Specifically, the `row_to_python()` method in the `MySQLConverter` class can convert all values in a row. Listing 3-5 shows the equivalent of the example in Listing 3-4, but this time using `row_to_python()` to handle the conversion.

Listing 3-5. Converting Query Results Using `MySQLConverter`. `row_to_python()`

```python
import mysql.connector
from mysql.connector.conversion import MySQLConverter

# Create connection to MySQL
db = mysql.connector.connect(
  option_files="my.ini", use_pure=True)

# Execute a query
result = db.cmd_query(
  """SELECT Name, CountryCode,
          Population
      FROM world.city
     WHERE Population > 9000000
     ORDER BY Population DESC"""
)

# Fetch the rows
(cities, eof) = db.get_rows()

# Initialize the converter
converter = MySQLConverter(
  db.charset, True)

# Print the rows found
print(__file__ + " - Using MySQLConverter:")
print("")
print(
  "{0:15s}   {1:7s}   {2:3s}".format(
    "City", "Country", "Pop"
  )
)
```

```
for city in cities:
  values = converter.row_to_python(
    city, result["columns"])
  print(
    "{0:15s}    {1:^7s}    {2:4.1f}".format(
      values[0],
      values[1],
      values[2]/1000000.0
    )
  )

db.close()
```

The important parts of the example in Listing 3-5 are those involving the MySQLConverter class. First, the class is imported; then the class is instantiated when the result set is ready to be printed; and finally, the rows are converted by using the row_to_python() method.

When the MySQLConverter class is instantiated, two arguments are required: the character set and whether Unicode is used in Python. Remember from Chapter 2 that it is possible to configure both when creating the connection. The character set is exposed through the charset property of the connection so, as before, that is used to ensure that a change of connection character set does not require code changes when converting the row. The MySQLConverter class knows how to handle utf8mb4, so there is no need to take care of that explicitly. There is no property for the use of Unicode in Python, so it is necessary to specify it explicitly.

With an instance of the MySQLConverter class available, the rows can be converted one at a time. The column information from the result of the cmd_query() call is passed as an argument along the values to be converted; this ensures that MySQL Connector/Python knows the data type for each column. The output is the same as for the example in Listing 3-4 except the information in the eof part has be removed:

```
listing_3_5.py - Using MySQLConverter

City              Country   Pop
Mumbai (Bombay)     IND      10.5
Seoul               KOR      10.0
São Paulo           BRA      10.0
Shanghai            CHN       9.7
Jakarta             IDN       9.6
Karachi             PAK       9.3
```

The examples thus far have fetched all rows in the result set and then used the rows. That is great for a small result, but it is not efficient for a large number of rows with large values.

Retrieving Rows – get_rows( ) With Limit

One option to limit the number of rows retrieved is to specify the number of rows to fetch as an argument to get_rows(). This can be done in one of two ways: either just give the number of rows as an argument on its own or explicitly as the count parameter. The number of rows specified is the maximum number of rows to read in the batch. While there are more rows to be read, eof will be set to None. If there are fewer rows available than requested, get_rows() will return what is left and set eof to include the end-of-file information. This is illustrated in Listing 3-6.

Listing 3-6. Fetching a Limited Number of Rows at a Time Using get_rows()

```
import mysql.connector
from mysql.connector.conversion import MySQLConverter

# Create connection to MySQL
db = mysql.connector.connect(
  option_files="my.ini", use_pure=True)
```

```python
# Execute a query
result = db.cmd_query(
  """SELECT Name, CountryCode,
          Population
      FROM world.city
     WHERE Population > 9000000
     ORDER BY Population DESC"""
)

# Initialize the converter
converter = MySQLConverter(
  db.charset, True)

# Fetch and print the rows
print(__file__
      + " - Using get_rows with limit:")
print("")
count = 0
(cities, eof) = db.get_rows(4)
while (cities):
  count = count + 1
  print("count = {0}".format(count))

  # Print the rows found in this batch
  print(
    "{0:15s}   {1:7s}   {2:3s}".format(
      "City", "Country", "Pop"
    )
  )
  for city in cities:
    values = converter.row_to_python(
      city, result["columns"])
```

```
  print(
    "{0:15s}    {1:^7s}    {2:4.1f}".format(
      values[0],
      values[1],
      values[2]/1000000.0
    )
  )
print("")

# Read the next batch of rows
if (eof == None):
  (cities, eof) = db.get_rows(count=4)
else:
  cities = []

db.close()
```

The first four rows are fetched with the row count just specified as the argument on its own:

```
(cities, eof) = db.get_rows(4)
```

The rest of the rows are read inside the loop:

```
  if (eof == None):
    (cities, eof) = db.get_rows(count=4)
  else:
    cities = []
```

It is necessary to check for the value of the eof part of the result set because the previous read may have fetched the last rows. Indeed, that happens here. The first pass through the loop prints the first four rows of the result, and the second pass the remaining two rows:

```
listing_3_6.py - Using get_rows with limit

count = 1
City                 Country   Pop
Mumbai (Bombay)        IND      10.5
Seoul                  KOR      10.0
São Paulo              BRA      10.0
Shanghai               CHN       9.7

count = 2
City                 Country   Pop
Jakarta                IDN       9.6
Karachi                PAK       9.3
```

One thing to be aware of with this use is that get_rows() reads a total of seven "rows:" the six rows that are the result of the query plus the eof information.

A special case of reading a limited number of rows at a time is to fetch one row. The read_row() method is available for that case as a wrapper around a call to get_rows() with count=1.

Retrieving Rows – get_row( )

There are two different strategies for fetching rows after executing a query with the cmd_query() method. Either several rows can be fetched at once using get_rows(), as has been shown thus far, or rows can be fetched one at a time using the get_row() method.

The advantage to just fetching one row at a time is that the application only stores that one row in memory at a time. This can be more efficient for large result sets even though it requires more calls to the get_row() method and more round trips for reading the data from MySQL Server.

Note   This is a little simplified. As you will see in the next chapter, cursors support buffering results (i.e. prefetching the result set). However, that is not supported when using the `cmd_query()` method directly.

Another potential advantage of `get_row()` is that it provides a different flow of the code. With `get_rows()`, the rows are first fetched and then the code iterates over the rows. On the other hand, when fetching one row at a time, it is possible to use `get_row()` directly in a loop, as shown in Listing 3-7. Which code flow is preferable depends on the situation and general style of the program.

Listing 3-7. Using `get_row()` to Read the Rows One by One

```
import mysql.connector
from mysql.connector.conversion import MySQLConverter

# Create connection to MySQL
db = mysql.connector.connect(
  option_files="my.ini", use_pure=True)

# Execute a query
result = db.cmd_query(
  """SELECT Name, CountryCode,
          Population
      FROM world.city
     WHERE Population > 9000000
     ORDER BY Population DESC"""
)
```

```
# Print the rows found
print(__file__ + " - Using get_row:")
print("")
converter = MySQLConverter(
  db.charset, True)
print(
  "{0:15s}   {1:7s}   {2:3s}".format(
    "City", "Country", "Pop"
  )
)
(city, eof) = db.get_row()
while (not eof):
  values = converter.row_to_python(
    city, result["columns"])
  print(
    "{0:15s}   {1:^7s}   {2:4.1f}".format(
      values[0],
      values[1],
      values[2]/1000000
    )
  )
  (city, eof) = db.get_row()
db.close()
```

Most of the code in Listing 3-7 is the same as in the earlier examples.
The difference is how the loop printing the result set is done. Here the
values for each city and the end-of-file information are obtained using the
get_row() method. The eof variable is None while there are more rows to
read. Then a while loop is used to keep fetching rows until eof is set to the
same value as for get_rows(). The output is

```
listing_3_7.py - Using get_row

City              Country  Pop
Mumbai (Bombay)     IND    10.5
Seoul               KOR    10.0
São Paulo           BRA    10.0
Shanghai            CHN     9.7
Jakarta             IDN     9.6
Karachi             PAK     9.3
```

Before moving on to cursors, it is worth considering the general nature of consuming results in MySQL Connector/Python.

Consuming Results

Thus far, the examples have just used get_rows() or get_row() to fetch the rows returned by the SELECT statements. That is all well and good when testing, but it is worth looking a little more into consuming results.

Whenever a query returns a result set, the rows must be consumed before another query can be executed. If the rows have not been consumed, an exception will occur:

```
mysql.connector.errors.InternalError: Unread result found
```

There are two ways to avoid the error:

- Read the rows with get_rows() or get_row(). All the rows as well as the eof package must be read.

- Enable the can_consume connection property when creating the connection.

Caution   Always ensure that all rows returned by a query are consumed either using one of the methods get_rows() or get_row() or by enabling can_consume when creating the connection.

You can check whether the can_consume option has been enabled by using the can_consume_results property of the connection. When can_consume is enabled, MySQL Connector/Python will call get_rows() internally if a new query is about to be executed and there still are unread rows.

How does the program know whether there are any unread rows left? The connection class keeps track of this through the unread_result property. When the last row of a result set is read, unread_result is set to False. The property is public accessible, so it is possible to use it, for example, together with get_rows().

The can_consume_results property is just one of many properties of the connection object. Several of the properties were mentioned in the previous chapter when I discussed how connections are created. Now, with a better understanding of how connections and query execution work, you can move on to cursors.

Tip   If there is a large amount of data to be consumed and the data is not needed, it can be faster to close the connection and reconnect compared to fetching the rows.

Cursors

Thus far, all of the examples in this chapter have exclusively used the methods and properties of the connection object to execute queries and fetch the resulting rows. Using the connection directly can be considered the low-level method. For actual programs, it is more common to choose the higher-level cursors, which provide a nicer way of working with queries.

Note   While the connection methods cmd_query(), get_rows(), and get_row() are rarely used directly, it is still useful to know how the methods work. It helps explain why cursors work the way they do and is useful when debugging issues.

Before it is possible to use the cursor to execute queries, it must be instantiated. This is the first topic in the journey through the use of cursors.

Instantiation

There are two ways to instantiate a cursor: either using the cursor() method of the connection object or using the MySQLCursor constructor directly. The two methods are illustrated with the following code snippet:

```
import mysql.connector
from mysql.connector.cursor import MySQLCursor

# Create connection to MySQL
db = mysql.connector.connect(
  option_files="my.ini", use_pure=True)

# Create a cursor using cursor()
cursor1 = db.cursor()
cursor1.close()

# Create a cursor using the constructor
cursor2 = MySQLCursor(db)
cursor2.close()

db.close()
```

> **Note**   This example is not the whole story. There are several cursor
> subclasses, and the one returned by db.cursor() depends on the
> cursor settings. More about that shortly.

As with the database connection itself, the cursor is closed using the
close() method of the cursor object. Closing the cursor when you are
done using it ensures that the reference back to the connection object is
deleted, thus avoiding memory leaks.

There are several different cursor classes. The one to use depends on
the requirements. The classes are

- MySQLCursor: This is the "plain" cursor class for
  unbuffered output converted to Python types. This is
  the default cursor class.

- MySQLCursorBuffered: This uses buffered result sets
  (see Chapter 4), but still converts the result set to
  Python types.

- MySQLCursorRaw: This returns the raw results as byte
  arrays similar to get_rows() in version 8.0.11 and
  earlier while not using buffering.

- MySQLCursorBufferedRaw: This returns the raw result
  set and enables buffering.

- MySQLCursorDict: The same as MySQLCursor, but the
  rows are returned as dictionaries.

- MySQLCursorBufferedDict: The same as
  MySQLCursorBuffered, but the rows are returned as
  dictionaries.

- MySQLCursorNamedTuple: The same as MySQLCursor,
  but the rows are returned as named tuples.

- `MySQLCursorBufferedNamedTuple`: The same as `MySQLCursorBuffered`, but the rows are returned as named tuples.

- `MySQLCursorPrepared`: For use with prepared statements. Prepared statements will be discussed at the end of the chapter.

An advantage of using the `cursor()` method is that you can provide arguments for the cursor and the method will return a cursor object using the appropriate cursor class. The supported arguments are

- `buffered`: Whether to buffer the result set in the application. The default is taken from the `buffered` option for the connection.

- `raw`: Whether to return the raw result sets instead of converting them to Python types. The default is taken from the `raw` option for the connection.

- `prepared`: Whether the cursor will be using prepared statements. Examples of this will be given in the "Handling User Input" section. The default is `None` (`False`).

- `cursor_class`: Specifies a custom cursor class to use. This custom class must be a subclass of the `CursorBase` class. The default is `None`. Custom classes are beyond the scope of this book.

- `dictionary`: Whether to return the rows as dictionaries. Cannot be combined with `raw` and `named_tuple`. The default is `None` (`False`).

- `named_tuple`: Whether to return the rows as named tuples. This option cannot be enabled if `raw` or `dictionary` is also enabled. The default is `None` (`False`).

Table 3-1 summarizes the supported combinations of options and the cursor class that is returned. In the header, the `dictionary` option has been abbreviated with "dict" and the `named_tuple` option with "tuple." The options left empty in the table can either be `False` or `None`.

Table 3-1. *Arguments for Cursor Objects*

buffered	raw	prepared	dict	tuple	Class
					MySQLCursor
True					MySQLCursorBuffered
	True				MySQLCursorRaw
True	True				MySQLCursorBufferedRaw
			True		MySQLCursorDict
True			True		MySQLCursorBufferedDict
				True	MySQLCursorNamedTuple
True				True	MySQLCursorBufferedNamedTuple
		True			MySQLCursorPrepared

If an unsupported combination of options is used, a `ValueError` exception is raised, for example:

```
ValueError: Cursor not available with given criteria:
dictionary, named_tuple
```

The rest of this section will cover the cursor execution flow and examples of instantiating and using cursors, starting with the execution flow.

MySQLCursor – Execution Flow

The usage of the `MySQLCursor` class is similar to what was used when executing queries directly from the connection class: the query is executed and then the rows are fetched.

The main method for executing queries is the execute() method, while there are three different methods for reading the rows returned by the query. The execute() and the row fetching methods and their relationship are summarized in Figure 3-2. Additionally, there are the executemany() and callproc() methods for executing queries. They are discussed in Chapter 4 together with stored_results(), which is used together with the callproc() method.

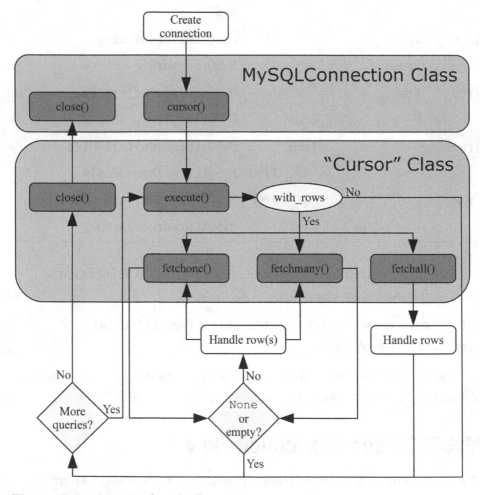

Figure 3-2. *A typical code flow using cursors*

The flow starts with the application creating a connection. The cursor() method is then used to create a cursor. There is not just one cursor class; rather, it is a family of classes depending on the exact nature of the cursor. Single queries, as discussed in this chapter, are executed using the execute() method.

The cursor classes have a property called with_rows that specifies whether there is a result set to handle. The rows can be fetched using one of three methods: fetchone(), fetchmany(), or fetchall(). Once all rows are fetched, the fetch method will return None or an empty result. The cursor can be reused to execute more queries. Once all queries have been executed, both the cursor and the connection are closed.

As with the flow chart showing how to use the connection methods, this is a simplified example. At the end of this section, it will be clearer how cursors work, and the next chapter will add more details.

MySQLCursor – Query Execution

For single queries other than for stored procedures, the execute() method is used; this includes support for executing multiple different queries in one call. The executemany() method can be used to execute the same query with different parameter sets.

The execute() method takes one required argument, the query to execute, as well as two optional arguments:

- operation: The query to execute. This argument is mandatory.

- params: Either a dictionary, list, or tuple of the parameters to use with the query. The "Handling User Input" section discusses the use of parametrized queries. The default is None.

- `multi`: When `True`, the operation is considered multiple queries separated by semicolons and `execute()` returns an iterator to make it possible to iterate over the result of each query. Chapter 4 includes examples of this. The default is `False`.

The rows returned by the query can be fetched using one of the following methods:

- `fetchall()`: Fetches all remaining rows. This is similar to the `get_rows()` method without any argument. `fetchall()` uses `get_rows()` for the connection to get all rows in one call for unbuffered cursors.

- `fetchmany()`: Fetches a batch of rows with the possibility to set the maximum number of rows to include in the batch. This is similar to using `get_rows()` with an argument. `fetchmany()` is implemented using `fetchone()`. The default is to read one row at a time.

- `fetchone()`: Reads one row at a time. This is the equivalent of the `get_row()` method, which is also used for unbuffered results.

Stored procedures can be executed using the `callproc()` method. The `stored_results()` is a related method that can be used when the stored procedure returns one or more result sets. Executing multiple queries and using stored procedures will be discussed in Chapter 4.

Note All rows must be fetched explicitly or by enabling `consume_ results` for the connection. An exception will be raised if unread rows are found and a new query is executed using the same cursor or the cursor is closed unless `consume_results` is enabled. It is also only possible to have one cursor for the connection with an unread result at a time.

Listing 3-8 shows a simple example of using a cursor to find the cities with more than nine million residents (the same query used in several of the cmd_query() examples).

Listing 3-8. Using a Cursor to Execute a SELECT Statement

```
import mysql.connector

# Create connection to MySQL
db = mysql.connector.connect(
  option_files="my.ini")

# Instantiate the cursor
cursor = db.cursor()

# Execute the query
cursor.execute(
  """SELECT Name, CountryCode,
          Population
      FROM world.city
     WHERE Population > 9000000
     ORDER BY Population DESC"""
)
```

```python
print(__file__
    + " - Using the default cursor:")
print("")
if (cursor.with_rows):
  # Print the rows found
  print(
    "{0:15s}   {1:7s}   {2:3s}".format(
      "City", "Country", "Pop"
    )
  )
  city = cursor.fetchone()
  while (city):
    print(
      "{0:15s}   {1:^7s}   {2:4.1f}".format(
        city[0],
        city[1],
        city[2]/1000000.0
      )
    )
    city = cursor.fetchone()

cursor.close()
db.close()
```

The first thing to note about the program is that the loop for printing the result is more compact compared to using get_row(). In the example in Listing 3-7, which is essentially the same example using cmd_query() and get_row(), the loop was 13 lines of code (including reading the first row); in the cursor example, the loop is 11 lines. The reason for this is that the MySQLCursor class automatically handles the conversion from the raw data to the Python types, irrespective of whether the pure Python or C Extension implementation is used, making it simpler to just loop over the rows and print them.

The second point is that the use of fetchone() and the loop condition are a little different compared to the example with get_rows(). The return value of fetchone() is just a tuple of the values for the row whereas get_rows() also includes the eof information. This means that the loop must terminate when fetchone() returns None.

The third point is that the with_rows property of the cursor is checked before fetching the rows. The with_rows property is True when the query returns rows. The value does not change even if all rows have been fetched; this is different from the unread_result property that was examined earlier for the connection object.

The output is the same as in the previous examples except for the heading:

```
listing_3_8.py - Using the default cursor
```

City	Country	Pop
Mumbai (Bombay)	IND	10.5
Seoul	KOR	10.0
São Paulo	BRA	10.0
Shanghai	CHN	9.7
Jakarta	IDN	9.6
Karachi	PAK	9.3

Since neither execute() nor the fetch methods include the eof information, how can that information be obtained? Let's find out.

MySQLCursor – Properties

An advantage of working with cursors is that it is no longer necessary to consider the eof information that cmd_query(), get_rows(), and get_row() return. Instead, the relevant information is available through properties of the cursor.

The properties that are available are

- `column_names`
- `description`
- `lastrowid`
- `rowcount`
- `statement`
- `with_rows`

All of the properties are read-only and contain information related to the latest query that was executed. Each of the properties will be briefly discussed in the following sections.

column_names

The `column_names` property includes the name of each column in the same order as their values. It is the same as the first element in the list for the columns in the result dictionary returned by the `cmd_query()` method.

The column names can, for example, be useful if a row should be converted into a dictionary using the column names as the keys:

```
row = cursor.fetchone()
row_dict = dict(
  zip(cursor.column_names, row)
)
```

Tip   If you want all of the results converted to dictionaries, then use the `MySQLCursorDict` cursor class instead. An example is provided in "The Dictionary and Named Tuple Cursor Subclasses" section.

---

description

The description property is equivalent to the entire columns element in the cmd_query() result dictionary. The value of the property is a list of tuples, such as the following (as printed using the pprint module):

```
[('Name', 254, None, None, None, None, 0, 1),
 ('CountryCode', 254, None, None, None, None, 0, 16393),
 ('Population', 3, None, None, None, None, 0, 1)]
```

The details of the values included in the tuples can be found in the "Query Metadata" section in Chapter 4.

lastrowid

The lastrowid can be used to get the last assigned ID after inserting it into a table with an auto-increment column. This is the same as the insert_id element of the OK package returned by cmd_query() for INSERT statements. If the statement inserts multiple rows, it is the ID of the first row that is assigned to lastrowid. If no ID is available, the value of lastrowid is None.

rowcount

The meaning of the rowcount property depends on the statement that was executed. For SELECT statements, it is the number of rows returned. For data modification language (DML) statements such as INSERT, UPDATE, and DELETE, it is the number of rows affected.

For unbuffered SELECT queries (the default), the row count will only be known after all rows have been fetched. In those cases, rowcount is initialized to -1, set to 1 when the first row is read, and then incremented as rows are fetched. That is, rowcount will be -1 until the first row has been fetched and afterwards will reflect the number of rows fetched up to the point of time when the property is read.

statement

The statement property holds the last query or queries to be executed. When parameter substitution is used (see the "Handling User Input" section), the statement property is set to the resulting query, making it useful for debugging.

with_rows

The with_rows property is a Boolean that is True when the query returns a result set. Unlike the unread_result property of the connection, with_rows is not set to False when all rows have been read.

The Dictionary and Named Tuple Cursor Subclasses

The other cursor classes that are available in addition to MySQLCursor, such as MySQLCursorDict, are all subclasses of the MySQLCursor class. This means that the behavior in general is the same for all of the cursor classes; the difference is the details of how they handle the result of SELECT statements, and for the MySQLCursorPrepared class, how the query is executed.

One scenario that can often come up is the requirement to obtain the query result as a dictionary rather than each row just being an (anonymous) tuple. In the recurring query used in several of the examples in this chapter, the city name has, for example, been found as city[0] or similar. Referencing the columns by their ordinal position makes it hard to understand the code, and it is error prone. Errors can easily arise by using the wrong column number or adding a column to the query.

A better solution is to refer to the column by its name. The MySQLCursorDict subclass can make the conversion from a tuple of values to a dictionary automatically. Listing 3-9 shows an example of how the cursor is created with the dictionary parameter set to True.

Listing 3-9. Using the MySQLCursorDict cursor Subclass

```
import mysql.connector

# Create connection to MySQL
db = mysql.connector.connect(
  option_files="my.ini")

# Instantiate the cursor
cursor = db.cursor(dictionary=True)

# Execute the query
cursor.execute(
  """SELECT Name, CountryCode,
          Population
       FROM world.city
     WHERE Population > 9000000
     ORDER BY Population DESC"""
)

print(__file__
      + " - Using the dictionary cursor:")
print("")
if (cursor.with_rows):
  # Print the rows found
  print(
    "{0:15s}   {1:7s}   {2:3s}".format(
      "City", "Country", "Pop"
    )
  )
```

```
  city = cursor.fetchone()
  while (city):
    print(
      "{0:15s}   {1:^7s}   {2:4.1f}".format(
        city["Name"],
        city["CountryCode"],
        city["Population"]/1000000
      )
    )
    city = cursor.fetchone()

cursor.close()
db.close()
```

The only differences from the previous example are that
dictionary=True is provided as an argument to db.cursor() and, when
printing the values, the columns values are referenced by column name,
for example city["Name"].

The MySQLCursorNamedTuple subclass works similarly:

```
...
cursor = db.cursor(named_tuple=True)
...
  city = cursor.fetchone()
  while (city):
    print(
      "{0:15s}   {1:^7s}   {2:4.1f}".format(
        city.Name,
        city.CountryCode,
        city.Population/1000000
      )
    )
    city = cursor.fetchone()
...
```

This concludes the discussion of cursors for now. The next chapter is on advanced query usage and it will include more discussion of cursors. However, before you get that far, a very important subject must be addressed: how to handle input provided by users.

Handling User Input

A common scenario in programs is that queries are generated based on input from users or other external sources. After all, a program with all static queries is rarely of much interest. It is critical how this input is handled. A failure to handle it properly can, in the best case, result in mysterious errors; in the worst case, it can result in data theft, lost data, and data corruption. This section discusses how to handle externally provided data correctly.

Caution   Never input information into the database without ensuring that it is handled such that it cannot change the meaning of the queries. Failing to do so can, for example, open the application to SQL injection attacks.

There are several ways to secure the program. The three ways that will be discussed are

- Validating the input

- Parametrizing the queries

- Using prepared statements

These three methods are the topics in the remainder of this chapter.

Validating the Input

Whenever the application reads data, it is important to validate the input. For example, if the application asks for the age in years, verify that the entered data is a positive integer, optionally with a check of whether the specified age is in the expected range. Not only does the validation help make the application safer, it also makes it easier to provide useful feedback to the user, which enhances the user experience.

Note   Client-side data validation, such as using JavaScript in web pages, is great for improving the user experience, but does not count as data validation for the application. The reason is that the user can override the validation performed on their side.

There is nothing unique to Python programming with respect to data validation. It is a common requirement irrespective of the programming language. How to do query parametrization is, however, specific to MySQL Connector/Python, which is the second line of defense.

Query Parameterization

A great way to defend the database against SQL injection attempts is to use parametrized queries. This will hand over the task of escaping and quoting the data to MySQL Connector/Python.

There are two ways of using parameter substitution with the cursor execute() method. The first is to provide a list or tuple with the values in the same order as they appear in the query. In this case, each parameter is represented with a %s in the query text. This is a useful way to provide the parameters if there only are a couple of parameters or for repeated use such as for an INSERT statement.

Tip   Specifying a single parameter inside parameters, like ("John Doe"), does not create a tuple; the end result is a scalar string. If you only have one parameter, either use a list or add a comma after the value, like ("John Doe",), to force the value into a tuple.

The other way is to provide a dictionary where each parameter is given a name (the key of the dictionary with the value being the parameter value). This is more verbose, but on the upside, it also makes for easier-to-read source code. This is particularly the case if the query includes several parameters. The parameters are specified in the query like %(name_of_parameter)s.

As an example, consider the following query:

```
SELECT *
  FROM world.city
 WHERE Name = ?
```

The question mark represents data that will be provided by the user of the application. Assume the user specifies the city name as 'Sydney' OR True. Listing 3-10 shows two different ways of handling that input using a dictionary for the parametrized query.

Listing 3-10. Handling User-Provided Data

```
import mysql.connector

input = "'Sydney' OR True"

# Create connection to MySQL
db = mysql.connector.connect(
  option_files="my.ini")

# Instantiate the cursor
cursor = db.cursor(dictionary=True)
```

```
# Execute the query without parameter
sql = """SELECT *
            FROM world.city
            WHERE Name = {0}""".format(input)
cursor.execute(sql)

cursor.fetchall()
print("1: Statement: {0}".format(
  cursor.statement))
print("1: Row count: {0}\n".format(
  cursor.rowcount))

# Execute the query with parameter
sql = """SELECT *
            FROM world.city
            WHERE Name = %(name)s"""
params = {'name': input}
cursor.execute(
  sql,
  params=params
)

cursor.fetchall()
print("2: Statement: {0}".format(
  cursor.statement))
print("2: Row count: {0}".format(
  cursor.rowcount))

cursor.close()
db.close()
```

The input is set in the `input` variable first in the program. Then the query is executed twice. In the first execution, the input is simply added in the query using the `format()` string method. In the second execution, the

input is added by setting the params option when calling the execute()
cursor method. After each execution, the executed statement and the
number of rows found are printed. The output is

```
1: Statement: SELECT *
            FROM world.city
         WHERE Name = 'Sydney' OR True
1: Row count: 4079

2: Statement: SELECT *
            FROM world.city
         WHERE Name = '\'Sydney\' OR True'
2: Row count: 0
```

Notice how the first execution ends up finding all 4079 rows in the
world.city table. The reason for this is that the WHERE clause ends up
consisting of two parts: Name = 'Sydney' and True. Because of the OR
between the two conditions, all cities will end up matching because True
matches everything.

On the other hand, the second execution escapes the single quotes and
adds quotes around the whole string. So, no rows are found because no
city is named "'Sydney' OR True."

Caution   MySQL Connector/Python uses the Python data type to
determine how to insert the parameters into the query. So, it is not a
defense against the user providing data of the wrong type. To protect
against the wrong data types being used, data validation and/or
prepared statements must be used.

Using parametrization is not only good to ensure that the data is
quoted and escaped correctly. It also makes it easy to reuse queries, and
it is possible to use Python data types in the application and let MySQL

Connector/Python handle the proper conversion to MySQL data types. An example is dates. In Listing 3-11, a temporary table is first created, then a row is inserted including a date, and then the actual query executed is printed. This time the parameters are provided in a tuple.

Listing 13-11. Using Parameters with a datetime Value

```python
import mysql.connector
import datetime

# Create connection to MySQL
db = mysql.connector.connect(
  option_files="my.ini")

# Instantiate the cursor
cursor = db.cursor()

# Create a temporary table
sql = """
CREATE TEMPORARY TABLE world.tmp_person (
  Name varchar(50) NOT NULL,
  Birthday date NOT NULL,
  PRIMARY KEY (Name)
)"""
cursor.execute(sql)

sql = """
INSERT INTO world.tmp_person
VALUES (%s, %s)
"""
params = (
  "John Doe",
  datetime.date(1970, 10, 31)
)
```

```
cursor.execute(sql,params=params)

print("Statement:\n{0}".format(
  cursor.statement))

cursor.close()
db.close()
```

The output of the print statement is:

```
Statement:
INSERT INTO world.tmp_person
VALUES ('John Doe', '1970-10-31')
```

So the parameter substitution ensured that the date of October 31, 1970 was expressed correctly as `'1970-10-31'` in the query sent to MySQL.

A method that is related to parameter optimization is prepared statements. This is the last method of defense that will be discussed.

Prepared Statements

Prepared statements can be very useful when working with databases because they have some advantages over the more direct ways of executing queries that have been used thus far. Two of the advantages are improved performance when a query is reused and protection against SQL injection.

From the point of view of MySQL Connector/Python, there is little difference between using parameterization or prepared statements. In fact, other than creating a different cursor subclass, the usage from the application point of view is identical.

Behind the scenes, there are subtle differences, though. The first time a query is executed, the statement is prepared; that is, the statement is submitted to MySQL Server with place holders, and MySQL Server prepares the statement for future use. Then the cursor sends a command to tell MySQL Server to execute the prepared statement along with

127

the parameters to use for the query. There are two advantages of this approach:

- MySQL Server does as much of the preparation of the query during the prepare phase as possible. This means that for subsequent executions, there is less work required, and only the parameters need to be sent over the network, so the performance is improved.

- MySQL Server resolves which tables and columns are required for the query, so it is able to ensure the submitted parameters are handled according to the data type of the column. This prevents SQL injection.

Note   With respect to performance, the one thing to watch out for is that if the query is only executed once, there is no performance gain. On the other hand, there will be an extra round trip to MySQL Server, so the performance of using a prepared statement will be worse than executing the query directly. The more time a prepared statement is reused, the more the performance will benefit.

The exact method used to prepare and execute the prepared statements depends on whether the pure Python or C Extension implementation of MySQL Connector/Python is used. The pure Python implementation uses the PREPARE and EXECUTE statements (see https:// dev.mysql.com/doc/refman/en/sql-syntax-prepared-statements. html). The C Extension uses the binary protocol, which is more efficient. The use of the C Extension with prepared statements requires using the _mysql_connector module, which is discussed in Chapter 4.

Listing 3-12 shows an example of using the same query, except for the country code, to find the three most populous cities in the United States and India.

Listing 13-12. Using Prepared Statements

```
import mysql.connector

# Format strings
FMT_QUERY = "Query {0}:\n" + "-"*8
FMT_HEADER = "{0:18s}   {1:7s}   {2:3s}"
FMT_ROW = "{0:18s}   {1:^7s}   {2:4.1f}"

# Define the queries
SQL = """
SELECT Name, CountryCode, Population
  FROM world.city
 WHERE CountryCode = %s
 ORDER BY Population DESC
 LIMIT 3"""

# Create connection to MySQL
db = mysql.connector.connect(
  option_files="my.ini", use_pure=True)

cursor = db.cursor(prepared=True)

# Execute the query finding the top
# three populous cities in the USA and
# India.
count = 0
for country in ("USA", "IND"):
  count = count + 1;
  print(FMT_QUERY.format(count))

  cursor.execute(SQL, (country,))

  if (cursor.with_rows):
    # Print the result.
```

```
    print(FMT_HEADER.format(
      "City", "Country", "Pop"))
    city = cursor.fetchone()
    while (city):
      print(FMT_ROW.format(
        city[0],
        city[1],
        city[2]/1000000
      ))
      city = cursor.fetchone()

  print("")

cursor.close()
db.close()
```

This example is very similar to earlier examples except that the cursor is created with prepared=True. The main difference is that there is no support for named parameters, so %s is used. The output of the program is

```
Query 1:
--------
City                   Country    Pop
New York                 USA      8.0
Los Angeles              USA      3.7
Chicago                  USA      2.9

Query 2:
--------
City                   Country    Pop
Mumbai (Bombay)          IND     10.5
Delhi                    IND      7.2
Calcutta [Kolkata]       IND      4.4
```

There is no support when using prepared statements for converting the rows into a dictionary or named tuple. This makes it somewhat harder to use prepared statements. Finally, the `callproc()` and `stored_results()` methods (see the "Stored Procedures" section in Chapter 4) are not implemented. The upside is improved protection against SQL injection, so it is worth going through the extra work.

Note   The prepared statement cursor is more basic than the other cursor subclasses. There is no support for data conversion for strings, dictionaries, named tuples, and the stored procedures methods. If prepared statements are used regularly, it worth considering a custom cursor class that adds support for these features.

Summary

This chapter went through the basics of executing queries using MySQL Connector/Python. You started out using the methods available for the connection object:

- `cmd_query()` to execute queries

- `get_rows()` to fetch multiple rows (by default all rows) when the query generated a result set

- `get_row()` to fetch one row at a time

These methods can be considered the low-level methods. At a higher level, the cursor classes provide support for executing queries while offering support for converting the result automatically to Python types and other features. The cursor methods discussed were

- `execute()` to execute queries

- `fetchone()`, `fetchmany()`, and `fetchall()` for reading the result sets

Finally, you learned how to handle user input. It is very important that all input is validated, and parameterization is used to protect against SQL injections. Parameterization can be performed using cursors. Enabling prepared statements in the cursor provides additional protection because it is MySQL Server handling the parameters with the knowledge of the target data types. Prepared statements can also improve performance when the same base query is executed repeatedly.

There is still much more to query execution in MySQL Connector/ Python, so the next chapter will continue with more advanced examples.

CHAPTER 4

Advanced Query Execution

In the previous chapter, you looked at the basics of executing queries. This chapter explores additional features related to query execution. It starts out by looking into the options of executing multiple queries in one API call and then moves on to features such as buffered results, calling stored procedures, and loading data in CSV files.

The second half of the chapter focuses on the connection properties, how to execute transactions, using the default database property to avoid specifying the database name explicitly for each table, and working with time zones. It also offers an overview of how to use the column information available after queries. The chapter concludes with a discussion of the C Extension.

Tip There are a number of example programs in this chapter. All example programs that appear in a listing are available for download. See the discussion of example programs in Chapter 1 for more information about using the example programs.

© Jesper Wisborg Krogh 2018
J. W. Krogh, *MySQL Connector/Python Revealed*,
https://doi.org/10.1007/978-1-4842-3694-9_4

Multi-Query Execution

In the previous chapter, all calls to the cmd_query() and execute() methods involved a single query. It is, however, also possible to execute multiple queries with one call to MySQL Connector/Python.

Note   While it may seem like a simplification to submit multiple queries at a time and the performance in some cases can be improved, there are also downsides. Particularly, it can be harder to follow what is going on when reading the source code of the program. So, make sure to use the support for multiple query execution with care.

There is support for multiple queries both using the connection object and cursors. Assuming the connection object is named db and the cursor is named cursor, the methods that have support for handling multiple queries are

- db.cmd_query_iter(): This works similarly to the cmd_query() method, except it returns a generator that can be used to fetch the result of each of the queries. The method is only available in the pure Python implementation.

- cursor.execute(): When the multi argument is enabled, the execute() method of a cursor can also execute multiple queries. This is the equivalent of cmd_query_iter() and a generator for the results is returned.

- cursor.executemany(): This method takes a template (query with parameter placeholders) and a list of sets of parameters. There is no support for having results returned.

The three methods will be the topic of the rest of this section, starting with the execution of several queries using the cmd_query_iter() and execute() methods, then moving on to queries based on a template using executemany(), and finally the special case of inserting multiple rows into a table using executemany().

Multiple Queries with Support for Results

The equivalent of the methods used in the previous chapter but with support for executing multiple queries is the cmd_query_iter() method of the connection object and the execute() method of the cursor object (the same as used for single queries). In both cases, a generator for the results (not rows!) is returned.

The flow of executing queries in this way is illustrated in Figure 4-1.

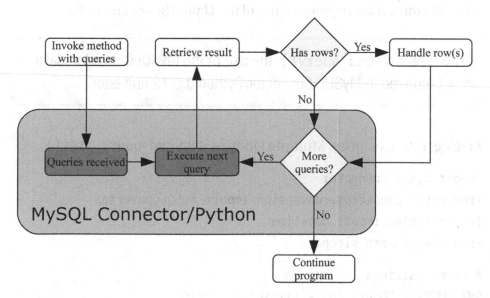

Figure 4-1. *Flow of executing multiple queries at a time*

Figure 4-1 shows that the queries are sent to MySQL Server one by one. When MySQL Server is done executing the query, the result is sent back to the application. Once all rows are read, MySQL Connector/Python automatically sends the next query. This means that enabling buffering (discussed later in this chapter in the "Buffered Results" section) can be useful with multi-statement execution.

The details of cmd_query_iter() and execute() with multi = True will be discussed in turn in the next subsections.

Connection - cmd_query_iter( )

The cmd_query_iter() method works similar to the cmd_query() method. The main difference is that cmd_query_iter() returns a generator that can be used to fetch the results instead of returning the result directly.

Listing 4-1 shows an example where cmd_query_iter() is used to select the three most populous cities of the United States and India.

Note As with cmd_query(), the use of the MySQLConverter class is not required in MySQL Connector/Python 8.0.12 and later.

Listing 4-1. Executing Multiple Queries with cmd_query_iter()

```
import mysql.connector
from mysql.connector.conversion import MySQLConverter
from datetime import datetime
from time import sleep

# Format strings
FMT_QUERY = "Query {0} - {1}:\n" + "-"*19
FMT_HEADER = "{0:18s}    {1:7s}    {2:3s}"
FMT_ROW = "{0:18s}    {1:^7s}    {2:4.1f}"
```

```
# Create connection to MySQL
db = mysql.connector.connect(
  option_files="my.ini", use_pure=True)

# Prepare the converter
converter = MySQLConverter(db.charset, True)

# Define the queries
sql1 = """
SELECT Name, CountryCode, Population
  FROM world.city
 WHERE CountryCode = 'USA'
 ORDER BY Population DESC
 LIMIT 3"""
sql2 = "DO SLEEP(3)"
sql3 = """
SELECT Name, CountryCode, Population
  FROM world.city
 WHERE CountryCode = 'IND'
 ORDER BY Population DESC
 LIMIT 3"""
queries = [sql1, sql2, sql3]

# Execute the queries and obtain the
# iterator
results = db.cmd_query_iter(";".join(queries))

# Iterate through the results
count = 0
for result in results:
  count = count + 1;
  time = datetime.now().strftime('%H:%M:%S')
  print(FMT_QUERY.format(count, time))
```

```
if ('columns' in result):
  # It is one of the SELECT statements
  # as it has column definitions.
  # Print the result.
  print(FMT_HEADER.format(
    "City", "Country", "Pop"))
  (city, eof) = db.get_row()
  while (not eof):
    values = converter.row_to_python(
      city, result["columns"])
    print(FMT_ROW.format(
      values[0],
      values[1],
      values[2]/1000000.0
    ))
    (city, eof) = db.get_row()
else:
  # Not a SELECT statement
  print("No result to print")

sleep(2)
print("")

db.close()
```

The first thing to notice is that the connection is established using pure_python = True. The cmd_query_iter() method is one of the cases where it is necessary to use the pure Python implementation because the method is not available in the C Extension implementation.

After the connection has been established, the format strings for the later outputs are defined, and the three queries that will be executed are defined. After executing the queries, there is a loop over each result. If the result dictionary includes column information, then there are rows to fetch. Otherwise, it is another type of query (for example INSERT or, as here, a DO statement).

Note   The `with_rows` property of cursors also works by checking whether there is column information in the result dictionary.

Two sleeps are inserted: the second query performs a sleep of three seconds on the MySQL Server side, and at the end of each loop handling the results, there is a sleep of two seconds in the Python code. This allows you to see from the output the flow of the queries and fetching of results. The output is

```
Query 1 - 16:24:58:
-------------------
City                 Country    Pop
New York                 USA    8.0
Los Angeles              USA    3.7
Chicago                  USA    2.9

Query 2 - 16:25:01:
-------------------
No result to print

Query 3 - 16:25:03:
-------------------
City                 Country    Pop
Mumbai (Bombay)          IND    10.5
Delhi                    IND    7.2
Calcutta [Kolkata]       IND    4.4
```

The first query completed the execution at 16:24:58. The second query is the three-second sleep, which is also the delay until the result of the query is ready. Since there also is a two-second sleep in the Python code after handling the result of the first query, it shows that the second query is executing while the application is "working" after reading the result of the first query.

This also shows one of the advantages of using the multi-query methods: if the queries are slow and possibly the application also needs some time to handle the result, it can improve the overall performance because the application can move on to processing the query result while the next query is executing.

Next up is how to perform the same task using a cursor instead.

Cursor – execute( )

Executing multiple queries at a time using a cursor is very similar to executing a single query. In both cases, the execute() method is used. The main differences are that the multi argument is set to True and that a generator is returned. The queries are submitted in one string with the queries separated by a semicolon, just like with cmd_query_iter().

Passing parameters to the queries is supported; however, all parameters must be in a single tuple, list, or dictionary. This makes it less useful to use the multi-query execution when parameters are required; instead, several single query executions are recommended in those cases.

Tip   If it the same query template is used for all the queries, and there is no result set to handle, then the executemany() method discussed next is a useful alternative to execute() with multi = True.

Listing 4-2 shows the example that corresponds to the previous cmd_query_iter() one, but this time using a cursor. The sleeps in the Python code and the printing of timestamps have been removed since they would work the same.

Listing 4-2. Using a Cursor to Execute Multiple Queries

```
import mysql.connector

# Format strings
FMT_QUERY = "Query {0}:\n" + "-"*8
FMT_HEADER = "{0:18s}    {1:7s}   {2:3s}"
FMT_ROW = "{0:18s}    {1:^7s}    {2:4.1f}"

# Create connection to MySQL
db = mysql.connector.connect(
  option_files="my.ini")

# Define the queries
sql_select = """
SELECT Name, CountryCode, Population
  FROM world.city
 WHERE CountryCode = %s
 ORDER BY Population DESC
 LIMIT 3"""
sql_do = "DO SLEEP(3)"
queries = [sql_select, sql_do, sql_select]

# Execute the queries and obtain the
# iterator
cursor = db.cursor()
results = cursor.execute(
  ";".join(queries),
  params=("USA", "IND"),
  multi=True
)

# Iterate through the results
count = 0
```

```
for result in results:
  count = count + 1;
  print(FMT_QUERY.format(count))
  if (result.with_rows):
    # It is one of the SELECT statements
    # as it has column definitions.
    # Print the result.
    print(FMT_HEADER.format(
      "City", "Country", "Pop"))
    city = cursor.fetchone()
    while (city):
      print(FMT_ROW.format(
        city[0],
        city[1],
        city[2]/1000000
      ))
      city = cursor.fetchone()
  else:
    # Not a SELECT statement
    print("No result to print")

  print("")

cursor.close()
db.close()
```

There are only few surprises in the code. The main thing is that, as discussed, the params argument is a single tuple shared for all queries. In this case, it is reasonably simple to keep track of the parameters in the queries, but in general this can become difficult and error prone. So, if parameter substitution is required, it is in most cases better to use multiple executions of single queries, or if the use case permits, use the cursor executemany() method.

> **Caution**   Using parameter substitution with multi-query execution is error prone. Consider executing the queries one by one, or if no result set is returned and the same template is used for all queries, use the cursor executemany() method.

The output of the script is similar to the previous example:

```
Query 1:
--------
City                    Country     Pop
New York                USA         8.0
Los Angeles             USA         3.7
Chicago                 USA         2.9

Query 2:
--------
No result to print

Query 3:
--------
City                    Country     Pop
Mumbai (Bombay)         IND         10.5
Delhi                   IND         7.2
Calcutta [Kolkata]      IND         4.4
```

Multiple Queries Based on a Template

In some cases, it is necessary to execute the same query over and over but using different parameters. For that use case, the executemany() method exists.

The main downside of executemany() is that there is no support for returning result sets. After each query execution, it is checked whether there are any rows to fetch; if so, all rows are fetched but not saved. Even the return value is always None.

Listing 4-3 shows a simple example where several cities have population changes. Since the basic query is the same, executemany() is a good candidate for this task. To make it easier to see which cities are updated, the city name, district, and country code are spelled out. However, in real applications, if the primary key (the ID column for the city table) is known, it is a better identifier of the rows to update because it will require fewer locks and better performance.

Tip   Aim to look up rows using the primary key or at least another index when possible. The more specific an index is, the fewer rows will be searched and the less locks will be held. This applies to all queries selecting, updating, or deleting rows.

Listing 4-3. Using executemany() to Update Several Rows

```
import mysql.connector

# Create connection to MySQL
db = mysql.connector.connect(
  option_files="my.ini", use_pure=True)
cursor = db.cursor()

# Definte the query template and the
# parameters to submit with it.
sql = """
UPDATE world.city
   SET Population = %(population)s
 WHERE Name = %(name)s
```

```
        AND CountryCode = %(country)s
        AND District = %(district)s"""
params = (
  {
    "name": "Dimitrovgrad",
    "country": "RUS",
    "district": "Uljanovsk",
    "population": 150000
  },
  {
    "name": "Lower Hutt",
    "country": "NZL",
    "district": "Wellington",
    "population": 100000
  },
  {
    "name": "Wuhan",
    "country": "CHN",
    "district": "Hubei",
    "population": 5000000
  },
)

# Get the previous number of questions
# asked to MySQL by the session
cursor.execute("""
  SELECT VARIABLE_VALUE
    FROM performance_schema.session_status
  WHERE VARIABLE_NAME = 'Questions'""")
tmp = cursor.fetchone()
questions_before = int(tmp[0])
```

```
# Execute the queries
cursor.executemany(sql, params)
print("Row count: {0}".format(
  cursor.rowcount))
print("Last statement: {0}".format(
  cursor.statement))

# Get the previous number of questions
# asked to MySQL by the session
cursor.execute("""
  SELECT VARIABLE_VALUE
    FROM performance_schema.session_status
   WHERE VARIABLE_NAME = 'Questions'""")
tmp = cursor.fetchone()
questions_after = int(tmp[0])

print("Difference in number of"
  + " questions: {0}".format(
    questions_after-questions_before
))

db.rollback()
cursor.close()
db.close()
```

First, the template is defined. In this case, named parameters are used to make it possible to use a sequence of dictionaries of the parameters. It makes for more verbose code, but also code that is easier to read and understand.

Then the executemany() method is called and the number of rows modified is printed. In this case, three rows are updated. Before and after the executemany() call, the number of questions asked by the connection is fetched from the performance_schema.session_status table. This is used to show how many queries are sent to MySQL Server during the executemany() call. The rowcount and statement properties of the cursor are used to get some information about the call to executemany(). It is the use of the statement property that is the reason for use_pure = True when the connection is created; when using the C Extension, the statement property is not supported when queries are executed with executemany() except for extended inserts.

Tip   In MySQL Server 5.6 and earlier, change the performance_ schema.session_status table to the information_schema. session_status table.

Finally, the transaction is rolled back to leave the city table as before the start of the example. This is only done so that all examples will use the same known state of the data; plus it means you can re-execute the example and get the same result. Transactions are discussed in the "Transactions" section later in this chapter. The output of the program is

```
Row count: 3
Last statement: UPDATE world.city
    SET Population = 5000000
 WHERE Name = 'Wuhan'
       AND CountryCode = 'CHN'
       AND District = 'Hubei'
Difference in number of questions: 4
```

The output shows that executemany() updated three rows (and then later rolled back), and the last executed statement updated the population of the city of Wuhan. The difference in the number of questions asked before and after is four: three for the three update statements, and one for querying for the number of questions asked.

As shown, the queries are executed one by one by executemany() calling the execute() method. So, there is no performance advantage compared to looping over the queries in the application itself. There is one exception, however: INSERT statements.

Extended Inserts

MySQL supports a feature called *extended inserts*. Usually when inserting multiple rows into a table, it's done as a series of INSERT statements:

```
CREATE TEMPORARY TABLE world.t1 (
  id int unsigned NOT NULL,
  val varchar(10),
  PRIMARY KEY (id)
);
INSERT INTO world.t1 VALUES (1, 'abc');
INSERT INTO world.t1 VALUES (2, 'def');
INSERT INTO world.t1 VALUES (3, 'ghi');
SELECT * FROM world.t1;
+----+------+
| id | val  |
+----+------+
|  1 | abc  |
|  2 | def  |
|  3 | ghi  |
+----+------+
```

This can be converted to a single statement that uses extended inserts:

```
DELETE FROM world.t1;
INSERT INTO world.t1
VALUES (1, 'abc'),
       (2, 'def'),
       (3, 'ghi');
```

```
SELECT * FROM world.t1;
+----+------+
| id | val  |
+----+------+
|  1 | abc  |
|  2 | def  |
|  3 | ghi  |
+----+------+
```

Extended inserts can greatly improve the performance of bulk inserts compared to single inserts, particularly if autocommit is enabled (see the "Transactions" section for more about autocommit).

MySQL Connector/Python has built-in support for generating extended INSERT statements by the use of the executemany() method. When it is detected that the template matches an INSERT statement, a single statement inserting all the required rows is generated. Listing 4-4 shows an example of inserting three rows into the world.t1 temporary table.

Listing 4-4. Using executemany() to Insert Several Rows

```
import mysql.connector

# Create connection to MySQL
db = mysql.connector.connect(
  option_files="my.ini"
)
cursor = db.cursor()

# Create a temporary table for this
# example
cursor.execute("""
  CREATE TEMPORARY TABLE world.t1 (
    id int unsigned NOT NULL,
    val varchar(10),
    PRIMARY KEY (id)
  )""")
```

```python
# Definte the query template and the
# parameters to submit with it.
sql = """
INSERT INTO world.t1 VALUES (%s, %s)"""
params = (
  (1, "abc"),
  (2, "def"),
  (3, "ghi")
)
# Get the previous number of questions
# asked to MySQL by the session
cursor.execute("""
  SELECT VARIABLE_VALUE
    FROM performance_schema.session_status
   WHERE VARIABLE_NAME = 'Questions'""")
tmp = cursor.fetchone()
questions_before = int(tmp[0])
# Execute the query
cursor.executemany(sql, params)
print("Row count = {0}".format(
  cursor.rowcount))
print("Last statement: {0}".format(
  cursor.statement
))
# Get the previous number of questions
# asked to MySQL by the session
cursor.execute("""
  SELECT VARIABLE_VALUE
    FROM performance_schema.session_status
   WHERE VARIABLE_NAME = 'Questions'""")
tmp = cursor.fetchone()
questions_after = int(tmp[0])
```

```
print("Difference in number of"
  + " questions: {0}".format(
    questions_after-questions_before
))
cursor.close()
db.close()
```

The example is basically identical to the previous one except it is an INSERT statement and a temporary table is created for the data to be inserted into. The output this time is

```
Row count = 3
Last statement: INSERT INTO world.t1 VALUES (1, 'abc'),(2,
'def'),(3, 'ghi')
Difference in number of questions: 2
```

The row count is still three, but now the last statement includes all three rows: the three INSERT statements have been rewritten to a single statement inserting all three rows. This is also reflected in the number of questions, which is two less than it was for the UPDATE example.

This concludes the topic of multiple queries for now. There will be a brief additional discussion in the "Transactions" section. Now it is time to look at some of the other features of cursors; first up is buffered results.

Buffered Results

A special feature of cursors is that it is possible to have MySQL Connector/ Python automatically fetch the result set after a query and buffer it so it can be used later. Buffering the result frees up the resources from MySQL Server as quickly as possible but adds requirements to the application instead. This makes buffering most useful where the application handles small result sets. The buffering cursor can be combined with the dictionary or named_tuple options.

One advantage of buffered cursors over non-buffered cursors is that it is possible to have two cursors for the same connection active at the same time even if they include result sets. For a non-buffered cursor, attempting to execute a query through the same connection before all rows have been fetched results in an exception. Since a buffering cursor automatically fetches the rows and makes the fetch methods read from the buffer, as far as MySQL Server is concerned, the connection is free to be used again.

Two examples where this feature can be useful are

- Executing two or more SELECT statements where it makes sense to handle the returned rows side by side. Often it is better to rewrite those queries to a single query using JOINs, but occasionally there can be reasons to use more but simpler queries.

- Reading rows from one query and then using the rows in another query. Again, it may be better to combine the queries but, for example, if a row is read so it can be updated and the business logic is not available in the database, then it can be useful to use two cursors.

Note   Buffering allows for executing a new query in the same cursor before handling the result set. However, it will cause the old result set to be discarded.

Listing 4-5 shows an example where both buffering and conversion to a dictionary are enabled. There are two cursors: cursor1 reads the Australian cities and cursor2 updates the population by increasing it by 10%. The business logic in this case is so simple, it would be better to have done it in one query, but a similar approach can be used where the logic for updating the row is more complex.

Listing 4-5. Using a Buffering Cursor to Update Rows

```python
import mysql.connector
from math import ceil

# The SQL UPDATE statement that will be
# used in cursor2.
SQL_UPDATE = """
  UPDATE world.city
    SET Population = %(new_population)s
  WHERE ID = %(city_id)s"""

# Function to increase the population
# with 10%
def new_population(old_population):
  return int(ceil(old_population * 1.10))

# Create connection to MySQL
db = mysql.connector.connect(
  option_files="my.ini")

# Instantiate the cursors
cursor1 = db.cursor(
  buffered=True, dictionary=True)
cursor2 = db.cursor()

# Execute the query to get the
# Australian cities
cursor1.execute(
  """SELECT ID, Population
      FROM world.city
    WHERE CountryCode = %s""",
  params=("AUS",)
)
```

```
city = cursor1.fetchone()
while (city):
  old_pop = city["Population"]
  new_pop = new_population(old_pop)
  print("ID, Old => New: "
    + "{0}, {1} => {2}".format(
    city["ID"], old_pop, new_pop
  ))
  cursor2.execute(
    SQL_UPDATE,
    params={
      "city_id": city["ID"],
      "new_population": new_pop
    }
  )
  print("Statement: {0}".format(
    cursor2.statement))
  city = cursor1.fetchone()
db.rollback()
cursor1.close()
cursor2.close()
db.close()
```

First, the logic for updating the population is defined. In this case, it is a simple function that increases the argument with 10% and then rounds the result up to the nearest integer.

The two cursors are defined. cursor1 reads the rows that will be updated, so it must be a buffering cursor. In this case, it has also been decided to have the rows returned as a dictionary. cursor2 performs the updates while the rows from cursor1 are read. It does not matter in this example whether cursor2 is a buffering or non-buffering cursor because it does not return any rows.

After the SELECT query to find the ID and existing population of the Australian cities has been executed, there is a loop over the cities. For each city, the new population is calculated and the UPDATE statement is executed. The city ID, the before and after populations, and the UPDATE statement are all printed as output. The output for the first three cities is

```
ID, Old => New: 130, 3276207 => 3603828
Statement: UPDATE world.city
    SET Population = 3603828
  WHERE ID = 130
ID, Old => New: 131, 2865329 => 3151862
Statement: UPDATE world.city
    SET Population = 3151862
  WHERE ID = 131
ID, Old => New: 132, 1291117 => 1420229
Statement: UPDATE world.city
    SET Population = 1420229
  WHERE ID = 132
...
```

Caution   The queries for the two cursors must be executed within the same transaction (happens by default) to ensure the right result. Otherwise another connection may update the population between the SELECT and the UPDATE. However, the rows are locked for as long as the transaction is active, so be careful that the execution of the loop does not take a long time, or it may cause other queries to time out or deadlocks may occur.

The last cursor-specific feature to discuss is the support for stored procedures.

Stored Procedures

Stored procedures have characteristics that mean they must be treated differently for some use cases. Specifically, they can return values through the argument list and a single query calling a stored procedure can return multiple result sets. Under the hood, the cmd_query_iter() method of the connection is used together with one internal buffered cursor per result set.

Caution   Because buffered cursors are used to handle the results sets of a stored procedure, the memory usage on the application side can be higher than expected. Use the stored procedure support with care if large results are returned.

The cursor methods that can be used to execute stored procedures are

- callproc(): This is the method used to execute the stored procedure. The return value is a tuple with the parameters passed to the procedure.

- stored_results(): This method is a generator for iterating over the result sets returned by a stored procedure invoked with callproc().

The easiest way to understand how the two procedures work is to consider an example. For this purpose, the min_max_cities() procedure in Listing 4-6 will be used.

Listing 4-6. The min_max_cities() Procedure

```
DELIMITER $$
CREATE PROCEDURE world.min_max_cities(
    IN in_country char(3),
    INOUT inout_min int,
    OUT out_max int
```

```
)
SQL SECURITY INVOKER
BEGIN
  SELECT MIN(Population),
         MAX(Population)
    INTO inout_min, out_max
    FROM world.city
   WHERE CountryCode = in_country
         AND Population >= inout_min;
  SELECT *
    FROM world.city
   WHERE CountryCode = in_country
         AND Population >= inout_min
   ORDER BY Population ASC
   LIMIT 3;

  SELECT *
    FROM world.city
   WHERE CountryCode = in_country
         AND Population >= inout_min
   ORDER BY Population DESC
   LIMIT 3;
END$$
DELIMITER ;
```

The procedure finds the minimum and maximum populations of
the cities of a given country, where the city population must be at least a
certain amount. Then all data for the three cities fulfilling the minimum
population requirement is selected, and finally the same for the three most
populous cities. The procedure takes three arguments:

- in_country: The country code by which to filter cities.
  This argument is read-only inside the procedure.

- inout_min: On input, it is the minimum population
  the cities must have. On output, it is the minimum
  population of the cities fulfilling the requirement.

- out_max: On output, it contains the population of
  the most populous city that has at least inout_min
  residents. The input value is discarded.

In total, this procedure uses all of the features of the stored procedure
implementation in MySQL Connector/Python cursors. The procedure can
be installed in a similar way to how the world sample database was installed:

```
shell$ mysql --user=pyuser --password \
          --host=127.0.0.1 --port=3306 \
          --execute="SOURCE listing_4_6.sql"
```

The command assumes the mysql command-line client is the
execution search path and that the file listing_4_6.sql with the
procedure definition is in the current working directory. On Windows, the
same command can be used, but all of the arguments must be on the same
line. An example of using the procedure from within the mysql command-
line client is shown in Listing 4-7.

Listing 4-7. Using the world.min_max_cities Procedure

```
mysql> SET @MIN = 500000;
Query OK, 0 rows affected (0.00 sec)

mysql> CALL world.min_max_cities('AUS', @MIN, @MAX);
+-----+-----------+-------------+------------------+------------+
| ID  | Name      | CountryCode | District         | Population |
+-----+-----------+-------------+------------------+------------+
| 134 | Adelaide  | AUS         | South Australia  |    978100  |
| 133 | Perth     | AUS         | West Australia   |   1096829  |
| 132 | Brisbane  | AUS         | Queensland       |   1291117  |
+-----+-----------+-------------+------------------+------------+
```

```
3 rows in set (0.01 sec)

+-----+-----------+-------------+------------------+------------+
| ID  | Name      | CountryCode | District         |Population  |
+-----+-----------+-------------+------------------+------------+
| 130 | Sydney    | AUS         | New South Wales  |   3276207  |
| 131 | Melbourne | AUS         | Victoria         |   2865329  |
| 132 | Brisbane  | AUS         | Queensland       |   1291117  |
+-----+-----------+-------------+------------------+------------+
3 rows in set (0.01 sec)

Query OK, 0 rows affected (0.02 sec)

mysql> SELECT @MIN, @MAX;
+--------+---------+
| @MIN   | @MAX    |
+--------+---------+
| 978100 | 3276207 |
+--------+---------+
1 row in set (0.00 sec)
```

Listing 4-8 shows the corresponding Python program that calls the procedure using the callproc() method and then reads the result sets using the stored_results() method.

Listing 4-8. Using the Cursor Stored Procedure Methods

```
import mysql.connector

# Format strings
FMT_QUERY = "Query {0}:\n" + "-"*8
FMT_HEADER = "{0:18s}   {1:3s}"
FMT_ROW = "{0:18s}   {1:4.1f}"
```

```python
# Create connection to MySQL
db = mysql.connector.connect(
  option_files="my.ini")
cursor = db.cursor()

# Execute the procedure
return_args = cursor.callproc(
  "world.min_max_cities",
  ("AUS", 500000, None)
)

# Print the returned arguments
print("""Country ..........: {0}
Min Population ...: {1:8d}
Max Population ...: {2:8d}
""".format(*return_args))

# Iterate over the result sets and print
# the cities and their population
# Convert the rows to dictionaries to
# avoid referencing the columns by
# ordinal position.
count = 0
for result in cursor.stored_results():
  count = count + 1;
  print(FMT_QUERY.format(count))
  if (result.with_rows):
    # It is one of the SELECT statements
    # as it has column definitions.
    # Print the result.
    print(FMT_HEADER.format("City", "Pop"))
    city = result.fetchone()
    while (city):
```

```
        city_dict = dict(
          zip(result.column_names, city))

        print(FMT_ROW.format(
          city_dict["Name"],
          city_dict["Population"]/1000000
        ))
        city = result.fetchone()
    print("")

cursor.close()
db.close()
```

After establishing the connection and setting up the format strings for printing the output, the procedure is invoked using the `callproc()` method. The `args` argument (second argument) must include one element for each argument taken by the procedure, even if some of the arguments are only used as out arguments. The return value is a tuple with one element per argument passed to procedure. For arguments that are only sent to the procedure, the original value is used in the return tuple.

Tip   The returned arguments will by default retain the data type defined in the procedure (unless `raw=True` for the cursor, in which case they are returned as `arraybytes`). It is, however, also possible to explicitly specify the MySQL data type, for example (`0, 'CHAR'`). See `https://dev.mysql.com/doc/refman/en/cast-functions.html` for the available types.

The last part of the program iterates over the results returned by `stored_results()`. The loop is similar to what was used with the other multi-result set method. The output looks like the following:

```
Country ..........: AUS
Min Population ...:   978100
Max Population ...:  3276207

Query 1:
--------
City              Pop
Adelaide          1.0
Perth             1.1
Brisbane          1.3

Query 2:
--------
City              Pop
Sydney            3.3
Melbourne         2.9
Brisbane          1.3
```

With stored procedures in place, there is only one type of query left to discuss: loading data stored as comma-separated values (CSV).

Loading Data Using a CSV File

A popular way to transport data between systems is files with comma-separated values (CSV). This is a standard way to store data and there is wide support for it, from exporting spreadsheets to database backups. Loading the data stored in a CSV file is also a relatively efficient way to bulk load data.

Note   While the C in CSV suggest the data is comma-separated, it is common to use the tab character, space, semicolon, or other characters as a separator. In fact, MySQL uses a tab as the default separator.

The MySQL statement to load data is the LOAD DATA INFILE
command. There is no native support for this command in MySQL
Connector/Python, but there are still some special considerations. There
are essentially two ways to use the LOAD DATA INFILE: loading a file located
on the host where MySQL Server is installed or loading a file from the
application side. In either case, the statement is executed as any other
single statement using the connection cmd_query() method or the cursor
execute() method.

Loading a Server-Side File

Loading a file located on the host where MySQL Server is installed is the
method used when executing LOAD DATA INFILE without any modifier.
The main things to be aware of are that the MySQL user must have the
FILE privilege and the CSV file cannot be located in any random location.

The paths where LOAD DATA INFILE is allowed to read files from are
limited by the secure_file_priv option (https://dev.mysql.com/doc/
refman/en/server-system-variables.html#sysvar_secure_file_priv)
for MySQL Sever. Only paths in the path specified by secure_file_priv or
below it can be used. The secure_file_priv option also specifies where
the SELECT … INTO OUTFILE statement can export data to. The current
value of secure_file_priv can, for example, be found using the following
query:

```
mysql> SELECT @@global.secure_file_priv;
+---------------------------+
| @@global.secure_file_priv |
+---------------------------+
| C:\MySQL\Files\           |
+---------------------------+
1 row in set (0.00 sec)
```

In recent MySQL Server versions, `secure_file_priv` defaults to `NULL`, which disables both imports and exports except when installed on Linux using native packages (where it defaults to `/var/lib/mysql-files`) or using MySQL Installer on Windows (where it defaults to `C:\ProgramData\ MySQL\MySQL Server 8.0\Uploads\` or similar).

The `secure_file_priv` option can only be changed by updating the MySQL configuration file (by convention, `my.ini` on Windows and `my.cnf` on other platforms). For example:

```
[mysqld]
secure_file_priv = C:\MySQL\Files
```

After the MySQL configuration file has been updated, a restart of MySQL Server is required for the change to take effect. At this time, it is possible to load data using the `LOAD DATA INFILE` command. Before discussing an example of loading data, let's look at the alternative to loading a file from the MySQL Server side: loading a file that is local to the application.

Loading an Application-Side File

The local version is used when the `LOCAL` keyword is added to the command: `LOAD DATA LOCAL INFILE`. On the MySQL Server side, the option `local_infile` (`https://dev.mysql.com/doc/refman/en/server-system-variables.html#sysvar_local_infile`) specifies whether the feature is allowed. In MySQL Server 5.7 and earlier, it is enabled by default; in version 8.0 and later, it is disabled by default.

In MySQL Connector/Python, the option `allow_local_infile` specifies whether loading local files is allowed. In all recent MySQL Connector/Python versions, `allow_local_infile` is enabled by default. The option is set when the connection is created or with the connection `config()` method.

Tip From a security perspective, it is best to disable support for reading data files from the application side. That is, it is recommended to set `local_infile = 0` on the MySQL Server side (the default in MySQL Server 8.0 and later) and `allow_local_infile = False` in the MySQL Connector/Python program unless the feature is really required. One potential issue of allowing local files to be read is that a bug in a web application can end up allowing the user to retrieve any file the application can read. See `https://dev.mysql.com/doc/refman/en/load-data-local.html` for more about the security implications of loading local files.

The rest of this section will go through an example with the main focus on the local variant but with some notes on how to turn it into the server-side case.

Load Data Example

The LOAD DATA INFILE statement is quite versatile because it can handle different delimiters, quoting styles, line endings, etc. A complete guide to the statement is beyond the scope of this book, but it is worth taking a look at an example. The code listing will use the application-side variant; however, the server side is very similar and it is left as an exercise to load the file from the server side.

Tip For the complete documentation of LOAD DATA INFILE, see `https://dev.mysql.com/doc/refman/en/load-data.html`.

The example will load the file testdata.txt, located in the same directory as where the Python program is executed. The data will be loaded into the world.loadtest table. The content of the file is

```
# ID, Value
1,"abcdef..."
2,"MySQL Connector/Python is fun"
3,"Smileys require utf8mb4"
4, 🐬
```

The last value is the dolphin emoji (U+1F42C). Since the dolphin is one of the emojis requiring four bytes in UTF-8 (0xF09F90AC), it is necessary to use the utf8mb4 character set in MySQL (the default in MySQL 8.0 and later). The world.loadtest table can be created with the following statement:

```
CREATE TABLE world.loadtest (
  id int unsigned NOT NULL PRIMARY KEY,
  val varchar(30)
) DEFAULT CHARACTER SET=utf8mb4;
```

As this is loading a local file, you must enable the local_infile option in MySQL Server. This can be done using the following statement:

```
mysql> SET GLOBAL local_infile = ON;
Query OK, 0 rows affected (0.00 sec)
```

This enables the setting without a need to restart MySQL; however, it does not persist the change.

With the data, table, and server-side setting ready, the program in Listing 4-9 can be used to load the data into the table. The file endings used for the file in the example are assumed to be Unix newlines. If Windows newlines are used, the LOAD DATA LOCAL INFILE statement must be changed to \r\n or \r (depending on the application that wrote the file) instead of \n for the LINES TERMINATED BY argument.

Listing 4-9. Loading Data with LOAD DATA LOCAL INFILE

```python
import mysql.connector

FMT_HEADER = "{0:2s}    {1:30s}    {2:8s}"
FMT_ROW = "{0:2d}    {1:30s}    ({2:8s})"

# Create connection to MySQL
db = mysql.connector.connect(
  option_files="my.ini",
  allow_local_infile=True
)
cursor = db.cursor(dictionary=True)

# Clear the table of any existing rows
cursor.execute("DELETE FROM world.loadtest")

# Define the statement and execute it.
sql = """
LOAD DATA LOCAL INFILE 'testdata.txt'
    INTO TABLE world.loadtest
CHARACTER SET utf8mb4
   FIELDS TERMINATED BY ','
          OPTIONALLY ENCLOSED BY '"'
   LINES TERMINATED BY '\n'
   IGNORE 1 LINES"""
cursor.execute(sql)

print(
  "Number of rows inserted: {0}".format(
  cursor.rowcount
))
print("")

sql = """
```

```
SELECT id, val, LEFT(HEX(val), 8) AS hex
  FROM world.loadtest
 ORDER BY id"""
cursor.execute(sql)

if (cursor.with_rows):
  # Print the rows found
  print(
    FMT_HEADER.format(
      "ID", "Value", "Hex"
    )
  )
  row = cursor.fetchone()
  while (row):
    print(
      FMT_ROW.format(
        row["id"],
        row["val"],
        row["hex"]
      )
    )
    row = cursor.fetchone()
# Commit the transaction
db.commit()
cursor.close()
db.close()
```

The connection is created with the allow_local_infile option
explicitly set to True. This can seem unnecessary; however, it shows the
clear intention to load a local file and insert the content into a table. Note
that MySQL client programs such as the mysql command-line client have
disabled the option corresponding to allow_local_infile by default

in MySQL Server 8.0. It may be that the connectors including MySQL Connector/Python will make the same change at some point in the future, so enabling `allow_local_infile` explicitly will make upgrades easier in the future.

The first thing that is done after the connection and cursor have been created is to delete all the existing data in the `world.loadtest` table. This is done in case the program is run multiple times; the `DELETE` statement ensures the table is always empty before the data is loaded.

The data is then loaded using the `LOAD DATA LOCAL INFILE` statement. The exact arguments to use depend on the CSV file that is being loaded. It is recommended to always specify the character set of the file so that the data is read correctly.

Tip   Always specify the character set the data has been saved with so that MySQL can interpret the data correctly.

After the data has been loaded, the number of rows inserted is printed using the `cursor.rowcount` property, and the content of the table is selected and printed. Be aware that not all terminal programs can print the dolphin emoji, so it may look like a question mark, some other place-holder character, or even no character at all. This is the reason the first four bytes of the value are also printed in hexadecimal notation, so it is possible to verify that the value is the correct one. The output looks like

```
Number of rows inserted: 4

ID   Value                          Hex
 1   abcdef...                      (61626364)
 2   MySQL Connector/Python is fun  (4D795351)
 3   Smileys require utf8mb4        (536D696C)
 4   ?                              (F09F90AC)
```

If you want to try the server-side variant, then you need to ensure the user has the FILE privilege:

```
mysql> GRANT FILE ON *.* TO pyuser@localhost;
Query OK, 0 rows affected (0.40 sec)
```

On the other hand, you no longer need to enable the allow_local_infile option. Additionally, you will have to remove the LOCAL keyword in the LOAD DATA INFILE statement and change the path to point to the location of the file server-side, for example:

```
LOAD DATA INFILE 'C:/MySQL/Files/testdata.txt'
    INTO TABLE world.loadtest
CHARACTER SET utf8mb4
  FIELDS TERMINATED BY ','
        OPTIONALLY ENCLOSED BY '"'
   LINES TERMINATED BY '\n'
  IGNORE 1 LINES
```

This concludes the tour of various non-trivial ways to execute queries. It is time to look at connection properties.

Connection Properties

There are several properties that provide information about the status of the connection or the behavior when executing queries. These properties range from setting the default database (schema) and character set for the queries to information on whether there are rows to be consumed, as discussed in the previous chapter. The properties are part of the connection object and are summarized in Table 4-1.

Table 4-1. *The Connection Properties*

Property	Type	Data Type	Description
autocommit	RW	Boolean	Whether the auto-commit mode is enabled for the connection. Using the property causes the SELECT @@session.autocommit query to be executed on the MySQL Server.
can_consume_results	RO	Boolean	Is True when results are automatically consumed if a new query is executed before the previous rows have been fetched. The corresponding connection configuration option is consume_results.
charset	RO	String	The character set used for the connection. Use the set_charset_collation() method to change the character set and/or collection used.
collation	RO	String	The collection used for the connection. Use the set_charset_collation() method to change the character set and/or collection used.
connection_id	RO	Integer	The connection ID assigned to the connection by MySQL Server. This property was used in Chapter 2 to verify the connection had been created.

(continued)

Table 4-1. (*continued*)

Property	Type	Data Type	Description
database	RW	String	The current default database (schema) for the connection or None if no default database is set. Referencing the property executes SELECT DATABASE() on the server. Setting the property executes the USE statement. Alternatively, the default database can be changed using the cmd_init_db() method.
get_warnings	RW	Boolean	Whether warnings are automatically retrieved when using a cursor.
in_transaction	RO	Boolean	Whether the connection is currently in a transaction.
python_charset	RO	String	The Python equivalent of the MySQL character set. The difference between the two is that the utf8mb4 and binary character sets are returned as utf8 in Python.
raise_on_warnings	RW	Boolean	Whether a warning is converted to an exception when using a cursor. When the value is changed, the value of get_warnings is automatically set to the same value as for raise_on_warnings.

(*continued*)

Table 4-1. (*continued*)

Property	Type	Data Type	Description
server_host	RO	String	The hostname used to connect to MySQL Server. The corresponding connection configuration option is host.
server_port	RO	Integer	The TCP/IP port used to connect to MySQL Server. The corresponding connection configuration option is port.
sql_mode	RW	String	The SQL mode currently in use. Reading the property causes the following query to be executed: SELECT @@session.sql_mode. Setting the SQL mode executes a SET statement. It is recommended to specify a new SQL mode using a list of modes from the SQLMode constants class. The returned value is a string with the values separated by commas.
time_zone	RW	String	The time zone used for the connection. This affects the values returned for timestamp data types. Reading the property executes the query SELECT @@session.time_zone. Assigning a new time zone executes a SET statement.

(*continued*)

Table 4-1. (*continued*)

Property	Type	Data Type	Description
unix_socket	RO	String	The path to the Unix socket used to connect to MySQL Server.
unread_result	RW	Boolean	Whether there are rows to be read from the previous query. **Warning:** Do not set this property. The write support is meant for cursors only.
user	RO	String	The user currently used for the connection. The cmd_change_user() method of the connection can be used to change the user, default schema, and character set.

The Type column specifies whether the property is read-only (RO) or it possible to both read and write to the property (RW). Some of the read-only options have a special method to change their value; when this is the case, the method is mentioned in the description. For example, the character set and collation-related properties can be updated through the set_charset_collation() method, as shown in Chapter 2. With the exception of the properties connection_id, in_transaction, python_charset, and unread_result, the properties can all be set when creating the configuration. The name of the configuration option is the same as the property name except where it is mentioned in the description.

The following sections will include examples of some of the properties. First, transactions will be discussed, including the relationship between the autocommit and in_transaction properties. Later sections will discuss specifying a default database and using time zones.

Transactions

Transactions are a very important concept when using databases. A transaction groups several queries together and ensures that all are either committed or rolled back. They also allow isolation so, for example, the changes made by one transaction will not be visible to other transactions until the changes have been committed.

TRANSACTIONS – WHAT IS ACID?

ACID stands for atomicity, consistency, isolation, and durability. Perhaps one of the most important concepts in database theory, it defines the behavior that database systems must exhibit to be considered reliable for transaction processing.

Atomicity means that the database must allow modifications of data on an "all or nothing" basis for transactions that contain multiple commands. That is, each transaction is atomic. If a command fails, the entire transaction fails, and all changes up to that point in the transaction are discarded. This is especially important for systems that operate in highly transactional environments, such as the financial market. Consider for a moment the ramifications of a money transfer. Typically, multiple steps are involved in debiting one account and crediting another. If the transaction fails after the debit step and doesn't credit the money back to the first account, the owner of that account will be very angry. In this case, the entire transaction from debit to credit must succeed, or none of it does.

Consistency means that only valid data will be stored in the database. That is, if a command in a transaction violates one of the consistency rules, the entire transaction is discarded, and the data is returned to the state they were in before the transaction began. Conversely, if a transaction completes successfully, it will alter the data in a manner that obeys the database consistency rules.

Isolation means that multiple transactions executing at the same time will not interfere with one another. This is where the true challenge of concurrency is most evident. Database systems must handle situations in which transactions cannot violate the data (alter, delete, etc.) being used in another transaction. There are many ways to handle this. Most systems use a mechanism called locking that keeps the data from being used by another transaction until the first one is done. Although the isolation property does not dictate which transaction is executed first, it does ensure they will not interfere with one another.

Durability means that no transaction will result in lost data nor will any data created or altered during the transaction be lost. Durability is usually provided by robust backup-and-restore maintenance functions. Some database systems use logging to ensure that any uncommitted data can be recovered on restart.[1]

There are two connection properties related to transactions. The `autocommit` option specifies whether transactions are committed automatically; the `in_transaction` property reflects whether the connection is in the middle of a transaction.

Note MySQL has two transactional storage engines: `InnoDB`, which is the default in MySQL Server, and `NDBCluster`, which is included with the MySQL Cluster product.

An example of the effect of the `autocommit` option can be seen from the example in Listing 4-10 where the value of the `in_transaction` property is examined with the `autocommit` property first disabled and then enabled.

---

[1]Thanks to Dr. Charles Bell for contributing this sidebar.

Listing 4-10. The Effect of the autocommit Property

```
import mysql.connector

# Create connection to MySQL
db = mysql.connector.connect(
  option_files="my.ini")
cursor = db.cursor()

# Initialize the stages (ordered)
stages = [
  "Initial",
  "After CREATE TABLE",
  "After INSERT",
  "After commit()",
  "After SELECT",
]

# Initialize dictionary with one list
# per stage to keep track of whether
# db.in_transaction is True or False
# at each stage.
in_trx = {stage: [] for stage in stages}

for autocommit in [False, True]:
  db.autocommit = autocommit;

  in_trx["Initial"].insert(
    autocommit, db.in_transaction)

  # Create a test table
  cursor.execute("""
CREATE TABLE world.t1 (
  id int unsigned NOT NULL PRIMARY KEY,
  val varchar(10)
)"""
  )
```

```
  in_trx["After CREATE TABLE"].insert(
    autocommit, db.in_transaction)

  # Insert a row
  cursor.execute("""
INSERT INTO world.t1
VALUES (1, 'abc')"""
  )

  in_trx["After INSERT"].insert(
    autocommit, db.in_transaction)

  # Commit the transaction
  db.commit()

  in_trx["After commit()"].insert(
    autocommit, db.in_transaction)

  # Select the row
  cursor.execute("SELECT * FROM world.t1")
  cursor.fetchall()

  in_trx["After SELECT"].insert(
    autocommit, db.in_transaction)

  # Commit the transaction
  db.commit()

  # Drop the test table
  cursor.execute("DROP TABLE world.t1")

cursor.close()
db.close()

fmt = "{0:18s}   {1:^8s}   {2:^7s}"
print("{0:18s}   {1:^18s}".format(
  "", "in_transaction"))
```

```
print(fmt.format(
  "Stage", "Disabled", "Enabled"))
print("-"*39)
for stage in stages:
  print(fmt.format(
    stage,
    "True" if in_trx[stage][0] else "False",
    "True" if in_trx[stage][1] else "False",
  ))
```

The main part of the example consists of a loop where the `autocommit` property is first disabled (the default) and then enabled. In the loop, a series of statements are executed:

1. A test table is created.

2. A row is inserted into the test table.

3. The `commit()` method is called.

4. The row is selected from the test table.

5. The `commit()` method is called.

6. The test table is dropped.

The value of the `in_transaction` is captured before the first step and after each of the first four steps. The output of the program is

```
                            in_transaction
Stage                   Disabled    Enabled
---------------------------------------------
Initial                 False       False
After CREATE TABLE      False       False
After INSERT            True        False
After commit()          False       False
After SELECT            True        False
```

In both iterations the initial value of in_transaction is False. The value stays False after creating the table; this is because MySQL does not support schema changes inside a transaction. It becomes more interesting after the INSERT and SELECT statements. When autocommit = False, in_transaction is True until commit() is called. When autocommit is enabled, there is never an ongoing transaction after the statement has finished executing.

This difference in behavior is important to be aware of when coding applications that use MySQL for the data storage. If autocommit is disabled, you must ensure you commit or roll back your transactions when you are done with them. Otherwise the changes will not be visible to other connections, locks will keep preventing other connections from making changes to the rows, and there will be a (potentially large) overhead for all connections because the storage engine must keep track of the various versions of the data. If autocommit is enabled, you must start an explicit transaction when you need to group multiple statements, so they behave as an atomic change.

Note   Data definition language (DDL) statements such as CREATE TABLE always perform an implicit commit if there is an ongoing transaction.

It is still possible to use multi-statement transactions even if autocommit is enabled. In that case, it is necessary to explicitly start a transaction and commit or rollback the transaction when the transaction has completed. There is no built-in support for savepoints (except when using the X DevAPI as discussed in Chapter 6). There are three methods to control transactions:

- `start_transaction()`: Starts a transaction. This is only required when `autocommit` is enabled. It is possible to set whether to start the transaction with a consistent snapshot, the transaction isolation level, and whether the transaction is read-only. The arguments will be discussed later.

- `commit()`: Commits an ongoing transaction. The method does not accept any arguments.

- `rollback()`: Rolls back an ongoing transaction. Like the `commit()` method, `rollback()` does not accept any arguments.

The `commit()` and `rollback()` methods work the same way irrespective of the value for the `autocommit` setting. The `start_transaction()` method is mostly used when `autocommit` is enabled; however, it can also be used with `autocommit` disabled to get better control of how the transaction behaves.

There are three optional arguments when starting a transaction:

- `consistent_snapshot`: Takes a Boolean value and specifies whether a consistent snapshot will be created at the time the `start_transaction()` method is called. The default is `False`, which means the snapshot (if the transaction isolation level is REPEATABLE READ) will be created when the first query is executed after the start of the transaction. Enabling `consistent_snapshot` is the same as using WITH CONSISTENT SNAPSHOT with the START TRANSACTION statement. Consistent snapshots are only supported by tables using the InnoDB storage engine.

- `isolation_level`: The transaction isolation level to use for the transaction. The default is REPEATABLE READ. Only InnoDB tables support setting the transaction isolation level. Note that for tables using the NDBCluster storage engine, the specified isolation level is ignored, and the READ COMMITTED transaction isolation level will always be used.

- `readonly`: If it is known that the transaction will never modify any data, the `readonly` argument can be set to allow InnoDB to optimize the transaction. The default is `False`.

Tip   For more information about transaction settings, see also the description for the SET TRANSACTION statement in the MySQL Server manual and references therein: `https://dev.mysql.com/doc/refman/en/set-transaction.html`. A detailed description of the transaction isolation levels can be found in `https://dev.mysql.com/doc/refman/en/innodb-transaction-isolation-levels.html`.

So, a transaction is started either implicitly by having `autocommit` disabled or by explicitly calling `start_transaction()`. In either case, the transaction is completed using either `commit()` to persist the changes and make them visible to other connections or `rollback()` to abandon the changes. The flow of a typical transaction can be seen in Figure 4-2.

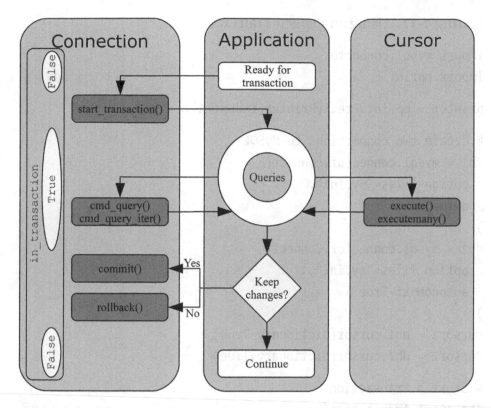

Figure 4-2. *The flow of a typical transaction*

The Boolean values in yellow (light grey) ellipsoids to the left in the connection are the value of the in_transaction property at the different stages. After the transaction starts, one or more queries are executed using either the connection object or a cursor (or a combination). Note that the status of the transaction is always a connection matter, but queries can be executed either in the connection itself or in a cursor.

An example of using an explicit transaction can be seen in Listing 4-11. In the example, a row is inserted into the world.city table and then selected again before the transaction is rolled back. To illustrate the difference between implicitly committed transactions and using an explicit transaction, autocommit is enabled for the connection and the in_transaction property is inspected between the INSERT and SELECT statements.

Listing 4-11. Using an Explicit Transaction

```
import mysql.connector
import pprint

printer = pprint.PrettyPrinter(indent=1)

# Create two connections to MySQL
db1 = mysql.connector.connect(
  option_files="my.ini",
  autocommit=True
)
db2 = mysql.connector.connect(
  option_files="my.ini",
  autocommit=True
)
cursor1 = db1.cursor(dictionary=True)
cursor2 = db2.cursor(dictionary=True)

# Start a transaction
db1.start_transaction()

# Insert a row
cursor1.execute("""
INSERT INTO world.city
VALUES (DEFAULT, 'Camelot', 'GBR',
        'King Arthur County', 2000)"""
)

print("\nin_transaction = {0}".format(
  db1.in_transaction))

id = cursor1.lastrowid
sql = """SELECT *
```

```
        FROM world.city
        WHERE id = {0}""".format(id)
cursor1.execute(sql)
cursor2.execute(sql)

# Fetch and print the rows
print("\nResult Set in Connection 1")
print("="*26)
result_set1 = cursor1.fetchall()
printer.pprint(result_set1)

print("\nResult Set in Connection 2")
print("="*26)
result_set2 = cursor2.fetchall()
printer.pprint(result_set2)

db1.rollback()
cursor1.close()
db1.close()

cursor2.close()
db2.close()
```

The program is quite straightforward. Two connections are created and then King Arthur's castle is inserted as a new city using the first of the connections. The world.city table has an auto-increment column as the primary key, so the first value is set to use the default (next available ID). The ID is retrieved from the lastrowid property of the cursor (or the insert_id element of the result dictionary of the INSERT statement if cmd_query() is used to insert the row), so it is possible to retrieve the row again using the primary key.

In-between the two statements, the value of in_transaction property is checked. Finally, the transaction is rolled back (and the inserted row is removed again). The second connection and cursor are used to query the same row from a separate connection. The output is similar to the following example (the ID will depend on how many rows have been inserted into the table, even if later rolled back):

```
Result Set in Connection 1
==========================
[{'CountryCode': 'GBR',
  'District': 'King Arthur County',
  'ID': 4080,
  'Name': 'Camelot',
  'Population': 2000}]

Result Set in Connection 2
==========================
[]
```

Notice how the second connection can't see the row. This is an example of how transactions provide isolation of the changes.

Tip   Unless there is a specific requirement to have `autocommit` disabled, it is often better to enable it. It makes it easier to see in the source code where multi-statement transactions are required, it saves round trips for the application with many one-statement transactions, and it allows InnoDB to automatically enable the read-only optimization for `SELECT` statements that do not use stored functions.

In the example, the table was referred to as `world.city`. That is, both the database name (`world`) and table name (`city`) were specified explicitly. It is possible to avoid specifying the database name every time by setting the default database. How to do this is discussed next.

MULTIPLE QUERY EXECUTION AND TRANSACTIONS

When autocommit is enabled, it is important to consider the impact of executing multiple statements in one cmd_query_iter(), execute(), or executemany() call. Except when multiple INSERT statements are rewritten to a single extended INSERT, each statement will be executed in its own transaction unless an explicit transaction is created. This is a fact that can easily be forgotten considering it is a single line of code.

To execute all of the queries in a single transaction, use the start_transaction() method of the connection to explicitly start a transaction:

```
import mysql.connector

# Create connection to MySQL
db = mysql.connector.connect(
  option_files="my.ini", autocommit=True)
cursor = db.cursor()

queries = [
  """UPDATE world.city
      SET Population = Population + 1
     WHERE ID = 130""",
  """UPDATE world.country
      SET Population = Population + 1
     WHERE Code = 'AUS'""",
]

db.start_transaction()
tests = cursor.execute(
  ";".join(queries), multi=True)
for test in tests:
  # Do something or pass if no action
  # is required.
  pass
db.rollback();
```

```
cursor.close()
db.close()
```

The example is also available in the Chapter_04/multi_stmt_ transaction.py file in the source code download for this book.

Default Database

In many applications, most or all queries are executed against tables in the same database. It may also be that the application can be used with several database names depending on the end user. An example is an online application that allows users to blog and the user can specify the name of the database where the tables for the installation are located. In such cases, it is convenient to be able to specify the database name in the configuration part of the application so all queries will be automatically executed against the configured database.

Note   In MySQL, *database* and *schema* are synonyms.

This is possible by setting the database option for the connection, either at the time the connection is created or by manipulating the property directly. An example of the use of a default database is shown in Listing 4-12.

Listing 4-12. Using a Default Database

```
import mysql.connector
from mysql.connector import errors

# Create connection to MySQL
db = mysql.connector.connect(
  option_files="my.ini",
  consume_results=True
)
```

```
# First query the city table without
# a default database
try:
  result = db.cmd_query(
    """SELECT *
        FROM city
        WHERE id = 130"""
  )
except errors.ProgrammingError as err:
  print(
    "1: Failed to execute query with "
    + "the error:\n   {0}".format(err)
  )
else:
  print("1: Query executed successfully")

# Then query the city table with
# a default database
db.database = "world"
try:
  result = db.cmd_query(
    """SELECT *
        FROM city
        WHERE id = 130"""
  )
except errors.ProgrammingError as err:
  print(
    "2: Failed to execute query with "
    + "the error:\n    {0}".format(err)
  )
else:
  print("2: Query executed successfully")

db.close()
```

The first query executes without having a default database configured. The result is that an exception occurs. After setting the default database to world, the second query succeeds. The output of executing the query is

```
1: Failed to execute query with the error:
   1046 (3D000): No database selected
2: Query executed successfully
```

Tip   It is also possible to change the default database using the cmd_init_db() connection method, for example cmd_init_db("world"). The difference is that setting the property executes a USE <database name> whereas cmd_init_db() sends a COM_INIT_DB command to MySQL Server. If you monitor MySQL using the Performance Schema, it makes a difference which method is used. The event name for USE is statement/sql/change_db and the statement is visible, whereas the event name is statement/com/Init DB for a COM_INIT_DB command.

This concludes the discussion about a default database, leaving one final topic related to connection properties to discuss: time zones.

Time Zones

Time zones are an important concept in the global world of today. Often it is desirable to display the time of an event in the user's local time zone, but this will be different for each user. This section will discuss how to use time zones in MySQL Connector/Python programs.

Before delving into the MySQL Connector/Python specifics of handling time zones, it is worth recapping how MySQL Server handles time zones. MySQL Server has two data types for handling values consisting both of a data and a time of day: datetime and timestamp. The datetime data type is used to store the date and time directly as it is given to MySQL; that is, the value is time zone-independent and the same value is always returned irrespective of the time zone. The timestamp data type provides a more compact storage format that always stores the value in UTC and returns the value according to the time zone set for the session. In neither case, a custom time zone is associated with the stored value. The two data types are summarized in Table 4-2.

Table 4-2. *MySQL Server Data Types Storing Both the Date and Time of Day*

Data Type	Time Zone Support	Date Range	Description
datetime	No	1000-01-01 to 9999-12-31	The data is stored as is. A workaround for the lack of time zone support is to explicitly convert the time to and from UTC when storing and reading it.
timestamp	Limited	1970-01-01 to 2038-01-19	The date and time (other than fractional seconds) are stored as an unsigned four-byte integer since the start of the Unix epoch time. The value is always stored in UTC using the session's time zone for the conversion.

In addition to the limited time zone support for the timestamp data type, there is the CONVERT_TZ() function (on the MySQL Server side; https://dev.mysql.com/doc/refman/en/date-and-time-functions. html#function_convert-tz). It takes a datetime value and converts it between two time zones. By default, there is support for time zones where the offset to UTC is specified explicitly (for example +10:00). Optionally, the time zone tables in the mysql database can be populated to add support for named time zones (such as Australia/Sydney). The named time zones also include information about changes to daylight saving time.

Tip   When using datetime columns, store the data in the UTC time zone and convert to the time zone required when using the data. By always storing the value in UTC, there is less chance of problems if the OS time zone or MySQL Server time zone is changed.

It can be a bit difficult to wrap one's head around time zones, so it is worth considering an example. Listing 4-13 is an example where the same value is inserted into a datetime and a timestamp column and then selected again using different time zone values. The time_zone property of the connection is used to change the time zone.

Listing 4-13. The Effect of the Time Zone

```
import mysql.connector
from datetime import datetime

# Create connection to MySQL
db = mysql.connector.connect(
  option_files="my.ini", use_pure=True)
cursor = db.cursor(named_tuple=True)
```

```
# Create a temporary table for this
# example
cursor.execute("""
  CREATE TEMPORARY TABLE world.t1 (
    id int unsigned NOT NULL,
    val_datetime datetime,
    val_timestamp timestamp,
    PRIMARY KEY (id)
  )""")

# Set the time zone to UTC
db.time_zone = "+00:00"

# Insert a date and time value:
#     2018-05-06 21:10:12
#     (May 6th 2018 09:10:12pm)
time = datetime(2018, 5, 6, 21, 10, 12)

# Definte the query template and the
# parameters to submit with it.
sql = """
INSERT INTO world.t1
VALUES (%s, %s, %s)"""

params = (1, time, time)

# Insert the row
cursor.execute(sql, params)

# Define output formats
# and print output header
fmt = "{0:9s}   {1:^19s}   {2:^19s}"
print(fmt.format(
  "Time Zone", "Datetime", "Timestamp"))
print("-"*53)
```

```python
# Retrieve the values using thee
# different time zones
sql = """
SELECT val_datetime, val_timestamp
  FROM world.t1
 WHERE id = 1"""

for tz in ("+00:00", "-05:00", "+10:00"):
  db.time_zone = tz
  cursor.execute(sql)
  row = cursor.fetchone()
  print(fmt.format(
    "UTC" + ("" if tz == "+00:00" else tz),
    row.val_datetime.isoformat(" "),
    row.val_timestamp.isoformat(" ")
  ))

# Use the CONVERT_TZ() function to
# convert the time zone of the datetime
# value
sql = """
SELECT CONVERT_TZ(
         val_datetime,
         '+00:00',
         '+10:00'
       ) val_utc
  FROM world.t1
 WHERE id = 1"""
cursor.execute(sql)
row = cursor.fetchone()
```

```
print("\ndatetime in UTC+10:00: {0}".format(
  row.val_utc.isoformat(" ")))

cursor.close()
db.close()
```

The date time value for May 5th, 2018 at 09:10:12pm is inserted into a temporary table with both a `datetime` and `timestamp` column. The time zone is set to UTC using the connection `time_zone` property when the row is inserted. The `datetime` and `timestamp` values are then selected with three different time zones set, and the `datetime` value is converted to UTC+10 using the `CONVERT_TZ()` function. The output is

```
Time Zone        Datetime              Timestamp
--------------------------------------------------------------
UTC              2018-05-06 21:10:12    2018-05-06 21:10:12
UTC-05:00        2018-05-06 21:10:12    2018-05-06 16:10:12
UTC+10:00        2018-05-06 21:10:12    2018-05-07 07:10:12

datetime in UTC+10:00: 2018-05-07 07:10:12
```

The value printed for the `datetime` column is always the same irrespective of the time zone. However, for the `timestamp` column, the value returned depends on the time zone. Only when the time zone is the same at the time of selecting the data as when the data was inserted is the returned `timestamp` value the same as what was inserted. So, when using `timestamp` columns, it is important to keep the time zone in mind.

Tip   For more information about MySQL time zone support and how to add the named time zones, see `https://dev.mysql.com/doc/refman/en/time-zone-support.html`.

This is the final example that involves the properties of the connection. There are several other utility methods, some of which will be discussed in the next section.

Other Connection Utility Methods

The connection object has several methods that can be used for a range of tasks such as checking whether the connection is still available, resetting the connection, and getting information about the server to which the application is connected. This section will briefly discuss the most useful utility methods.

Note   For a complete list of methods, see `https://dev.mysql.`
`com/doc/connector-python/en/connector-python-api-`
`mysqlconnection.html`.

The utility methods that will be discussed are summarized in Table 4-3. The scope of the methods is one of Connection and Server. The connection methods affect the connection or perform tests for the connection. The server methods can be used to get information about MySQL Server.

Table 4-3. *Some Useful Connection Utility Methods*

Method	Scope	Description
cmd_change_ user()	Connection	Changes the user as well as the database and character set related options.
cmd_reset_ connection()	Connection	Resets the user variables and session variables for the connection. Only works for MySQL Server 5.7 and later and is only available when using the pure Python implementation.
is_ connected()	Connection	Returns True if the connection is still connected to MySQL Server.
ping()	Connection	Verifies whether the connection is still available by pinging MySQL Server. Can optionally attempt to reconnect.
reset_ session()	Connection	Resets the user variables and session variables for the connection. Works for all MySQL Server versions and allows setting user and session variables after the reset.
cmd_ statistics()	Server	Returns a dictionary with statistics for the MySQL Server.
get_server_ info()	Server	Returns the MySQL Server version as a string. This includes any version suffixes such as "rc" that may apply. If there is no suffix, it indicates a GA release. Examples are "8.0.4-rc-log" and "8.0.11".
get_server_ version()	Server	Returns the MySQL Server version as a tuple of integers. Version suffixes are not included.

These methods will be discussed in the following subsections.

Connection Methods

The connection methods can be used to perform various actions to either affect the connection or to check whether the connection is still alive. The methods will be discussed in alphabetical order, except the reset_ session() method, which will be discussed together with cmd_reset_ connection().

cmd_change_user( )

The cmd_change_user() method can be used to change which user is used for the connection, the default database, the character set, and collation. All of the arguments are optional; arguments that are not set use their default value. The arguments and their default values are summarized in Table 4-4.

Table 4-4. *The Arguments for cmd_change_user( )*

Argument	Default Value	Description
username	(Empty string)	The username to connect with.
password	(Empty string)	The password to authenticate with.
database	(Empty string)	The new default database.
charset	45	The character set and collation. The value of 33 corresponds to the utf8mb4 (the 4-byte implementation) with the utf8mb4_general_ci collation. In MySQL Connector/Python 8.0.11 and earlier the default is 33 (utf8 - the 3-byte implementation - with the utf8_general_ci collation).

Notice that the username is specified with the username argument rather than the usual user argument. Additionally, the character set is set using the internal character set ID, which is an integer and also includes which collation is used. The character set ID can be found as the first element in the tuple returned by the CharacterSet.get_charset_info() method in the mysql.connector.constants module.

Tip If the goal is just to change the default database and/or the character set and collation, use the dedicated methods for those tasks. The default database can be changed by setting the database property or calling the cmd_init_db() method, as discussed earlier in the chapter. The character set and collation can be changed using the set_charset_collation() method, as discussed in Chapter 2.

An example of changing the user to become the root (administrator) user while setting the default database to world, the character set to utf8mb4, and the collation to utf8mb4_0900_ai_ci is

```
import mysql.connector
from mysql.connector.constants import CharacterSet

db = mysql.connector.connect(
  option_files="my.ini")

charset = CharacterSet.get_charset_info(
  "utf8mb4", "utf8mb4_0900_ai_ci")
db.cmd_change_user(
  username="root",
  password="password",
  database="world",
  charset=charset[0]
)

db.close()
```

Caution   This example hard codes the password to keep the example simple. Do not do so in actual programs because it lets too many people know the password and makes the code harder to maintain.

---

cmd_reset_connection() and reset_session( )

The cmd_reset_connection() is a lightweight method to unset all user variables (e.g. @my_user_variable) for the connection and ensure all session variables (e.g. @@session.sort_buffer_size) are reset to the global defaults. The method is lightweight because it does not require reauthenticating. The method does not take any arguments and only works in MySQL 5.7 and later when using the pure Python implementation. An example is

```
import mysql.connector

db = mysql.connector.connect(
  option_files="my.ini", use_pure=True)

db.cmd_reset_connection()

db.close()
```

The reset_session() method is related (and uses cmd_reset_connection() under the hood) but allows you to set user and session variables after the reset. Another advantage of reset_connection() is that it works with all versions of MySQL Server and with the C Extension implementation. For server versions that support cmd_reset_connection(), this is used to avoid reauthenticating; for older server versions, reset_session() falls back on the more expensive reauthentication approach. An example of using reset_connection() is

```
import mysql.connector

db = mysql.connector.connect(
  option_files="my.ini")

user_variables = {
  "employee_id": 1,
  "name": "Jane Doe",
}
session_variables = {
  "sort_buffer_size": 32*1024,
  "max_execution_time": 2,
}
db.reset_session(
  user_variables=user_variables,
  session_variables=session_variables
)

db.close()
```

This sets the @employee_id and @name user variables to the values of 1 and Jane Doe, respectively. The session uses a sort buffer that is at most 32kiB large and SELECT queries are not allowed to take longer than two seconds. Both arguments are optional and default to setting no variables.

is_connected( )

The is_connected() method checks whether the connection is still connected to the database. It returns True or False, with True meaning the connection is still working. A simple example of using the method is

```
import mysql.connector

db = mysql.connector.connect(
  option_files="my.ini")
```

```
if (db.is_connected()):
  print("Is connected")
else:
  print("Connection lost")

db.close()
```

A related method is ping().

ping( )

The ping() method is similar to is_connected(). In fact, the ping() and is_connected() methods both use the same underlying (internal) method to verify whether the connection is available. There are a couple of differences, however.

Whereas the is_connected() method returns False if the connection is not available, ping() triggers an InterfaceError exception. Another difference is that the ping() method supports waiting for the connection to become available. It supports the arguments in Table 4-5.

Table 4-5. *The Arguments Supported by* ping()

Argument	Default Value	Description
reconnect	False	Whether to attempt to reconnect if the connection is not available.
attempts	1	The maximum number of times to try reconnecting. Use a negative value to try an infinite number of times.
Delay	0	The delay in seconds between completing the previous reconnection attempt and trying the next. As the connection attempt itself takes time, the total time per attempt will be larger than the value specified.

An example of pinging for the connection to become available again with at most five attempts to reconnect and each attempt separated by one second is

```
import mysql.connector
from mysql.connector import errors

db = mysql.connector.connect(
  option_files="my.ini")

try:
  input("Hit Enter to continue.")
except SyntaxError:
  pass

try:
  db.ping(reconnect=True, attempts=5, delay=1)
except errors.InterfaceError as err:
  print(err)
else:
  print("Reconnected")
db.close()
```

The input() function allows you to shut down MySQL before proceeding to pinging the server. If MySQL Server becomes available again before the attempts are exhausted, *Reconnected* is printed. Otherwise, an InterfaceError exception occurs after some time when five attempts to reconnect have been exhausted, for example:

```
Can not reconnect to MySQL after 5 attempt(s): 2003 (HY000):
Can't connect to MySQL server on '127.0.0.1' (10061)
```

The message tells the number of attempts made and the reason the connection failed. The details will depend on the platform, whether the C Extension is used, and why MySQL Connector/Python cannot connect.

This is the last connection-related utility method that will be discussed. However, there are some methods related to the server that are worth discussing.

Server Information Methods

There are three methods to obtain statistics about the server or the server version. The information can also be obtained through normal SQL statements, but the dedicated methods can be useful because they require less parsing.

The cmd_statistics() method returns a dictionary with a few metrics about the operation of the server, for example the number of times the tables have been flushed, the number of questions (queries) asked, and the uptime.

The get_server_info() method returns the server version as a string. This can be useful if the application logs the version of the database it is connected to.

The last method is get_server_version(), which returns the server version as a tuple with each of the three components as an element. This can be useful, for example, when verifying whether the server is new enough to have a certain feature.

The following code example demonstrates how the three methods can be used:

```
import mysql.connector
import pprint

# Print the result dictionary
printer = pprint.PrettyPrinter(indent=1)

# Create connection to MySQL
db = mysql.connector.connect(
  option_files="my.ini")
```

```
print("cmd_statistics\n" + "="*14)
statistics = db.cmd_statistics()
printer.pprint(statistics)

print("\nget_server_info\n" + "="*15)
server_info = db.get_server_info()
printer.pprint(server_info)

print("\nget_server_version\n" + "="*18)
server_version = db.get_server_version()
printer.pprint(server_version)
if (server_version >= (8, 0, 2)):
  print("Supports window functions")

db.close()
```

The output depends on how long it has been since MySQL Server was started, the workload on the instance, and the MySQL Server version. An example of the output generated by the code is

```
cmd_statistics
==============
{'Flush tables': 2,
 'Open tables': 66,
 'Opens': 90,
 'Queries per second avg': Decimal('0.034'),
 'Questions': 71,
 'Slow queries': 0,
 'Threads': 2,
 'Uptime': 2046}

get_server_info
===============
'8.0.11'
```

```
get_server_version
==================
(8, 0, 11)
Supports window functions
```

A related topic is the metadata that is available for the columns returned in SELECT and SHOW statements. This is the next topic to explore.

Column Information

When a query that asks for data to be returned, typically a SELECT statement, is executed, the dictionary returned by the connection cmd_query() method includes details about each of the columns in the result set. When a cursor is used, the description property includes the same information. You have already seen examples of using the column information when converting the results to Python types. Much of the information is not trivial to use, so this section will look into how the information can be easily converted into a more accessible format.

The column information for a row in the world.city table using the pure Python implementation is

```
[('ID', 3, None, None, None, None, 0, 16899),
 ('Name', 254, None, None, None, None, 0, 1),
 ('CountryCode', 254, None, None, None, None, 0, 16393),
 ('District', 254, None, None, None, None, 0, 1),
 ('Population', 3, None, None, None, None, 0, 1)]
```

The information is a list with one tuple per column. There are eight elements of each the tuple:

- The name of the column

- The field type (this is an integer)

- The display size

- The internal size

- The precision of the column

- The scale of the column

- Whether the column values can be NULL (0 is used for False, 1 for True)

- MySQL-specific flags specified as an integer

The display size, internal size, precision of the column, and the scale of the column are always set to None. As you can see from the example output, the column name is easy to use, but the field type and the MySQL-specific flags need mappings. The rest of the section will discuss how to convert the field type and the flags into names.

Field Types

The field type integers originate from MySQL Server and are defined in the source code (the include/mysql.h.pp file in the MySQL Server 8.0 source code). MySQL Connector/Python includes the FieldType.get_info() function (in the constants.py file) to convert the types to human-readable names. The example in Listing 4-14 shows how the integer field types can be mapped into names.

Listing 4-14. Mapping the Field Types

```
import mysql.connector
from mysql.connector import FieldType

# Create connection to MySQL
db = mysql.connector.connect(
  option_files="my.ini")
cursor = db.cursor()
```

```python
# Create a test table
cursor.execute(
  """CREATE TEMPORARY TABLE world.t1 (
    id int unsigned NOT NULL PRIMARY KEY,
    val1 tinyint,
    val2 bigint,
    val3 decimal(10,3),
    val4 text,
    val5 varchar(10),
    val6 char(10)
  )"""
)

# Select all columns (no rows returned)
cursor.execute("SELECT * FROM world.t1")

# Print the field type for each column
print("{0:6s}    {1}".format(
  "Column", "Field Type"))
print("=" * 25);
for column in cursor.description:
  print("{0:6s}    {1:3d} - {2}".format(
    column[0],
    column[1],
    FieldType.get_info(column[1])
  ))

# Consume the (non-existing) rows
cursor.fetchall()

cursor.close
db.close()
```

After the connection is made, the temporary table world.t1 is created. The table has seven columns of various data types. Next, a SELECT query is executed to get the result dictionary including the column information. The dictionary is used to print the field type both as an integer and as a string. The output of executing the code is

```
Column    Field Type
===========================
id           3 - LONG
val1         1 - TINY
val2         8 - LONGLONG
val3       246 - NEWDECIMAL
val4       252 - BLOB
val5       253 - VAR_STRING
val6       254 - STRING
```

MySQL Column Flags

The other piece of information available that can be converted into names is the MySQL column flags (also called field flags). The column flags are defined in MySQL Server in the include/mysql_com.h header file in the source. The information included in the flag includes whether the column is a primary key, whether it allows NULL values, etc. The latter is how the "allow NULL" value in the column description is derived (from protocol.py in the MySQL Connector/Python installation):

```
~flags & FieldFlag.NOT_NULL,  # null_ok
```

As the definition shows, the column flags are defined in the FieldFlag class in constants.py and they can be used with the bitwise and operator (&) to check whether a given flag is set. Unlike the columns types, there is no readymade function to get the flags for a given column, so it is necessary to determine the flags yourself. Listing 4-15 shows an example of how to do this.

Listing 4-15. Checking Whether Field Flags Are Set for a Column

```
def get_column_flags(column_info):
  """Returns a dictionary with a
  dictionary for each flag set for a
  column. The dictionary key is the
  flag name. The flag name, the flag
  numeric value and the description of
  the flag is included in the flag
  dictionary.
  """
  from mysql.connector import FieldFlag

  flags = {}
  desc = FieldFlag.desc
  for name in FieldFlag.desc:
    (value, description) = desc[name]
    if (column_info[7] & value):
      flags[name] = {
        "name": name,
        "value": value,
        "description": description
      }

  return flags

# Main program
import mysql.connector

# Create connection to MySQL
db = mysql.connector.connect(
  option_files="my.ini")
cursor = db.cursor()
```

```
# Create a test table
cursor.execute("""
CREATE TEMPORARY TABLE world.t1 (
  id int unsigned NOT NULL auto_increment,
  val1 bigint,
  val2 varchar(10),
  val3 varchar(10) NOT NULL,
  val4 varchar(10),
  val5 varchar(10),
  PRIMARY KEY(id),
  UNIQUE KEY (val1),
  INDEX (val2),
  INDEX (val3, val4)
)"""
)

# Select all columns (no rows returned)
cursor.execute("SELECT * FROM world.t1")

# Print the field type for each column
print("{0:6s}    {1}".format(
  "Column", "Field Flags"))
print("=" * 74);
all_flags = {}
for column in cursor.description:
  flags = get_column_flags(column)

  # Add the flags to the list of
  # all flags, so the description
  # can be printed later
  # for flag_name in flags:
  all_flags.update(flags)
```

```python
    # Print the flag names sorted
    # alphabetically
    print("{0:6s}    {1}".format(
      column[0],
      ", ".join(sorted(flags))
    ))

print("")

# Print description of the flags that
# were found
print("{0:18s}    {1}".format(
  "Flag Name", "Description"))
print("=" * 53);
for flag_name in sorted(all_flags):
  print("{0:18s}    {1}".format(
    flag_name,
    all_flags[flag_name]["description"]
  ))

# Consume the (non-existing) rows
cursor.fetchall()

cursor.close
db.close()
```

The most interesting part of the program is the get_column_flags() function. The function loops over all known flags and uses the bitwise and operator to check whether the flag is set. FieldFlag.desc is a dictionary with the flag name as the key. For each flag there is a tuple with the number value as the first element and a description and the second element. The FieldFlag class also has a constant with the name the same as the flag name, for example FieldFlag.PRI_KEY for the "is part of the primary key" flag.

The flag names are printed in alphabetical order for each column, and at the end the description is printed for each flag that has been used. The output from MySQL 8.0.11 using the C Extension is

```
Column   Field Flags
================================================================
id       AUTO_INCREMENT, GROUP, NOT_NULL, NUM, PART_KEY,
         PRI_KEY, UNSIGNED
val1     GROUP, NUM, PART_KEY, UNIQUE_KEY
val2     GROUP, MULTIPLE_KEY, NUM
val3     GROUP, MULTIPLE_KEY, NOT_NULL, NO_DEFAULT_VALUE, NUM
val4     GROUP, NUM
val5

Flag Name               Description
================================================================
AUTO_INCREMENT          field is a autoincrement field
GROUP                   Intern: Group field
MULTIPLE_KEY            Field is part of a key
NOT_NULL                Field can't be NULL
NO_DEFAULT_VALUE        Field doesn't have default value
NUM                     Field is num (for clients)
PART_KEY                Intern; Part of some key
PRI_KEY                 Field is part of a primary key
UNIQUE_KEY              Field is part of a unique key
UNSIGNED                Field is unsigned
```

The PART_KEY flag is only included when the C Extension implementation is used.

This concludes the discussion of the column information. There is one remaining topic: the MySQL Connector/Python C Extension.

The C Extension

Thus far, most examples have not specified whether to use the implementation of MySQL Connector/Python written purely in Python or the one using the C Extension. While the pure Python implementation has advantages such as being able to easily look at the code executed by the connector, it has some disadvantages with respect to performance. To overcome that, there is the MySQL Connector/Python C Extension.

Depending on the platform and how MySQL Connector/Python has been installed, the C Extension may or may not have been included automatically. For example, on Windows using MySQL Installer and the latest supported Python version, it is included, but using RPM packages on Red Hat Enterprise Linux (RHEL) or Oracle Linux requires an extra RPM package to be installed.

The main benefit of using the C Extension is performance. There are particularly two use cases where the C Extension can be beneficial compared to the pure Python implementation:

- Handling large result sets

- Using prepared statements, particularly if a large amount of data needs to be transferred

The C Extension provides an interface from the Python part of the connector to the MySQL C client library. For queries returning large result sets, it is an advantage to handle the memory-intensive parts in a C library. Additionally, the MySQL C client library has the advantage that is supports prepared statements implemented using the binary protocol.

Tip   In most cases, it is recommended to enable the C Extension for anything but simple scripts. That said, the pure Python implementation can be useful for debugging programs.

There are two ways to switch to the C Extension:

- **The `mysql.connector.connect()` function**: Call the function with the use_pure connection option set to `False`. This is the default in MySQL Connector/Python 8.0.11 and later. An advantage is that the API stays the same.

- **The `_mysql_connector` module**: Import the _mysql_ connector module instead of `mysql.connector`. The advantage is that the C Extension API is used directly, thus removing the overhead of the wrapper methods. The disadvantage is that the API is different.

Tip   Using the `mysql.connector.connect()` function is the simplest way to use the C Extension. On the other hand, using the `_mysql_connector` module can give better performance.

The rest of this section provides an example of using each of the two methods to access the C Extension.

The mysql.connector.connect( ) Function

The simplest way to get to use the C Extension is to use the `mysql.connector.connect()` function. All that is required if you have an existing MySQL Connector/Python application is to change how the connection is created.

Caution   While there are in general only small differences between the pure Python and C Extension implementation when using the `mysql.connector` module, you must do exhaustive testing if you change the implementation used for an existing application. This includes upgrading to MySQL Connector/Python version 8.0 from an earlier version.

Listing 4-16 shows how to use the C Extension. Once the connection is created, a query is executed and the result is printed.

Listing 4-16. Using the C Extension by Setting use_pure = False

```
import mysql.connector

# Create connection to MySQL
db = mysql.connector.connect(
  option_files="my.ini",
  use_pure=False
)

# Instantiate the cursor
cursor = db.cursor(dictionary=True)

# Execute the query
cursor.execute(
  """SELECT Name, CountryCode,
             Population
       FROM world.city
      WHERE Population > 9000000
      ORDER BY Population DESC"""
)

print(__file__ + " - Setting use_pure = False:")
print("")
if (cursor.with_rows):
  # Print the rows found
  print(
    "{0:15s}   {1:7s}   {2:3s}".format(
      "City", "Country", "Pop"
    )
  )
```

```
city = cursor.fetchone()
while (city):
  print(
    "{0:15s}   {1:^7s}    {2:4.1f}".format(
      city["Name"],
      city["CountryCode"],
      city["Population"]/1000000.0
    )
  )
  city = cursor.fetchone()
cursor.close()
db.close()
```

There is just one difference compared with similar previous programs where the default implementation was used: the use_pure variable is set to False to request the C Extension. The output of the program is

```
listing_4_16.py - Setting use_pure = False:
```

City	Country	Pop
Mumbai (Bombay)	IND	10.5
Seoul	KOR	10.0
São Paulo	BRA	10.0
Shanghai	CHN	9.7
Jakarta	IDN	9.6
Karachi	PAK	9.3

Note   Remember that when the C Extension is used, the mysql.
connector.connect() function must be used to create the
connection. The reason is that the decision of whether to use the C
Extension or not decides which connection class to instantiate.

If it is attempted to pass use_pure as an option to either of the CMySQLConnection() or MySQLConnection() classes or their connect() methods, an attribute error occurs:

```
AttributeError: Unsupported argument 'use_pure'
```

The _mysql_connector Module

The alternative way to use the C Extension is to explicitly import the _mysql_connector module. When the _mysql_connector module is used directly, the usage is similar to using the C client library. So, if you are used to writing C programs that use MySQL, this will be familiar, although not identical. Listing 4-17 shows the equivalent of the preceding example, but this time using the _mysql_connector module.

Listing 4-17. Using the C Extension by Importing the _mysql_ connector Module

```
import _mysql_connector

# Create connection to MySQL
connect_args = {
  "host": "127.0.0.1",
  "port": 3306,
  "user": "pyuser",
  "password": "Py@pp4Demo",
};

db = _mysql_connector.MySQL()
db.connect(**connect_args)
charset_mysql = "utf8mb4"
charset_python = "utf-8"
db.set_character_set(charset_mysql)
```

```
# Execute the query
db.query(
  """SELECT Name, CountryCode,
           Population
       FROM world.city
      WHERE Population > 9000000
      ORDER BY Population DESC"""
)

print(__file__ + " - Using _mysql_connector:")
print("")
if (db.have_result_set):
  # Print the rows found
  print(
    "{0:15s}   {1:7s}   {2:3s}".format(
      "City", "Country", "Pop"
    )
  )
  city = db.fetch_row()
  while (city):
    print(
      "{0:15s}   {1:^7s}   {2:4.1f}".format(
        city[0].decode(charset_python),
        city[1].decode(charset_python),
        city[2]/1000000.0
      )
    )
    city = db.fetch_row()

db.free_result()
db.close()
```

The first thing to notice is that unlike the other examples in this chapter, the connection arguments are not read from a configuration file. The support for reading the options from a configuration file is a feature of the Python part of MySQL Connector/Python and thus not supported when _mysql_connector module is used directly.

The second thing is that the character set is set explicitly, and it is necessary to set the character set using the set_character_set() method. The reason is that the connect() method only supports a subset of the connection options that MySQL Connector/Python otherwise supports. The rest of the options must be set using dedicated methods such as the set_character_set() method.

The third thing is that using the methods of the _mysql_connector. MySQL class is similar to using the connection methods (like cmd_query()) for executing the query and handling the result set. However, the method names are different. With this, it is also necessary to handle the result values explicitly. The string values are returned as bytes, though the population is returned as an integer.

The fourth thing is that it is necessary to free the result using the free_result() method, when the program is done handling the result. This is also similar to using the C client library.

The output of the program is

```
listing_4_17.py - Using _mysql_connector:
```

City	Country	Pop
Mumbai (Bombay)	IND	10.5
Seoul	KOR	10.0
São Paulo	BRA	10.0
Shanghai	CHN	9.7
Jakarta	IDN	9.6
Karachi	PAK	9.3

> **Tip**   The `_mysql_connector` module will not be discussed in any more detail. For the full documentation of the C Extension API, see `https://dev.mysql.com/doc/connector-python/en/connector-python-cext-reference.html`.

Summary

This chapter covered several features of query execution and the connection object in MySQL Connector/Python. It began by looking at executing multiple queries in a single API call, including handling multiple result sets and using extended inserts. Additionally, the use of buffered results, calling stored procedures, and loading data from CSV files were discussed.

The second half the chapter focused on connection properties, transactions, setting the default database, and time zones. The chapter ended with a discussion of the C Extension. The C Extension is recommended for most cases. When enabling the C Extension by setting `use_pure = False` in the `mysql.connector.connect()` function, the API is the same as for the pure Python implementation, making it relatively simple to change between the two implementations.

It is time to take a break from the focus on queries and take a look at advanced connection features such as connection pools and failover configuration.

CHAPTER 5

Connection Pooling and Failover

In the two previous chapters, you went through the workings of MySQL Connector/Python from a query point of view. It is time to change the topic a bit and look at some of the more advanced connection features: connection pooling and failover.

Tip There are several example programs in this chapter. All example programs that appear in a listing are available for download. See the discussion of example programs in Chapter 1 for more information about using the example programs.

Connection Pooling – Background

Connection pooling makes it possible to have a number of connections that the application can draw on for its queries. This is useful in multi-threaded applications, where queries end up being executed in parallel. By using a pool, it is possible to control the number of concurrent connections and it reduces the overhead because it is not necessary to create a new connection for each task.

© Jesper Wisborg Krogh 2018
J. W. Krogh, *MySQL Connector/Python Revealed*,
https://doi.org/10.1007/978-1-4842-3694-9_5

While creating a connection in MySQL is relatively fast, particularly for applications doing many quick queries and if the network to MySQL is stable, using persistent connections can save enough time to make it worthwhile to implement a connection pool. On the other hand, if you are writing a program for the Internet of Things (IoT) with an unstable network connection and the program will only execute a few queries each minute, it is better to create a new connection each time.

There are two classes used with a connection pool. The classes are

- `pooling.MySQLConnectionPool`

- `pooling.PooledMySQLConnection`

This section will look at the two classes, their methods, and properties. The next section will discuss the more practical side of connection pools.

Note   It is not possible to use the C Extension with a connection pool. The `use_pure` option will be ignored when calling the `mysql.connector.connect()` function with a combination of connection pool settings and `use_pure`.

The pooling.MySQLConnectionPool Class

The `pooling.MySQLConnectionPool` class is the main class defining the pool. This is the class where connections are added, configured, and retrieved when the application needs to execute a query.

In addition to the constructor, there are three methods and one property that are used with the `pooling.MySQLConnectionPool` class. They are summarized in Table 5-1.

Table 5-1. *Summary of the* pooling.MySQLConnectionPool *Class*

Name	Type	Description
MySQLConnectionPool	Constructor	The constructor for creating a connection pool.
add_connection()	Method	Adds or returns a connection to the pool (i.e. increases the number of connections in the pool with one).
get_connection()	Method	Fetches a connection from the pool.
set_config()	Method	Configures the connections in the pool.
pool_name	Property	The name of the pool. This can be set when instantiating the pool.

A connection pool is first created by invoking the constructor. This can either happen directly or indirectly through the mysql.connector. connect() function. When the application needs a connection, it can fetch one by calling the get_connection() method.

Caution   The add_connection() method is used internally to return a connection to the pool. It can also be called externally with a connection of the MySQLConnection class. (Connections using the C Extension are not supported.) However, adding a new connection to the pool does not actually increase the size of the pool. So, the result is that all of the connections can no longer be returned to the pool, and a PoolError exception with the error "Failed adding connection; queue is full" is returned.

If necessary, the configurations can be reconfigured using the set_config() method. Unlike standalone connections, like those used in the previous chapters, the configuration cannot be changed directly for the connection. If that was possible, it would no longer be guaranteed that all connections in the pool were identically configured. Since it is not known by the application which connection is returned, it would be very unfortunate if the configuration differed from connection to connection. If you need connections with different configurations, create one pool per configuration.

Tip   It is possible to have more than one pool. This can, for example, be used to have different connection configurations available. One use case is for read-write splitting, so writes go to a replication master (source) and reads to a replication slave (replica).

There is no official method to disconnect the connections in the pool. The constructor and methods will be discussed in more detail when they are used in the examples later in this section. However, first let's look at the other half using connection pools: the connections.

The pooling.PooledMySQLConnection Class

The connections retrieved from a connection pool are instances of the pooling.PooledMySQLConnection class rather than the MySQLConnection or the CMySQLConnection classes. In most aspects, a pooled connection behaves the same way as a standalone connection, but there are a couple of differences.

The two most important differences are that the close() and config() methods have been changed. The close() method does not actually close a pooled connection, but rather returns it to the pool. Since all connections in the pool must have the same configuration, the config() method will return a PoolError exception.

In addition to the changed behavior of the close() and config() methods, there is the pool_name property. This is the same as for the pooling.MySQLConnectionPool class and can be used to confirm which pool the connection is from. This can be useful where a connection is passed to another function or method.

Configuration Options

The configuration of a connection pool is controlled by three options, which all have the prefix pool_. These options allow you to set the name and size, and control whether the connection is reset when returned to the pool. The options are summarized in Table 5-2. It is not possible to change any of the settings after the pool has been created.

Table 5-2. *Options for Configuring a Connection Pool*

Name	Default Value	Description
pool_name	Auto generated	The name of a connection pool. By default, the name is generated by joining the values of the host, port, user, and database connection options. The name can be at most pooling.CNX_POOL_MAXNAMESIZE (defaults to 64) characters long and is allowed to use alphanumeric characters as well as the following characters: ., _, :, -, *, $, and #.
pool_reset_session	True	When True, the session variables are reset when the connection is returned to the pool.
pool_size	5	The number of connections to hold in the pool. The value must be at least 1 and at most pooling.CNX_POOL_MAXSIZE (defaulting to 32).

All connection pools have a name. If a name is not explicitly set when creating the pool, a name will be automatically generated by joining the values of the host, port, user, and database connection options. If neither of the options is set in the keyword arguments, an PoolError exception is raised. Options set through an option file are not considered when generating the name.

Tip   It is recommended to explicitly configure the pool name. This ensures that changes to the configuration do not change the pool name. If you have multiple pools, give them unique names to avoid confusion. Remember that even if the pool name is not used in your current code, it may be required later.

The pool_reset_session option controls whether the session variables are reset when a connection is returned to the pool. Resetting means unsetting all user variables (e.g. @my_user_variable) and ensuring all session variables (e.g. @@session.sort_buffer_size) have the same value as the global default. There are two limitations to resetting the connection in MySQL Server 5.6 and earlier:

- The reset is done by reconnecting.

- Compression (the compress option) is not supported.

In most cases, it is recommended to reset the connection because it ensures that the state of the connection is always the same when it is fetched from the pool.

Tip   Unless there is an explicit requirement to keep the state of the connections, always use pool_reset_session = True (the default) to ensure that the state of the connections is known when fetching them from the pool.

The number of connections in the pool is specified using the `pool_size` option. The default is to create the pool with five connections, but it is possible to have up to `pooling.CNX_POOL_MAXSIZE` connections. The `pooling.CNX_POOL_MAXSIZE` property defaults to 32.

In addition to the three connection pool options, the other connections options required for the connections must be specified in the same way as for standalone connections. The non-pool-related options can also be set for the connections in an existing pool by using the `set_config()` method, which works in the same way as the `config()` method for a standalone connection. The next section includes an example of using the `set_config()` method.

Now that the basics of the two connection pool classes and the configuration have been discussed, let's find out how to use them.

Using Connection Pools

It is finally time to be more practical and start using connection pools. This section will first show how to create a connection pool and then show examples of fetching and returning connections. The second half of the section will discuss query execution and reconfiguration of the connections when using a connection pool.

Creating a Connection Pool

When using connection pools, the first step is to create the pool. As mentioned, there are two different ways to create a pool: it can be done implicitly or explicitly.

To implicitly create a connection pool, use the `mysql.connector.connect()` function as for creating standalone connections. Whenever at least one of the connection pool options are present, a pool will be created if no pool with the same name already exists and a connection of the pooling.PooledMySQLConnection class is returned. If a pool with the same pool name exists, a connection from that pool is returned. An example is

```
import mysql.connector

db = mysql.connector.connect(
  option_files="my.ini",
  pool_name="test_connect",
)

print("Pool name: {0}".format(db.pool_name))
```

The advantage of the indirect method is that it is more similar to creating standalone connections. The disadvantage is that it that you have less control of the pool compared to using the pooling.MySQLConnectionP ool class.

The alternative is to create a connection pool explicitly by instantiating the pooling.MySQLConnectionPool class, for example:

```
from mysql.connector import pooling

pool = pooling.MySQLConnectionPool(
  option_files="my.ini",
  pool_name="test_constructor",
)

print("Pool name: {0}".format(pool.pool_name))
```

The advantage of creating a pool this way is that it gives access to reconfiguring the connections.

When invoking the pooling.MySQLConnectionPool constructor directly, all of the connection pool options are optional. If the pool is created using the mysql.connector.connect() function, at least one of the options must be specified.

Once the connection pool has been created, connections can be retrieved from the pool and returned to the pool. Let's look at how that is done.

Using Connection Pool Connections

Obviously, the main purpose of a connection pool is to have connections available for use. So, let's look a bit more into retrieving and returning connections as well as how to use them.

The way a connection is fetched depends on how the pool was created. For a pool created using the mysql.connector.connect() function, connections are retrieved using the mysql.connector.connect() function again with the same pool name as when the pool was created. On the other hand, for pools created explicitly by invoking the pooling.MySQLConnecti onPool constructor, connections are fetched using the get_connection() method.

Caution   Do not attempt to mix the two ways of fetching connections. If the mysql.connector.connect() function is used with the same pool name as for a pool created using the constructor, a second pool is created.

Using the mysql.connector.connect() Function

When the pool is created using the mysql.connector.connect() function, the first connection is returned immediately and additional connections are fetched invoking the function again with the same pool name. Any options passed to mysql.connector.connect() other than the pool_name option are ignored.

Figure 5-1 shows the general workflow when using a connection pool with two connections and a pool created with the mysql.connector.connect() function.

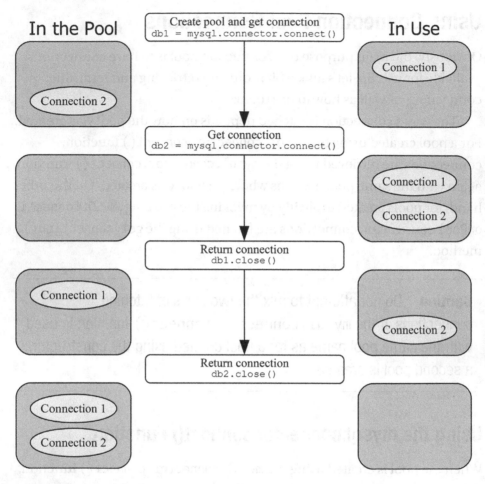

Figure 5-1. *The workflow when using the* `mysql.connector.`
`connect()` *function*

In the middle of the figure are the commands executed in the
application. A connection pool with two connections is created at the start.
A connection can either be in the pool awaiting the application to fetch it
(the connections to the left) or in use in the application (the connections
to the right).

You can see that the steps of creating the pool and fetching the first connection out the pool are combined into one call to the `mysql.connector.connect()` function. Subsequent connections can be fetched in the same way. Once the application is done with the connection, it is returned to the pool by closing it. The connection can be reused if needed by fetching it from the pool again (not shown in the figure).

Listing 5-1 shows an example of using the `mysql.connector.connect()` function to manage a connection pool.

Listing 5-1. Managing a Connection Pool with `mysql.connector.connect()`

```python
import mysql.connector
from mysql.connector.errors import PoolError

print(__file__ + " - connect():")
print("")

# Create a pool and return the first
# connection
db1 = mysql.connector.connect(
  option_files="my.ini",
  pool_size=2,
  pool_name="test",
)

# Get a second connection in the same pool
db2 = mysql.connector.connect(
  pool_name="test")

# Attempt to get a third one
try:
  db3 = mysql.connector.connect(
    pool_name="test")
```

```
except PoolError as err:
  print("Unable to fetch connection:\n{0}\n"
    .format(err))

# Save the connection id of db1 and
# return it to the pool, then try
# fetching db3 again.
db1_connection_id = db1.connection_id
db1.close()

db3 = mysql.connector.connect(
  pool_name="test")

print("Connection IDs:\n")
print("db1   db2   db3")
print("-"*15)
print("{0:3d}   {1:3d}   {2:3d}".format(
    db1_connection_id,
    db2.connection_id,
    db3.connection_id
  )
)

db2.close()
db3.close()
```

Initially a connection is fetched in the same way as for a standalone connection. The only difference is that the connection pool is enabled by setting at least one of the connection pool options; in this case, both the pool_size and pool_name options are set. The connection is an instance of the pooling.PooledMySQLConnection class.

The db2 connection is fetched in a similar way. The pool_name option is the only thing set here, and it is the only required option. However, it is fine to keep the original options if that makes the code easier to write; any extra options are simply ignored, provided they are valid options, when fetching additional connections from the pool.

234

When a third connection is attempted, a `PoolError` exception occurs. The exception has been imported from `mysql.connector.errors` near the top of the example. The exception occurs because the pool has been exhausted. Returning the db1 connection to the pool allows you to get db3. Finally, the three connection IDs are printed:

```
listing_5_1.py - connect():
```

```
Unable to fetch connection:
Failed getting connection; pool exhausted
```

```
Connection IDs:
```

```
db1   db2   db3
---------------
324   325   324
```

The actual IDs will differ from the example output because they depend on how many connections have been made since MySQL was last restarted. The important thing is that the output confirms that db3 ends up with the connection ID previously used by db1.

Using the get_connection() Method

The code used when working directly with the connection pool is somewhat different from using the `mysql.connector.connect()` function; however, the functionality is essentially the same. A connection is fetched with the `get_connection()` method. The returned connection is an instance of the `pooling.PooledMySQLConnection` class just as when using the `mysql.connector.connect()` function. Figure 5-2 shows the basic workflow for a pool with two connections.

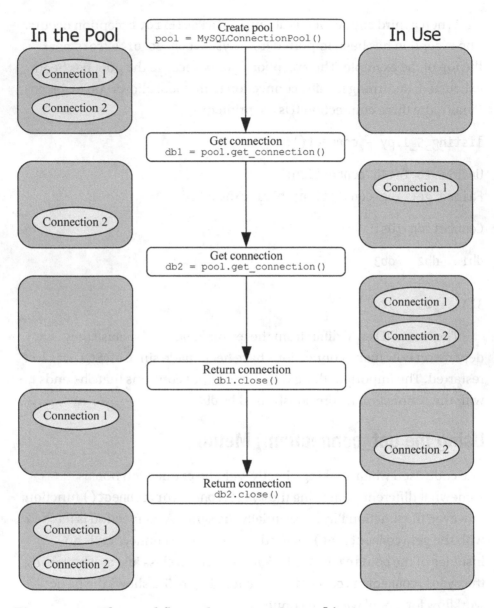

Figure 5-2. *The workflow when using the pooling.*
MySQLConnectionPool class

The connection pool with two connections is created explicitly using the pooling.MySQLConnectionPool constructor pooling.MySQLConnectionPool:constructor. Initially both connections are in the pool. Each time a connection is needed by the application, it is fetched using the get_connection() method of the pool object. Once the application is done with the connection, it is returned to the pool by closing it. The equivalent of the previous example can be seen in Listing 5-2.

Listing 5-2. Managing a Connection Pool Using the pool Object Directly

```
from mysql.connector import pooling
from mysql.connector import errors

print(__file__ + " - MySQLConnectionPool():")
print("")

pool = pooling.MySQLConnectionPool(
  option_files="my.ini",
  pool_name="test",
  pool_size=2,
)

# Fetch the first connection
db1 = pool.get_connection()

# Get a second connection in the same pool
db2 = pool.get_connection()

# Attempt to get a third one
try:
  db3 = pool.get_connection()
except errors.PoolError as err:
  print("Unable to fetch connection:\n{0}\n"
    .format(err))
```

```
# Save the connection id of db1 and
# return it to the pool, then try
# fetching db3 again.
db1_connection_id = db1.connection_id
db1.close()

db3 = pool.get_connection()

print("Connection IDs:\n")
print("db1    db2    db3")
print("-"*15)
print("{0:3d}    {1:3d}    {2:3d}".format(
    db1_connection_id,
    db2.connection_id,
    db3.connection_id
  )
)

db2.close()
db3.close()
```

The connection pool is created explicitly and the connections are retrieved using the get_connection() method of the pool object, but otherwise the example is identical to the one using the mysql.connector. connect() function. When the pool is exhausted and a connection is attempted, a PoolError exception occurs again, and connections are returned to the pool using the close() method of the connection object.

The output is similar to the output when the mysql.connector. connect() function was used to create the pool. Again, the actual IDs will differ. An example output is

```
listing_5_2.py - MySQLConnectionPool():
```

Unable to fetch connection:
Failed getting connection; pool exhausted

Connection IDs:

```
db1    db2    db3
---------------
350    351    350
```

Now that you know how to create and return connections, let's move on to what is ultimately the most important purpose of connections: to execute queries.

Executing Queries

Creating connection pools and fetching and returning the connection can be fun to play with, but a connection that is not used for queries is not worth much. While the connection is out of the pool, it can be used like any regular connection, except that the config() method does not work and the close() method returns the connection to the pool rather than closing the connection.

In order to execute queries, all of the other features discussed in Chapter 3 and Chapter 4 can be used (except the C Extension). Listing 5-3 shows an example of executing a simple SELECT query using a cursor.

Listing 5-3. Executing a Query in a Connection Pool Connection

```
from mysql.connector import pooling
pool = pooling.MySQLConnectionPool(
  option_files="my.ini",
  pool_name="test",
)
```

```python
db = pool.get_connection()

cursor = db.cursor(named_tuple=True)
cursor.execute("""
SELECT Name, CountryCode, Population
  FROM world.city
 WHERE CountryCode = %s""", ("AUS",))

if (cursor.with_rows):
  # Print the rows found
  print(
    "{0:15s}   {1:7s}   {2:10s}".format(
      "City", "Country", "Population"
    )
  )
  city = cursor.fetchone()
  while (city):
    print(
      "{0:15s}   {1:^7s}   {2:8d}".format(
        city.Name,
        city.CountryCode,
        city.Population
      )
    )
    city = cursor.fetchone()
cursor.close()
db.close()
```

The program is straightforward. After the connection has been created, a connection is fetched. The query is executing in a cursor using named tuples. When the query result has been handled, the cursor is closed, and the connection is returned to the pool. As you can see, there is nothing special in the example compared with the queries in the previous chapters, other than the fact that the connection came out of a pool. The output of executing the program is

City	Country	Population
Sydney	AUS	3276207
Melbourne	AUS	2865329
Brisbane	AUS	1291117
Perth	AUS	1096829
Adelaide	AUS	978100
Canberra	AUS	322723
Gold Coast	AUS	311932
Newcastle	AUS	270324
Central Coast	AUS	227657
Wollongong	AUS	219761
Hobart	AUS	126118
Geelong	AUS	125382
Townsville	AUS	109914
Cairns	AUS	92273

The final thing to consider for connection pools is how to reconfigure the connections in the pool and the impact it has on the connections.

Reconfiguring the Connections

When you use a standalone connection like in Chapters 3 and 4, the concept of reconfiguring it is simple. The reconfiguration happens in the same execution flow as where the connection is used for queries. It is different, however, for pooled connections because some connections will be in the pool and others will be outside doing work. Changing the configuration for a connection used somewhere else in the application can cause undefined behavior and can cause queries to suddenly be executed as another user or on another MySQL Server instance than expected.

The way MySQL Connector/Python handles a reconfiguration request is that for a given connection it is only reconfigured when it is inside the pool. For connections in use at the time of the reconfiguration request, the change to the configuration is postponed until it is returned to the pool.

Listing 5-4 shows an example of reconfiguring the connections in a connection pool with two connections. One of the connections (db1) is outside the pool at the time of the call to set_config(), whereas the other (db2) is inside the pool.

Listing 5-4. Using the set_config() Method

```python
from mysql.connector import pooling

pool = pooling.MySQLConnectionPool(
  option_files="my.ini",
  pool_name="test",
  pool_size=2,
)

print("{0:18s}: {1:3s}   {2:3s}".format(
  "Stage", "db1", "db2"
))
print("-"*29)
fmt = "{0:18s}: {1:3d}   {2:3d}"
db1 = pool.get_connection()
db2 = pool.get_connection()
print(
  fmt.format(
    "Initially",
    db1.connection_id,
    db2.connection_id
  )
)
```

```
# Return one of the connections before
# the reconfiguration
db2.close()

# Reconfigure the connections
pool.set_config(user="pyuser")

# Fetch db2 again
db2 = pool.get_connection()
print(
  fmt.format(
    "After set_config()",
    db1.connection_id,
    db2.connection_id
  )
)

# Return the db1 connection to the pool
# and refetch it.
db1.close()
db1 = pool.get_connection()
print(
  fmt.format(
    "After refetching",
    db1.connection_id,
    db2.connection_id
  )
)

db1.close()
db2.close()
```

A connection pool is first created. Two connections are then retrieved (exhausting the pool) and the connection IDs are printed. The db2 connection is returned before the reconfiguration, whereas db1 stays in use. After reconfiguring the connection, the connection IDs are printed again. In this case, there is not actually any change to the configuration, but that does not affect how MySQL Connector/Python behaves. Finally, the db1 connection is returned to the pool and retrieved again, and the connection ID is printed a last time. The output is similar to

```
Stage             : db1   db2
------------------------------
Initially         : 369   370
After set_config(): 369   371
After refetching  : 372   371
```

A change in connection ID means the old connection was closed, the connection configuration was updated, and the connection reestablished. You can see from the output that the connection ID of the db1 connection does not change by the call to set_config(). Connections already fetched from the pool will not have the configuration updated until it is returned to the pool. Connections sitting in the pool, like the one used with db2, will be updated immediately. After the db1 connection goes back in the pool and is fetched again, the connection ID is changed, reflecting the reconnect that happened when the configuration was updated.

This concludes the discussion of connection pools. There is another advanced topic for connections: failover configuration. It will be the final topic of the chapter.

Connection Failover

Many applications today need to be available 24x7. However, it is still necessary to be able to perform maintenance on the database backend, for example in order to upgrade the operating system or MySQL Server.

There may also be an outage due to hardware issues or a problem with the database. How is the application going to stay online when the database instance is not available? The answer is to perform a failover to another MySQL Server instance with the same data.

There are several ways to implement high availability for an application. This is a large and interesting topic and many books have been written about it. So, it is not possible to discuss it in detail in this book. One option, however, is directly related to MySQL Connector/Python: the possibility of the connector to automatically fail over when the primary database is not available.

This section will go through how the built-in failover in MySQL Connector/Python works. The first topic is configuration, then how to use failover in the application code, and finally there will be an example.

Note It can be easy to think that all that is required to implement failover is to configure it. However, for the failover to work properly, the application must be coded with failovers in mind. There will be more information in the "Coding for Failover" section.

Failover Configuration

Configuring the application to use the failover feature in MySQL Connector/Python is the simplest part of using failover. There is just one option to consider: the `failover` option.

The `failover` option takes a tuple (or list) with a dictionary for each MySQL Server instance to consider when creating a connection. The dictionaries must have the connection options that are unique for that instance. Common connection options can be set as normal. If an option is specified both in the argument list to the `mysql.connector.connect()` function and in a `failover` dictionary, the value in the `failover` dictionary takes precedence.

The `failover` option supports a subset of the connection options. Only the options that are directly related to specifying where to connect to, which user, and connection pool options are allowed. The complete list of supported options is

- user
- password
- host
- port
- unix_socket
- database
- pool_name
- pool_size

In general, it is preferable to keep the options as similar as possible for all of the MySQL Server instances because it reduces the chance of ending up with errors that are hard to debug. For example, if the user name is different, it increases the possibility that a change to the privileges ends up being different between the instances.

An example of creating a connection with failover is

```python
import mysql.connector

primary_args = {
    "host": "192.168.56.10",
}
failover_args = {
    "host": "192.168.56.11",
}
```

```
db = mysql.connector.connect(
  option_files="my.ini",
  failover=(
    primary_args,
    failover_args,
  )
)
```

In this example, the standard my.ini file is used to set the common options for the two instances. The only option set in the failover option is the host for each of the instances. MySQL Connector/Python will try to connect to the instances in the order they are listed, so the first one listed will be the primary instance and the second one the failover instance. It is possible to add more instances if required.

Note   The order in which the MySQL Server instances are added to the failover tuple matters. MySQL Connector/Python will try to connect to the instances in order starting with the first one listed.

The only time the instances listed in the failover option are considered is when a new connection is requested. That is, if first a connection is created successfully and it only fails later, MySQL Connector/Python will not automatically reconnect, neither to the old instance nor one of the other instances. The detection of a failed connection and establishing a new connection must be explicitly coded in the application. Similarly, the application must handle the case when it has run out of instances to connect to.

Coding for Failover

As mentioned, the hard part of working with failover is to make the application work with them. MySQL Connector/Python provides the framework to connect to the first available instance, but it is up to the application to ensure it is used to improve the availability.

When a connection fails, MySQL Connector/Python will never reconnect automatically. This is the case irrespective of whether the connection was made with or without the `failover` option. The reason for this is that it is in general not safe to just reconnect and continue as if nothing happened. For example, the application may be in the middle of a transaction when the disconnect happens, in which case it will be necessary to go back to the start of the transaction.

This means that the developer must check for errors when using a connector. Error handling in general is a topic of Chapter 9. With respect to failover, the important thing is to check whether it is really a connection error; otherwise, there is little point in initializing a failover. Some common possibilities of connection errors that can occur after the connection has been created are listed in Table 5-3.

Table 5-3. *Common Connection-Related Errors*

Errno	Errno – Define Symbol	Error Message
(None)	(None)	MySQL Connection not available
1053	ER_SERVER_SHUTDOWN	Server shutdown in progress
2005	CR_SERVER_LOST_EXTENDED	Lost connection to MySQL server at '...', system error: ...
2006	CR_SERVER_GONE_ERROR	MySQL server has gone away
2013	CR_SERVER_LOST	Lost connection to MySQL server during query

The error "MySQL Connection not available" occurs when it is attempted to use the connection in a non-query manner, for example when creating a cursor after the connection has been lost. When the error number is available, it can be found in the errno property of the exception. The define symbols are available in the mysql.connector.errorcode module and can be used to make it easier to see which error the error number is compared against.

If there are several application instances that all use the same MySQL Server instances and they write to the database, it is also important to ensure that either none of the application instances fail over or all do. If some application instances end up writing to one database instance and other application instances to another database instance, the data can end up being inconsistent. In a case with multiple application instances, it may be better to implement failover using a proxy such as MySQL Router or ProxySQL that directs connections to the correct MySQL Server instance.

Tip   To avoid inconsistent data, make sure that failover MySQL instances have the super_read_only option set until they are meant to accept writes. The super_read_only option is available in MySQL Server 5.7 and later. Earlier versions only offer the weaker read_only option that does not block a user with the SUPER privilege from writing to the instance.

Testing is also more important than normal when failover is involved. Ensure you test various failure conditions including forcefully killing MySQL Server while the application is executing queries and introducing network failures. Additionally, add some failures that should not result in a failover, such as lock wait timeouts. This is the only way to verify that the application is able to handle failures correctly.

To round up the discussion of using the failover feature, let's look at an example that incorporates some of the things discussed so far.

Failover Example

It can be hard to wrap your head around all of the things that must be considered in an application that uses failover. Hopefully an example will help make things clearer.

For the example to work, there must be two MySQL Server instances. In a real-world application, it's normal to have the database instances on different hosts, so it is possible to fail over even if the whole host is shut down. However, for this example, it is fine to have two instances on the same host using different TCP ports, paths to the data directory (the `datadir` options) and other database-specific files, and on Linux and Unix different Unix socket paths (the `socket` option).

Tip   There are different options for running multiple instances on one machine depending on your operating system and how you have installed MySQL. See `https://dev.mysql.com/doc/refman/en/multiple-servers.html` and references therein for instructions both for Microsoft Windows and Unix/Linux. If you are using systemd to manage MySQL on Linux, see also `https://dev.mysql.com/doc/refman/en/using-systemd.html`.

The example assumes both instances are on the local host (`127.0.0.1`) with the primary instance using port 3306 (as in all the previous examples) and the failover instance using port 3307. See Listing 5-5.

Listing 5-5. Using the Failover Feature

```
import mysql.connector
from mysql.connector import errorcode
from mysql.connector import errors
```

```python
def connect():
    """Connect to MySQL Server and return
    the connection object."""
    primary_args = {
        "host": "127.0.0.1",
        "port": 3306,
    }
    failover_args = {
        "host": "127.0.0.1",
        "port": 3307,
    }
    db = mysql.connector.connect(
        option_files="my.ini",
        use_pure=True,
        failover=(
            primary_args,
            failover_args,
        )
    )
    return db

def execute(db, wait_for_failure=False):
    """Execute the query and print
    the result."""
    sql = """
SELECT @@global.hostname AS Hostname,
       @@global.port AS Port"""

    retry = False
    try:
        cursor = db.cursor(named_tuple=True)
```

```
  except errors.OperationalError as err:
    print("Failed to create the cursor."
      + " Error:\n{0}\n".format(err))
    retry = True
  else:
    if (wait_for_failure):
      try:
        input("Shut down primary now to"
          + " fail when executing query."
          + "\nHit Enter to continue.")
      except SyntaxError:
        pass
      print("")

    try:
      cursor.execute(sql)
    except errors.InterfaceError as err:
      print("Failed to execute query"
        + " (InterfaceError)."
        + " Error:\n{0}\n".format(err))
      retry = (err.errno == errorcode.CR_SERVER_LOST)
    except errors.OperationalError as err:
      print("Failed to execute query"
        + " (OperationalError)."
        + " Error:\n{0}\n".format(err))
      retry = (err.errno == errorcode.CR_SERVER_LOST_EXTENDED)
    else:
      print("Result of query:")
      print(cursor.fetchall())
    finally:
      cursor.close()

  return retry
```

```
# Execute for the first time This should
# be against the primary instance
db = connect()
retry = True
while retry:
  retry = execute(db)
  if retry:
    # Reconnect
    db = connect()
print("")

# Wait for the primary instance to
# shut down.
try:
  input("Shut down primary now to fail"
      + " when creating cursor."
      + "\nHit Enter to continue.")
except SyntaxError:
  pass
print("")

# Attempt to execute again
retry = True
allow_failure = True
while retry:
  retry = execute(db, allow_failure)
  allow_failure = False
  if retry:
    # Reconnect
    db = connect()
db.close()
```

The connection is created in the connect() function. The main reason for putting this into its own function is that it is necessary to explicitly reconnect when a failure happens, so it is convenient to have the connection-related code isolated and reusable.

This is also the reason for the execute() function that creates a cursor and executes a query to get the hostname and port of the MySQL Server instance the program is connected to. The execution code includes try statements to test whether the operations succeeded and, if not, whether the query should be retried after a reconnect (and possible failover).

The example assumes both the primary and failover MySQL Server instances are available at the start. When the connection is first created, it will be against the primary instance because it is listed first in the failover option. Once the query against the primary instance has completed, the execution will pause, making it possible to shut down the primary instance if the failure should happen when the next cursor is created.

When the execution continues (after pressing *Enter*), the query will be attempted again. If the primary instance has been shut down, creating the cursor will fail and the error will be printed. Otherwise, a new pause will be created because wait_for_failover is set to True the first time the execute() function is called in the second round. If the primary instance is shut down at this time, the error will occur when trying to execute the actual query. In that case, the error number is compared to what is expected to make sure it is indeed a connection issue that caused the failure.

When the connection failure has been detected, the code will attempt to reconnect. This time mysql.connector.connect() will fail over to the failover instance. It is then possible to execute the query.

The output when the failure happens when the cursor is created is

```
Result of query:
[Row(Hostname='MY-COMPUTER', Port=3306)]

Shut down primary now to fail when creating cursor.
Hit Enter to continue.
```

```
Failed to create the cursor. Error:
MySQL Connection not available.
```

```
Result of query:
[Row(Hostname='MY-COMPUTER', Port=3307)]
```

The error received is an OperationalError exception with no error number. Notice how the port number changed after the connection failure, showing that the program is now connected to the failover instance.

The second case where the error occurs when attempting to execute the query has different exceptions and errors depending on the platform. On Microsoft Windows, the output is

```
Result of query:
[Row(Hostname='MY-COMPUTER', Port=3306)]
```

```
Shut down primary now to fail when creating cursor.
Hit Enter to continue.
```

```
Shut down primary now to fail when executing query.
Hit Enter to continue.
```

```
Failed to execute query (OperationalError). Error:
2055: Lost connection to MySQL server at '127.0.0.1:3306',
system error: 10053 An established connection was aborted by
the software in your host machine
```

```
Result of query:
[Row(Hostname='MY-COMPUTER', Port=3307)]
```

Here is another OperationalError exception, but with the error number set to 2055. On Linux, the error is

```
Failed to execute query (InterfaceError). Error:
2013: Lost connection to MySQL server during query
```

So, on Linux it is an `InterfaceError` exception with error number 2013. This shows that the details of the failure can depend on the platform as well. It can also depend on whether the pure Python implementation or the C Extension is used, so that must also be taken into account when coding.

Summary

In this chapter, you looked at two advanced connection features: connection pools and failover. They are not commonly used but can be useful for some applications.

The connection pool feature makes it possible for an application to retrieve connections out of the pool. This is particularly useful for multi-threaded applications where the pool can be used to reduce overhead and to limit the concurrency with which queries are executed.

The failover function makes MySQL Connector/Python go through each configured connection in turn to find the first one available. This can help improve availability, but it also requires additional work in the application. It is possible to combine the connection pool and failover features.

Except for error handling and troubleshooting (Chapter 9 and Chapter 10), this concludes the discussion of the traditional MySQL Connector/Python. In the next three chapters, you will look at how the X DevAPI that is exclusive to MySQL Connector/Python 8.0 can be used to work with MySQL Server as a document store.

PART III

The X DevAPI

CHAPTER 6

The X DevAPI

MySQL Server was originally released as an SQL database in 1995. SQL statements executed as shown in Chapters 2 and 3 are still by far the most common way to execute queries in MySQL, and the `mysql.connector` module uses the traditional protocol. There is, however, another way: the new X Protocol.

This chapter will start out with a brief introduction to the X Plugin (the back end) and the X DevAPI (the API used by the application) and the features in-between. The rest of the chapter will focus on the parts of the MySQL Connector/Python implementation of the X DevAPI that are common among the three main parts of the API: the MySQL Document Store, the create-read-update-delete (CRUD) interface to SQL tables, and SQL statements. This includes how to create a connection, common argument types, statement classes, and the result objects.

The next two chapters will go into detail on the rest of the API. Chapter 7 will show how to use the MySQL Document Store. Chapter 8 will show how to use the X DevAPI with SQL tables via the CRUD NoSQL methods and SQL statements. Error handling and troubleshooting are deferred until Chapters 9 and 10.

© Jesper Wisborg Krogh 2018
J. W. Krogh, *MySQL Connector/Python Revealed*,
https://doi.org/10.1007/978-1-4842-3694-9_6

Tip The MySQL X DevAPI is very new; it became GA with MySQL 8.0. This means that new features are still being worked on at a relative fast pace. If you can't find a certain feature, check the online API documentation at `https://dev.mysql.com/doc/dev/ connector-python/8.0/` to see if the feature has been added. You can also request new features at `https://bugs.mysql.com/`.

WHAT IS NOSQL?

There is no one definition of NoSQL that everyone agrees on. Does "No" mean "no, SQL is not used to define queries at all" or does "No" mean "not only?" Does "SQL" refer to the language used to write queries or to relational databases? Even within NoSQL there are large differences between the available products. Some are key-value stores, some store documents such as JSON documents, etc. In other words, it's not clear cut what NoSQL is, but one common thing is that you query the data using API methods rather than SQL statements.

Considering NoSQL from the MySQL point of view, using MySQL as a relational database and writing queries using the Structured Query Language (SQL) such as `SELET * FROM world.city` means it is clearly in the SQL regime. On the other hand, using the MySQL Document Store (storing data in JSON documents) and querying the data using the methods of the X DevAPI (the programming language features) to define the queries means it is in the NoSQL regime.

However, there is a grey zone in-between. The X DevAPI also supports querying SQL (relational) tables without writing SQL queries, and you can query a document in the Document Store using SQL statements. Whether these uses should be considered NoSQL or not can be discussed. In that sense, you can say that MySQL 8.0 with the Document Store and the X DevAPI is a "not only SQL" database.

The MySQL X Plugin

In MySQL Server 5.7.12, the MySQL X Plugin was introduced as a beta feature. It has since been given time to mature and is GA in MySQL Server 8.0. The X Plugin allows you to use MySQL using NoSQL in a similar way to other document stores in addition to traditional SQL statements.

There are several parts to the X Plugin to handle the various levels where it used. The parts are

- **The X Plugin**: This is the server-side implementation of the features. In MySQL 8.0.11 and later, it is a built-in plugin, so no actions are required to enable it.

- **The X Protocol**: The new protocol used for an application to communicate with the X Plugin. The default TCP port for the X Protocol is port 33060.

- **The X DevAPI**: This is the new API for use with the X Protocol.

- **The mysqlx Module**: The MySQL Connector/Python module with the implementation of the X DevAPI.

Additionally, there is the concept of the MySQL Document Store, which is the X Plugin, the X Protocol, the X DevAPI, and MySQL Shell (discussed shortly) together.

In order to be able to use the X Plugin, a new API named the X DevAPI was developed. It is available for several programming languages including Python, JavaScript (Node.js), PHP, .Net, C++, and Java. MySQL Shell is a new command-line client that to some extend can replace the traditional mysql command-line client. It supports the X DevAPI and can be used to execute queries using SQL statements, Python, and JavaScript. Additionally, MySQL Shell can be used to manage MySQL InnoDB Cluster using Python or JavaScript.

Communication between applications and the Document Store is done using the X Protocol. Because it is a new protocol compared to the traditional MySQL protocol, the Document Store uses its own port. The default port number is 33060; this can be changed using the `mysqlx_port` option.

The server-side part of the X DevAPI is implemented as a plugin to MySQL Server. The plugin is named the X Plugin. It is enabled by default in MySQL Server 8.0.11 and later; in fact, it has become a built-in plugin that cannot be removed, so it will always be present. The X Plugin is also available for older releases of MySQL; however, changes were made up to the time of 8.0.11 when MySQL 8.0 became generally available. So, make sure you are using MySQL 8.0.11 or later.

You can confirm that the plugin is active by querying the `PLUGINS` view in the `information_schema` database:

```
mysql> SELECT *
        FROM information_schema.PLUGINS
        WHERE PLUGIN_NAME = 'mysqlx'\G
*************************** 1. row ***************************
          PLUGIN_NAME: mysqlx
       PLUGIN_VERSION: 1.0
        PLUGIN_STATUS: ACTIVE
          PLUGIN_TYPE: DAEMON
  PLUGIN_TYPE_VERSION: 80011.0
       PLUGIN_LIBRARY: NULL
PLUGIN_LIBRARY_VERSION: NULL
        PLUGIN_AUTHOR: Oracle Corp
   PLUGIN_DESCRIPTION: X Plugin for MySQL
       PLUGIN_LICENSE: GPL
          LOAD_OPTION: ON
1 row in set (0.00 sec)
```

Notice here that the `PLUGIN_STATUS` is `ACTIVE`. If that is not the case, the most likely cause is that the X Plugin was disabled explicitly in the

MySQL configuration file (`my.ini` on Microsoft Windows, `my.cnf` on other platforms). Look for an option like

```
[mysqld]
mysqlx = 0
```

Instead of `mysqlx = 0`, you may also see `skip-mysqlx`. Remove this option, comment it out, or change it to `mysqlx = 1`. Since the X Plugin is enabled by default, the recommended way is to remove or comment it out.

You will learn some of the characteristics of the X features in this and the next two chapters. However, before you can start using the X DevAPI, you need a high-level overview of the `mysqlx` module.

The mysqlx Module

The X DevAPI support in Connector/Python is in its own separate module compared to the rest of MySQL Connector/Python. The module is called `mysqlx`. There are significant differences between the names and in the general use of the `mysqlx` module and the mysql.connector module. This may seem strange, but part of the idea of the X DevAPI is to have a relatively uniform API across the supported languages. This means if you are accustomed to using the X DevAPI in MySQL Connector/Python, it is easy to implement another project using, for example, MySQL Connector/Node.js.[1]

In order to get started using the X DevAPI for Python, you must import the `mysqlx` module:

```
import mysqlx
```

That's it. The next step is to create a session but let's first take a look at Figure 6-1, which shows how the `mysqlx` module is organized with respect to the classes that will be used in the remainder of the X DevAPI discussion.

---

[1]That said, each language keeps its characteristics, for example, with respect to naming conventions and whether setter and getter methods are used versus properties. So, there are some differences.

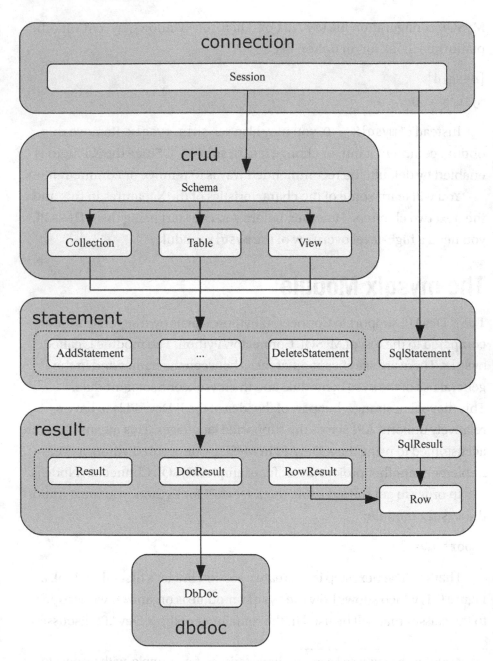

Figure 6-1. *The organization of the* `mysqlx` *module*

The classes are shown as the smaller yellow (light grey) boxes. The larger boxes surrounding the classes are the sub-module in which the class is located. For example, the Session class is located in mysqlx.connection.

Figure 6-1 also shows the general flow of the code execution. You start out with a session and can from the session object get a schema object to use with CRUD statements or an SQL statement. The flow for SQL statements is simple because that results in an SQL result which may returns rows.

The CRUD schema objects include collections, tables, and views. Collections are used with the Document Store whereas tables and views are used with SQL tables. The CRUD objects can be used to create a CRUD statement. These are the statements in the statement sub-module; in total, eight CRUD statement classes will be discussed. (The "..."-statement represents those classes not included in the figure.)

The CRUD statements end up with a "plain" result for queries without a result set. Statements that return data end with a document result for collections or a row result for SQL tables and views. A document result returns the data as DbDoc objects and a row result returns Row objects.

Feel free to return to this overview as you work through all of the parts. Before continuing to create a session let's discuss how commands are executed and the support for chaining them.

There are essentially two different ways to implement a series of commands: one line of code for each method and execute() (required for statements that have been defined and are ready for execution), or chaining the method calls. Consider a find statement where you want to define the fields to extract from the document, set a filter, and execute the query. With ellipses replacing the actual arguments, this query can be created, refined, and executed as

```
statement = collection.find()
statement.fields(...)
statement.where(...)
result = statement.execute()
```

Alternatively, the same query can be written as one chain, like so:

```
result = collection.find().fields(...).where(...).execute()
```

It is also possible to use a hybrid where part of the statement uses a chain and the other part doesn't, or you can use several shorter chains. This can be useful if you need to execute several queries that have a common base, but then have the filter or values changes.

One method is not more correct than the other. The one you use should be determined by the style of the code, requirements, and how the statement will be used. The next two chapters include examples of various ways to put the flow of commands together.

MYSQL SHELL

MySQL Shell is a new command-line client that provides several additional features compared to the traditional `mysql` command-line client. One of the features it includes is support for using the X DevAPI in Python. While MySQL Shell does not use MySQL Connector/Python and thus the `mysqlx` module is not 100% the same, you can use MySQL Shell to test the X DevAPI interactively.

An example that creates a session and executes a read request using MySQL Shell is

```
MySQL  Py > connect_args = {
    ...     'host'        : '127.0.0.1',
    ...     'port'        : 33060,
    ...     'user'        : 'pyuser',
    ...     'password'    : 'Py@pp4Demo',
    ... };
    ...
MySQL  Py > db = mysqlx.get_session(**connect_args)
MySQL  Py > schema = db.get_schema('world_x')
MySQL  Py > countries = schema.get_collection('countryinfo')
```

```
MySQL  Py > country = countries.get_one('AUS')
MySQL  Py >
MySQL  Py > fmt = "{0:13s} {1}"
MySQL  Py > print(fmt.format(
      ...    "Name ........:",
      ...    country["Name"]
      ... ))
      ...
Name ........: Australia
 MySQL  Py > print(fmt.format(
      ...    "Continent ...:",
      ...    country["geography"]["Continent"]
      ... ))
      ...
Continent ...: Oceania
```

Don't worry if the code does not make sense yet; this is what this and the next two chapters are about. At the end, it should all be clear. Chapter 10 will also look into using MySQL Shell as a tool during development.

Be aware that the example uses the world_x sample database, which is derived from the world sample database used in the earlier chapters. If you want to play with the world_x database, it can be downloaded from https://dev.mysql.com/doc/index-other.html.

Creating a Session

In the X DevAPI, a session corresponds to the connection object in the traditional MySQL Connector/Python mysql.connector module. It does not matter whether you want to create a session to use the Document Store, use the CRUD methods with SQL tables, or execute traditional SQL queries. This is one of the advantages of the X DevAPI: it combines the NoSQL and SQL worlds.

267

Tip   The primary use of the X DevAPI is the NoSQL CRUD methods. If you need more than basic SQL features, it is recommended to use the `mysql.connector` module as described earlier in this book. It is also possible to combine the use of the `mysqlx` and `mysql.connector` modules to get the best of both worlds.

A session is created using the get_session() method. The arguments passed to the function are used to configure the session. The definition of the function is

```
mysqlx.get_session(*args, **kwargs)
```

The connection arguments can be specified in one of two ways:

- Passing the options in the same way as when creating a connection in the mysql.connector module
- Creating an URI

Let's look at how to use each way, starting out by specifying the options explicitly. After the discussion of configuring the session, there will be examples of using the get_session() function to create the session.

Caution   Do not hard code the password into the application. This is neither safe nor practical. In general, it is best to keep the connection options outside the application. This also ensures that the connection options can be updated without updating the application.

Passing Individual Options

If you are used to coding with MySQL Connector/Python, the simplest way to specify the options is to pass them individually either as direct arguments or as a dictionary.

One important difference compared to the connections created in the previous chapters is that it is not possible to specify a MySQL configuration file. So, if you use the X DevAPI, it is recommended to store the options in a custom configuration file. The complete list of supported options can be seen in Table 6-1. The options are ordered alphabetically.

Table 6-1. *The X DevAPI Options for Creating a Session*

Name	Default Value	Description
auth	With SSL, Unix socket, and Windows named-pipe: PLAIN Otherwise, try MYSQL41 Finally, try SHA256_ MEMORY	auth takes one of three values: MYSQL41, SHA256_ MEMORY, or PLAIN. MYSQL41 should be used with the mysql_native_password authentication plugin. SHA256_MEMORY can be used to connect with an account using the sha2_caching_password authentication plugin without an SSL connection, provided that at least one connection has been made prior using SSL since the last restart of MySQL Server. PLAIN is used in most other cases but requires a secure connection, one that uses SSL, a Unix socket, or a Windows named-pipe. It is rarely necessary to set this option.
host	localhost	The hostname to connect to; the default is to connect to the local host.
password		The password to authenticate with; for the test user, it's Py@pp4Demo.
port	33060	The port MySQL is listening to for X DevAPI connections. Port 33060 is the standard MySQL X DevAPI port.

(*continued*)

Table 6-1. (*continued*)

Name	Default Value	Description
routers		List of dictionaries with the host and port keys defining possible MySQL instances to connect to. Optionally, the priority can also be set; the higher the value, the more likely the instance is used. If the priority is set for one instance, it must be set for all instances. If no priorities are given, the instances are used in the order they appear in the list. If the host option is specified in addition to routers, the host and port options are used to create an instance at the end of the routers list.
schema		The default schema (database) to use for the session. It is not required for the schema to already exist. The default schema only applies to the mysqlx.crud. Session.get_default_schema() method.
socket		Unix socket or Windows named-pipe.
ssl-ca		The path to the file containing the SSL certificate authority (CA).
ssl-crl		The path to the file containing the SSL certificate revocation lists.
ssl-cert		The path to the file containing the public SSL certificate.
ssl-key		The path to the file containing the private SSL key.

(*continued*)

Table 6-1. (*continued*)

Name	Default Value	Description
ssl-mode	REQUIRED	Which SSL mode to use. This is the same as for clients shipped with MySQL Server. It can take a range of values: DISABLED, PREFERRED, REQUIRED, VERIFY_CA, VERIFY_IDENTITY. The value VERIFY_IDENTITY is equivalent to the old ssl_verify_cert option. See also https://dev.mysql.com/doc/refman/en/encrypted-connection-options.html#option_general_ssl-mode.
use_pure	False	Whether to use the pure Python implementation (when use_pure = True) or the C Extension.
user		The username of the application user. Do not include the @ and the following hostname (that is, for the test user just specify pyuser).

As you can see from the list of options, there are not nearly as many as for the mysql.connector module. Most noticeable is that there are no character set options. The X DevAPI always uses utf8mb4.

Tip   If you data is stored using a different character set than utf8, utf8mb3, or utf8mb4, either convert it in the query or use the mysql.connector module.

The list of supported SSL options (except ssl-mode) is stored in the _SSL_OPTS constant in the mysqlx module, and the complete list of options can be found in the _SESS_OPTS constant. This makes it easy to get the list of options, for example, by using the following code:

```
import mysqlx

print("SSL options ...: {0}".format(
  mysqlx._SSL_OPTS
))
print("All options ...: {0}".format(
  mysqlx._SESS_OPTS
))
```

This code is an example of a difference between using the X DevAPI with MySQL Connector/Python and MySQL Shell. In MySQL Shell, the mysqlx module does not have these two properties, so the example will cause an exception. The output using MySQL Connector/Python 8.0.11 is

```
SSL options ...: ['ssl-cert', 'ssl-ca', 'ssl-key', 'ssl-crl']
All options ...: ['ssl-cert', 'ssl-ca', 'ssl-key', 'ssl-crl',
'user', 'password', 'schema', 'host', 'port', 'routers',
'socket', 'ssl-mode', 'auth', 'use_pure']
```

MySQL Connector/Python also supports specifying an URI with the connection options. Let's see how this is done.

Passing an URI

A common way to connect to a database is by creating an URI (Uniform Resource Identifier) that includes all of the connection options. An URI is also used to access a web site (all URLs (Uniform Resource Locators) are also URIs). Using an URI with database connections is also known from MySQL Connector/J (Java).

The basic form of an URI for the X DevAPI is

```
scheme://[user[:[password]]@]target[:port][/schema]
[?attribute1=value1][&attribute2=value2...]
```

The scheme is always `mysqlx` and can be left out (MySQL Connector/Python will add it if it is missing). At the time of writing, MySQL Connector/Python does not support escaping of characters in the URI (as is otherwise the norm), so some values are currently not supported.

Note   Because of the bug described in `https://bugs.mysql.com/89614`, some characters are not currently supported in the parameters. Most noticeable is that the @ character is not supported in passwords. If you want to test using an URI, you must change the password to not include the @ character until the bug has been fixed.

The target is either the socket option, the host option, or the host and port options separated with a colon. The attributes are any of the supported options other than `user`, `password`, `host`, `port`, `socket`, and `schema`.

As an example, consider creating a connection using the following arguments (in the order they appear in the URI):

- **user**: Pyuser

- **password**: PyApp4Demo

- **host**: 127.0.0.1

- **port**: 33060

- **schema**: py_test_db

- **ssl-mode**: REQUIRED

- **auth**: PLAIN

The resulting URI is

```
mysqlx://pyuser:PyApp4Demo@127.0.0.1:33060/py_test_db?ssl-mode=REQUIRED&auth=PLAIN
```

The rest of the discussion of the X DevAPI passes the connection options individually.

Connection Examples

The time has come to create an actual session that is connected to MySQL using the X DevAPI. In order to avoid coding the connection options into the examples, the configuration that is common to the examples in the remainder of this and the following two chapters will be stored in the `config` module.

See the following for the contents of the `config` module that is included with the source code for this book as `config.py`:

```
connect_args = {
  'host': '127.0.0.1',
  'port': 33060,
  'user': 'pyuser',
  'password': 'Py@pp4Demo',
};
```

Using the `config` module, the session can be created as follows:

```
import mysqlx
from config import connect_args

db = mysqlx.get_session(**connect_args)
```

When you are done using the session, it is recommended to close it to ensure the connection is terminated cleanly. This is achieved with the `close()` method:

```
import mysqlx
from config import connect_args

db = mysqlx.get_session(**connect_args)

...

db.close()
```

That's all there is to it. So, let's move on and start to use the X DevAPI session.

Working with the Session

The session object includes a few useful methods of its own. Remember that the session is the equivalent of the mysql.connector connection object, so it is at the session level that, for example, transactions are controlled. This section will go through these features. Additionally, the session also contains the methods used to manipulate a schema such as creating and dropping them. Working with schemas will be covered in the next section.

Transactions

The X DevAPI supports transactions for all actions other than those manipulating schema objects. This is the same as when using the mysql. connector module or any other way to interact with MySQL Server. The X DevAPI actually has better transactional support than the mysql. connector module because it supports savepoints in addition to the transactions themselves.

Note An important difference between mysqlx and mysql. connector is that autocommit. mysqlx inherits the value from the global default set in MySQL Server, and there is no way to change the value of it other than using an SQL statement. For this reason, it is recommended always to explicitly use transactions.

There are six methods to control transactions and savepoints. They are summarized in Table 6-2. The order of the methods is according to when they are used in a transaction.

Table 6-2. *Session Methods to Control Transactions*

Method	Argument	Description
start_transaction		Starts a transaction.
set_savepoint	name	Sets a savepoint. If the name is not specified, a name will be generated using the uuid. uuid1() function. The name of the savepoint is returned.
release_savepoint	name	Releases (the savepoint equivalent to a commit but without persisting the changes) the savepoint with the name specified.
rollback_to	name	Rolls back the changes made since the savepoint specified.
commit		Commits (persists) all changes made since the start_transaction() call.
rollback		Dismisses all changes made since the start_transaction() call. The use of a savepoint does not change the result of a rollback.

There will be examples of using transactions throughout the rest of the X DevAPI discussion. Before you get that far, there are a few session utility methods to discuss.

Other Session Methods

Let's discuss a few methods that are useful for various purposes. They mostly evolve around retrieving objects such as getting the underlying connection object or starting an SQL statement. The utility methods are summarized in Table 6-3 in alphabetical order. All returned objects are relative to the mysqlx module.

Table 6-3. *Session Utility Methods*

Method	Argument	Returns Object	Description
get_connection		connection. Connection	Retrieves the underlying connection.
is_open			Returns True or False depending on whether the connection is open.
sql	sql	statement. SqlStatement	Used for executing SQL queries. See also the "SQL Statements" section in Chapter 8.

Some of these methods will be used in the examples that follow later. One thing that is absent from this list of methods is how to proceed if you want to use the NoSQL CRUD methods. This is done by obtaining a schema object, which is the next thing to discuss, along with other schema methods.

Schemas

Schemas (schemata) are containers that can include tables or document collections. They are not used directly themselves and can in some way be seen as a kind of namespace. In the X DevAPI, schema objects are only needed when using the CRUD methods.

The methods to work with schemas are split among two classes. Methods for creating, dropping, and retrieving a schema exists in the mysqlx.Session class, whereas methods for using the schema or getting information about the schema are in the mysqlx.crud.Schema class. This section investigates these methods with the exception of methods related to manipulating collections and tables, which are the topic of the next two chapters. At the end of this section, there is an example that puts together the methods and properties discussed.

Schema Manipulation

When an application needs a schema, the first thing to do is to either create a new schema or retrieve an existing schema. Optionally, the schema may be dropped at the end if it is no longer needed.

The methods for performing these tasks have in common that they all exist in the mysqlx.Session class. The methods that will be discussed in this section are summarized in Table 6-4.

Table 6-4. *Session Schema Methods*

Method	Argument	Returns Object	Description
create_schema	name	crud.Schema	Creates a schema with the name specified as the argument.
drop_schema	name		Drops the schema specified by the name argument.
get_default_schema		crud.Schema	Returns the schema object for the schema specified when creating the session. If no default schema exists, a ProgrammingError exception occurs.
get_schema	name	crud.Schema	Returns the requested schema object. If no schema exists with the specified name, a Schema object is still returned.
get_schemas			Returns a list with the schema names the user has access to. This method is introduced in version 8.0.12.

Figure 6-2 shows how the schema sits in the workflow between the session and the object classes. The red (dark grey) boxes are examples of the methods that can be used to get from one class (large boxes) to another.

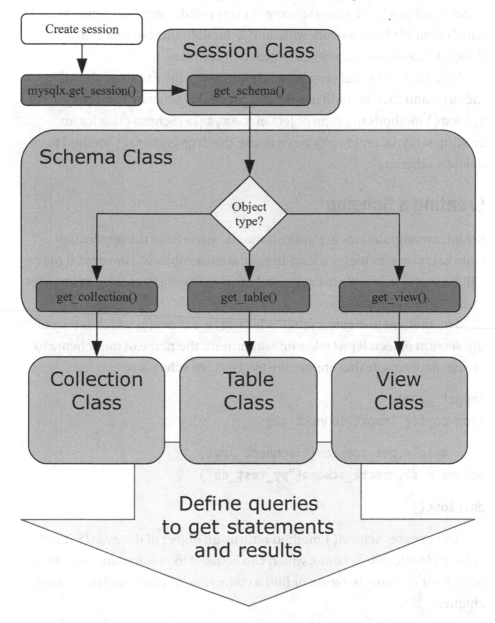

Figure 6-2. *Example of the workflow around the schema object*

Figure 6-2 starts out creating a session using the mysqlx.get_session() method, as discussed earlier in the chapter. The get_schema() method is then used to get a schema object. Another option is to use create_schema() for a new schema. At this point, there is a choice of which kind of object to work with, and from then on statements are defined. This is the subject of the next two chapters.

You will first look at creating a schema using the create_schema() method, and then you will use the get_default_schema() and get_schema() methods to get an object of the mysqlx.Schema class for an existing schema, and finally you will use the drop_schema() method to delete a schema.

Creating a Schema

Schema manipulations are not commonly made from the application code because schemas are long-living database objects. However, it may still be useful to be able to create and drop a schema from time to time, for example in a utility script.

The method to create a schema is create_schema(), which is part of the session object. It just takes one argument: the name of the schema to create. An example that creates the py_test_db schema is

```
import mysqlx
from config import connect_args

db = mysqlx.get_session(**connect_args)
schema = db.create_schema("py_test_db")

db.close()
```

The create_schema() method returns an object of the mysqlx.crud. Schema class for the schema, which can be used to manipulate the schema object, for example to create or find a collection, as discussed in the next chapter.

If you compare this with a CREATE SCHEMA SQL statement, there are two noticeable differences. First, there is no option to set the default character set for the schema. The default character set for a schema created with create_schema() is always the one specified with the character_set_server MySQL Server option. In the same way, the value of the collation_server MySQL Server option is used to specify the default schema collation.

The other difference is there is no equivalent to the IF NOT EXISTS clause of CREATE SCHEMA. Likewise, drop_schema() does not have an equivalent for IF EXISTS. Instead, create_schema() will succeed even if the schema already exists. In fact, the underlying SQL statement executed by the above example is

```
CREATE DATABASE IF NOT EXISTS `py_test_db`;
```

So, the IF NOT EXISTS clause will always be included. That does not mean it is recommended just to use create_schema() to get an existing schema. The CREATE DATABSE IF NOT EXISTS causes unnecessary overhead and it makes the intention of the code less clear. Instead, use one of the two dedicated methods to get a schema object for an existing schema.

Retrieving the Default Schema

The most common scenario in a real application is that the schema already exists and the application needs to get a schema object either to manipulate the schema or to go deeper down and get a collection or a table to work with. There are two ways to get a schema object in the X DevAPI: either to ask for the default schema specified when creating the session or to ask for it by schema name.

When the session is created, it is possible to specify the default schema using the schema option. To get the schema object for the default schema, you can use the get_default_schema() session method. As an example, consider a session that is created with the py_test_db schema as the default:

```
import mysqlx
from config import connect_args

db = mysqlx.get_session(
  schema="py_test_db",
  **connect_args
)

print("Retrieving default schema")
schema = db.get_default_schema()
print("Schema name: {0}"
  .format(schema.name)
)

db.close()
```

The connection is created with the schema='py_test_db' option added, and the schema object is then retrieved using the get_default_schema() method. Finally, the name of the schema is printed using the name property of the schema and the session is closed. The output is

```
Retrieving default schema
Schema name: py_test_db
```

The get_default_schema() method is a great way to retrieve the default schema, for example if the schema name is not known at the time the application is written. However, in other cases, it is necessary to retrieve a specific schema irrespective of the default schema. Let's see how this is done.

Retrieving a Schema by Name

Retrieving a specific schema by its name is similar to creating a new schema. The difference is that the get_schema() method is used instead of create_schema(). A single argument is required: name, which is a string with the name of the schema. Consider the following example to get the schema object for the py_test_db schema:

```python
import mysqlx
from config import connect_args

db = mysqlx.get_session(**connect_args)

print("Retrieving non-default schema")
schema = db.get_schema("py_test_db")
print("Schema name: {0}"
  .format(schema.name)
)

db.close()
```

After the session has been created, the schema is retrieved and the name is printed. This example is very similar to the previous one using get_default_schema(), except the name of the schema is specified at the time it is retrieved rather than at the time the session is created. The output of the example is the similar to the previous:

```
Retrieving non-default schema
Schema name: py_test_db
```

The final step of manipulating the schema is to drop a schema.

Dropping a Schema

Dropping a schema is done in a very similar way to creating it. The session includes the drop_schema() method, which takes the name of the schema to be removed. An example that drops the py_test_db schema used in this section is

```
import mysqlx
from config import connect_args

db = mysqlx.get_session(**connect_args)
db.drop_schema("py_test_db")

db.close()
```

The only difference here compared to the create_schema() example earlier in the section is that the drop_schema() method is used instead. Similar to creating a schema, no error occurs if the schema does not exist. That is, the underlying SQL statement is

```
DROP DATABASE IF EXISTS `py_test_db`;
```

As with the session, the mysqlx.crud.Schema class also has a few utility methods and two properties. They are the final things to consider for the schema objects.

Other Schema Methods and Properties

The mysqlx.Schema class includes a few methods as well as three properties that can be useful for checking the state of the schema object. They include information about the schema name, whether the schema exists, etc. Additionally, there are methods to get the underlying connection and session. All of this will be discussed here.

The schema methods that will be included in the discussion are summarized in Table 6-5. The objects returned are all relative to the `mysqlx` module. None of the methods take any arguments.

Table 6-5. *Schema Utility Methods*

Method	Returns Object	Description
exists_ in_database		Returns True or False depending on whether the schema exists.
get_connection	connection. Connection	Gets the underlying connection of the session.
get_name		Returns the name of the schema. This is the same as using the name property.
get_schema	crud.Schema	This returns the schema itself. This is the same as using the schema property. It is not commonly used in applications.
get_session	connection. Session	Returns the session object for the schema. This can be useful when a schema is passed as an argument to a function. In version 8.0.12 and later, the session can also be retrieved from the session property.

The most commonly used of the methods are those to get the name (get_name()) or to check whether the schema actually exists (exists_ in_database()). The name can also be obtained using the name property. Similarly, the session can be retrieved using either the get_session() method or in MySQL Connector/Python 8.0.12 and later the session property. Additionally, the schema itself is stored in the schema property; however, this is not usually used in applications.

Before moving on to discuss CRUD arguments, it is worth going through an example that combines the features discussed in this section.

Schema Example

Thus far, this has all been a bit abstract with minimal code examples. So, let's see an extended example that puts together several of the things discussed and shows how the methods and properties are related. Listing 6-1 uses a default schema and then uses the utility and schema manipulation methods to investigate and take actions.

Listing 6-1. Manipulating and Checking Schemas

```
import mysqlx
from config import connect_args

# Create the session
db = mysqlx.get_session(
  schema="py_test_db",
  **connect_args
)

# Retrieve the default schema
# (py_test_db)
py_schema = db.get_default_schema()
print("Schema name: {0} - Exists? {1}"
  .format(
    py_schema.name,
    py_schema.exists_in_database()
  )
)

# If py_test_db does not exist,
# create it
if (not py_schema.exists_in_database()):
  db.create_schema(py_schema.name)
```

```python
print("Schema name: {0} - Exists? {1}"
  .format(
    py_schema.name,
    py_schema.exists_in_database()
  )
)

# Get the world schema
w_schema = db.get_schema("world")
print("Schema name: {0} - Exists? {1}"
  .format(
    w_schema.name,
    w_schema.exists_in_database()
  )
)

# Get the session object of the world
# schema and see if it is the same as
# the db object.
w_session = w_schema.get_session()
print("db == w_session? {0}".format(
  db == w_session))

# Drop the py_test_db schema.
db.drop_schema(py_schema.name)
print("Schema name: {0} - Exists? {1}"
  .format(
    py_schema.name,
    py_schema.exists_in_database()
  )
)

db.close()
```

This example starts out by creating a session where the default schema is set to py_test_db and the get_default_schema() session method is used to get a schema object for the py_test_db schema. The name property and the exists_in_database() method of the schema object are used to print the name and whether it exists. This is repeated throughout the example whenever there are changes to the schema object.

If the py_test_db schema does not exist, then it is created. It is not actually necessary to check whether the schema does not exists before calling the create_schema() method, but it makes the intention clearer.

A second schema object is then retrieved, this time using the get_schema() method to get an object for the world schema. The session of the newly created w_schema object is retrieved using the get_session() method, and it is confirmed that the db and w_session objects are identical (as in their identities or memory addresses are identical).

Finally, the py_test_db schema is dropped again using the drop_schema() method, leaving the database in the same state as before the example (assuming the py_test_db schema did not exist at the start). Assuming the py_test_db does not exist and the world database from the previous chapters does exist, the output from running the example is

```
Schema name: py_test_db - Exists? False
Schema name: py_test_db - Exists? True
Schema name: world - Exists? True
db == w_session? True
Schema name: py_test_db - Exists? False
```

The output shows that py_test_db did not exist at the beginning, but after the create_schema() call it does. The world schema exists without being created because you loaded it manually in Chapter 1. When comparing the two copies of the session, you can see they are identical. Finally, after dropping the py_test_db schema, the exists_in_database() method returns False again.

To complete this chapter, you will look at three things that are common for the methods discussed in the next two chapters: first, the arguments used with CRUD methods.

CRUD Arguments

The CRUD methods that will be discussed in Chapter 7 and Chapter 8 all use a limited set of arguments. Rather than explaining again and again what these arguments mean, let's go through them now.

The CRUD methods use the following four argument types:

- documents
- document IDs
- conditions
- fields

The documents and document IDs are exclusive to the Document Store, whereas fields and conditions are shared between the two. The following discussion will look at each of the four argument types and go into the use of them.

Documents

The documents are the containers for the data that is stored in the Document Store. Inside MySQL the documents are stored as JavaScript Object Notation (JSON) documents. In Python, JSON can be represented as a dictionary where JSON objects are dictionary keys with a value. JSON arrays are created as a list in Python.

Tip   If you want to learn more about JSON documents some references are `https://json.org/`, `https://en.wikipedia.org/wiki/JSON`, and `https://dev.mysql.com/doc/refman/en/json.html`.

As an example, consider an employee named John Doe who is currently a team lead. He has a manager and he previously held roles as a developer (from 2010-2014) and senior developer (2014-2017). A document that represents this is

```
document = {
  "_id"        : "10001",
  "Name"       : "John Doe",
  "Manager_id" : "10000",
  "Title"      : "Team Lead",
  "Previous_roles": [
    {
      "Title"      : "Developer",
      "Start_year" : "2010",
      "End_year"   : "2014"
    },
    {
      "Title"      : "Senior Developer",
      "Start_year" : "2014",
      "End_year"   : "2017"
    },
  ]
}
```

The document starts with a dictionary and at the top level are all of the scalar facts about the employee such as name, manager, etc. The employee's history with the company is represented as a list with a dictionary for each of the roles the employee had previously.

The data inside the array does not need to have a structure. For example, if the favorite fruits for a person are stored, they can be represented as simple list with each fruit specified as a string.

One special field in the document is the _id element. This is the document ID, which is the unique identifier (primary key) of the document. Let's take a look at the document ID.

Document ID

The document ID is what MySQL uses to uniquely identify a document. It is also what is used as the primary key in the underlying storage. All documents must have a document ID. If it is not explicitly provided when connected to MySQL Server 8.0, it will be auto-generated.

The document ID is an (up to) 32-byte long binary string. If the ID is not provided, MySQL Server 8.0 will create one using three parts:

- **A prefix**: This is an unsigned integer in hexadecimal encoding. It is 0 except if it is set by the database administrator or MySQL Server is part of an InnoDB Cluster group. The prefix is stored in the mysqlx_ document_id_unique_prefix MySQL Server option.

- **A timestamp**: The time when the MySQL Server instance was last started in hexadecimal encoding.

- **An auto-increment counter**: This is an unsigned integer in hexadecimal encoding. The initial value is the value of the auto_increment_offset MySQL Server option, and it then increments with auto_increment_ increment per ID generated.

An example of an ID generated with `mysqlx_document_id_unique_prefix = 5678` is `162e5ae98778000000000000003`. The prefix is the first four hexadecimal digits (`162e`), followed by the timestamp; the `3` at the end shows it is the third ID generated after MySQL Server was last restarted.

The IDs generated this way are designed so they can be globally unique while also being optimized for the InnoDB storage engine and be cheap to generate. InnoDB performs optimally when monotonically incrementing primary keys are used. The auto-generated document IDs are optimized for this.

On the surface, a natural choice could have been an UUID, but they are not monotonically increasing. Even if you swap the high- and low-order time parts of an UUID, you will have interleaved values if there are application instances from multiple hosts connected. This is why the three-part ID was developed.

The next argument type to discuss is a condition.

Condition

A condition is used to filter which documents should be affected by an operation and is used both for CRUD methods with the Document Store and SQL tables. For read operations, only documents matching the filter are returned; for update and delete operations, the condition specifies which documents should be changed. The SQL equivalent of a condition is a `WHERE` clause. With the exception of `modify()` for a collection in version 8.0.12 and later, the methods accepting a condition as an argument also provide a `where()` method in their statement object that can be used instead.

The condition is fairly straightforward to write and uses the same syntax as a MySQL SQL `WHERE` clause. For example, to include all documents where the `Office` field is set to Sydney, the following condition can be used:

```
Office = 'Sydney'
```

One difference between SQL tables and documents is that where MySQL by default treats WHERE clauses as case insensitive when filtering on string data types, the Document Store is always case sensitive. The explanation of this is that JSON documents are stored as binary objects because otherwise it would not be possible to store arbitrary values in the documents.

Note   MySQL WHERE clauses and SQL tables by default perform a case insensitive match, but the Document Store is always case sensitive.

The final argument type is fields, which is used with CRUD methods to specify what to return or modify.

Fields

The fields argument, for example, specifies which fields to return in a select statement or which fields to set values for in an insert statement. The fields argument type is also used in some statement methods such as the FindStatement.fields() method. In the SQL language, a field is the same as a column.

Each field is represented as a string with the name of the field to include or set the value for. For JSON documents, the field is a JSON path to the location of the field within the JSON document. The document itself is represented by $. The path is then constructed by specifying the elements separated by a period (.). The leading $. is optional except when creating indexes on collections.

It is possible to use * as a wildcard. Specifying .* means all members of the object are matched. Alternatively, you can use the syntax [prefix]**{suffix} where the prefix is optional and the suffix is mandatory. This matches everything starting with the prefix and ending with the suffix.

For arrays, square brackets can be used to specify which elements to include. [N] returns the Nth element (0-based) of the array. Using [*] is the same as not specifying an index at all (i.e. the whole array is returned).

Tip   The rules for specifying a JSON path in MySQL are documented in `https://dev.mysql.com/doc/refman/en/json-path-syntax.html`.

The fields can be specified either as individual arguments, a tuple, or a list. The following three initializations of a select statement do the same thing:

```
stmt = city.select("Name", "District")

fields = ("Name", "District")
stmt = city.select(fields)

fields = ["Name", "District"]
stmt = city.select(fields)
```

This concludes the discussion about the arguments used with the CRUD methods. Next, you will look at the middle part of a query: the statement object.

Statements

Most of the methods that will be discussed in the next two chapters involve a statement object. This is used to refine the query and to execute it. The methods that on the surface do not involve statement objects, such as the `count()` methods, still use statements under the hood.

The statement object is where the bulk of the work with the query is done. You can, for example, use the statement object to set the filter condition for a find() query or limit the number of documents in the result. The statement classes that will be encountered in the next two chapters are summarized in Table 6-6.

Table 6-6. *Statement Classes*

Class	Scope	CRUD	Method
AddStatement	Collection	Create	add()
FindStatement	Collection	Read	find()
ModifyStatement	Collection	Update	modify()
RemoveStatement	Collection	Delete	remove()
InsertStatement	Table	Create	insert()
SelectStatement	Table	Read	select()
UpdateStatement	Table	Update	update()
DeleteStatement	Table	Delete	delete()
SqlStatement	SQL		sql()

The class is class in the mysqlx.statement module that is returned for the method. The scope specifies whether it is for collection-, table-, or SQL-based queries. The CRUD column shows the corresponding CRUD actions. Finally, the Method column lists the method used to create the statement.

The specific methods of the statements will be covered when the respective methods are discussed. There are, however, some features that are shared among all or several of the statements. These common methods are listed in Table 6-7.

Table 6-7. *Methods to Get Information About a Statement*

Method	Statements	Return Type	Description
get_binding_map	Read Update Delete	Dictionary	Returns a dictionary with the binding map.
get_bindings	Read Update Delete	List	Returns a list of the bindings. Each binding is represented by a dictionary with the name and value.
get_grouping	Read Update Delete	List	Returns the expressions used for grouping the result.
get_having	Read Update Delete	protobuf. Message object	Returns an object for the having filter.
get_limit_offset	Read Update Delete	Integer	Returns the offset for the limit.
get_limit_row_c ount	Read Update Delete	Integer	Returns the maximum number of documents to return from the query.
get_ projection_expr	Read Update Delete	List	Returns a list with the projection mappings of the fields.
get_sort_expr	Read Update Delete	List	Returns a list with the expressions used for sorting the result.

(continued)

Table 6-7. (*continued*)

Method	Statements	Return Type	Description
get_sql	Select	String	Returns the SQL statement as it looks with the current statement definition.
get_update_ops	Update	UpdateSpec object	Returns a list with the update operations.
get_values	Create	List	Returns a list of the values that the statement will create or has created.
get_where_expr	Read Update Delete	protobuf. Message object	Returns an object for the where filter.
is_doc_based	All	Boolean	Always returns True for a collection-based statements and False for table- and SQL-based statements.
is_ lock_exclusive	Read	Boolean	Returns True if an exclusive lock has been requested.
is_lock_shared	Read	Boolean	Returns True if a shared lock has been requested.
is_upsert	Create	Boolean	Returns True if the statement performs an upsert (that is, replace if the record already exists, otherwise add a new document) operation. It always returns False for insert statements. Chapter 7 includes an example of an upsert.

The `Statements` column shows which statement classes the method applies to. In most cases, the statement classes will be specified by the CRUD operations that have the method; for example, "Read" means the two read methods (`Collection.find()` and `Table.select()`) have it in the returned statement object. Two special values are "All," which means it applies to all of the statement types, and "Select," which means it only applies to `SelectStatement` objects (from `Table.select()`).

The `get_having()` and `get_where_expr()` methods return an object of the `mysqlx.protobuf.Message` class. The `get_update_ops()` method returns an object of the `mysqlx.statement.UpdateSpec` class. This book will not go into any details of how to use this class.

Once a statement has been executed, a result object is returned. The result object that is returned will depend on the statement class.

Results

When a query is executed, a result object is returned. The exact nature of the result object depends on the query and whether it is using a collection, SQL table, or is an SQL statement. This section will discuss the various result objects used with the X DevAPI.

For Document Store CRUD statements, an object of the `result.Result` class is returned for queries not returning any data, such as when adding documents. For queries returning data, an object of the `result.DocResult` class is returned. The only exception is the `count()` method, which returns the total number of documents in the collection directly as an integer.

For SQL tables, the pattern is similar, with the exception that the result object for a select statement is of the `result.RowResult` class. SQL statements always end up with a `result.SqlResult` object.

Table 6-8 summarizes which result object is returned for which method. How to get to the result and examples of using the result will be shown in the next two chapters.

Table 6-8. *Mapping of Statement Types to Result Objects*

Statement Type	Collections	Tables	SQL
CRUD – Create	Result	Result	
CRUD – Read	DocResult	RowResult	
CRUD – Update	Result	Result	
CRUD – Delete	Result	Result	
SQL			SqlResult

It is worth looking a bit closer at the four result classes. The following discussion will look at the result classes from a high level. Examples of using the results follow in the discussion of the CRUD and SQL methods.

result.Result

The result.Result class is used for CRUD statements where there is no result set and provides metadata about the query. For example, after inserting documents into a collection, it will include information about the number of documents inserted. It is used both for collection- and table-based statements.

Table 6-9 includes an overview of some of the most important methods of the result.Result class, including what they return. None of the methods take any arguments.

Table 6-9. *Important Methods of the* `result.Result` *Class*

Method	Returns Data Type	Description
`get_affected_items_count`	Integer	Returns the number of documents or rows affected by the query, such as how many documents were inserted or updated.
`get_autoincrement_value`	Integer	Returns the last auto-increment ID generated for a table insert statement. This is mostly useful when inserting a single row. It applies only to table objects.
`get_generated_ids`	List of strings	Returns all of the document IDs that have been inserted by the query into the collection. It applies only to collection objects.
`get_warnings`	List of tuples	Returns the warnings generated by the query.
`get_warnings_count`	Integer	Returns the number of warnings that occurred for the query.

These methods are similar to or provide similar data as what is also available for cursors in the `mysql.connector` module.

result.DocResult and result.RowResult

The `result.DocResult` and `result.RowResult` classes are used for `Collection.find()` and `Table.select()` methods, respectively. The classes work similarly to using a cursor in the `mysql.connector` module to work with a query result.

The most important methods of the `result.DocResult` and `result.RowResult` classes are summarized in Table 6-10. None of the methods take any arguments.

Table 6-10. Important Methods of the result.DocResult and result.RowResult Classes

Method	Returns Data Type	Description
fetch_all	List of documents	Returns all of the remaining documents in the result set. Each of the elements in the list is an instance of the mysqlx.dbdoc.DbDoc or mysql.result.Row class as described after the table.
fetch_one	Object	Returns the next document or row in the result set or None if all documents/rows have been retrieved. The object type returned is discussed after the table.
get_columns	List of objects	Returns the column information from the column property. It only exists for the result.RowResult class. Added in version 8.0.12.
get_warnings	List of tuples	Returns the warnings generated by the query.
get_warnings_count	Integer	Returns the number of warnings that occurred for the query.

In addition to the methods listed, there is the count property, which is set to the total number of documents retrieved using the fetch_all() method. The result.RowResult class furthermore includes the columns property, which includes similar information as the column information that was discussed in Chapters 3 and 4; in version 8.0.12 and later the columns can also be retrieved with the get_columns() method. The object type returned by fetch_one() and that makes up the list returned by fetch_all() depends on the statement type:

- `Collection.find()`: The object is of the `mysqlx.dbdoc.DbDoc` class

- `Table.select()`: The object of the `mysqlx.result.Row` class

In either case, the object behaves like a dictionary, so there are no special considerations required when using the returned documents.

The last result class that is used is `SqlResult`, which is used for all SQL statements.

result.SqlResult

The MySQL Connector/Python implementation of the X DevAPI does not distinguish between `SELECT` type queries and other queries when determining which type of result object to return for an SQL statement. It is always an object of the `result.SqlResult` class that is returned.

The most important methods of the `SqlResult` class have been summarized in Table 6-11.

Table 6-11. *Important Methods of the* `result.SqlResult` *Class*

Method	Argument	Returns Data Type	Description
`fetch_all`		List of rows	Returns all of the remaining rows in the result set. Each of the rows is an instance of the `mysql.result.Row` class.
`fetch_one`		`result.Row`	Returns the next row in the result set or None if all rows have been retrieved.

(continued)

Table 6-11. (*continued*)

Method	Argument	Returns Data Type	Description
get_ autoincrement_ value		Integer	Returns the last auto-increment ID generated, if the query was an insert statement. This is mostly useful when inserting a single row.
get_columns		List of objects	Returns the column information from the column property. Added in version 8.0.12.
get_warnings		List of tuples	Returns the warnings generated by the query.
get_ warnings_count		Integer	Returns the number of warnings that occurred for the query.
has_data		Boolean	Returns whether there is a result set for the query. For a SELECT query returning no rows, the value is False. Added in version 8.0.12.
index_of	col_name	Integer	Returns the numeric index of the column with the name specified.
next_result		Boolean	Reinitializes the result object to work with the next result set, when the query generated more than one result set. Returns True if there was another result to handle; otherwise False.

Additionally, the `SqlResult` class has two useful properties:

- **columns**: A list of the columns for the result

- **count**: The total number of items retrieved with the `fetch_all()` method

This concludes the discussion of the result classes used with the X DevAPI. They will appear again when you look at how to execute statements in the next two chapters.

Summary

This chapter provided an introduction to the MySQL X DevAPI. It started out with a brief overview of the X Plugin, X Protocol, X DevAPI, and the `mysqlx` module. For MySQL Connector/Python to be able to execute queries using the X DevAPI, it is necessary for the X Plugin to be installed in MySQL Sever. This is the case by default in MySQL Server 8.0.11 and later.

The rest of the chapter discussed the features that are common irrespectively of what part of the X DevAPI is used. A program starts by creating a session that can be used to create, get, and drop schemas. The schema objects are the next step when using CRUD methods. The final part of the workflow is to get the result object, so the result of the query can be checked or the result set used.

This chapter didn't cover the big piece in the middle, after creating the session and possibly obtaining the schema object. This is where the fun part exists (defining and executing statements) and this is what the next two chapters are all about. The next chapter looks at how to use the X DevAPI with the MySQL Document Store.

CHAPTER 7

The MySQL Document Store

As the name suggest, MySQL has traditionally been all about using SQL statements to execute queries. This is not just reflected in the language used to describe what the queries should do, but also in the underlying way the data is structured. The MySQL Document Store turns this upside down and provides not only a NoSQL database, but also uses JSON documents, like other document stores use for storing data.

The Document Store does not replace the SQL database. The two are meant to live side by side, so you can use whichever works the best for your application and data. You can even mix the two, so some data is stored in traditional SQL tables and other as documents.

This chapter will look into how you can use the MySQL Connector/Python and the X DevAPI to work with the MySQL Document Store.

The MySQL Document Store

The MySQL Document Store is part of the X Plugin that was introduced as a beta feature in MySQL Server 5.7.12 and became GA in MySQL Server 8.0. The Document Store stores the data as a JSON document but uses the InnoDB storage engine to provide features such as transactional support.

© Jesper Wisborg Krogh 2018
J. W. Krogh, *MySQL Connector/Python Revealed*,
https://doi.org/10.1007/978-1-4842-3694-9_7

Note   The Document Store is a big topic on its own and it is beyond
the scope of this book to give a comprehensive walkthrough. It is
recommended that you read more about it if you intend to use the
Document Store. Two excellent references are *Introducing the MySQL 8
Document Store* by Charles Bell (`https://www.apress.com/gp/`
`book/9781484227244`) and the *MySQL Reference Manual* (`https://`
`dev.mysql.com/doc/refman/en/document-store.html`).

While the details of the X Protocol and the Document Store will be
left as an exercise for the reader, there are a couple of characteristics that
are good to consider before continuing. As the name suggests, the data
is stored in documents. This means that unlike in a normal relational
schema, all "columns" are stored within the same data object.

In the Document Store, it is said that the documents are stored in a
collection. The documents use the JSON format. If you think of a row in
a regular MySQL table, the column names are the names of each object
inside the JSON document and the column values are the values of the
object. Unlike for an SQL table, there is no requirement for each document
("row") to have the same fields or contain the same type of data. The
documents are said to be part of a collection ("table" in SQL terminology).

Caution   As with other document stores, the MySQL Document
Store is schemaless. This may seem like a very attractive feature
from a development point of view; indeed, it makes it much easier to
add new types of data to the application. However, it also removes
the chance for the database layer to validate the data and check for
constraints. So, if you choose a schemaless data model, it is all up to
the developer to ensure data consistency.

All documents must have a unique key, which is always an object in the JSON document with the key _id. Indexes in general are supported by creating virtual columns on the table that holds the collection. The X DevAPI includes support for creating indexes for collections, and this is the preferred way to manipulate indexes. MySQL Shell is very useful if you need to create or drop an index for a collection.

Now let's take a look at the general workflow when working with collections in the Document Store.

Tip   There are a number of example programs in this chapter. All example programs that appear in a listing are available for download. See the discussion of example programs in Chapter 1 for more information about using the example programs. In general, changes are rolled back to allow for reexecuting the examples with the same result. An exception is when the sample data is loaded in Listing 7-3.

Workflow

The workflow was hinted at in the previous chapter, but it is worth looking at it in a bit more detail. Let's focus on how to work with collections. A collection is obtained through the schema, and statements are created from the collection. Finally, statements return results. Of course, there is more to it, which this section will go through. It will not be an exhaustive discussion; rather, it's meant to serve as an overview for the rest of the chapter.

The workflow starting with the schema and ending with the results can be seen in Figure 7-1. The main focus is on the steps of obtaining the collection and creating the statement. The details of refining and executing the statements are left out but will be discussed later in this chapter for each query method. The red (dark grey) boxes are the methods that are called.

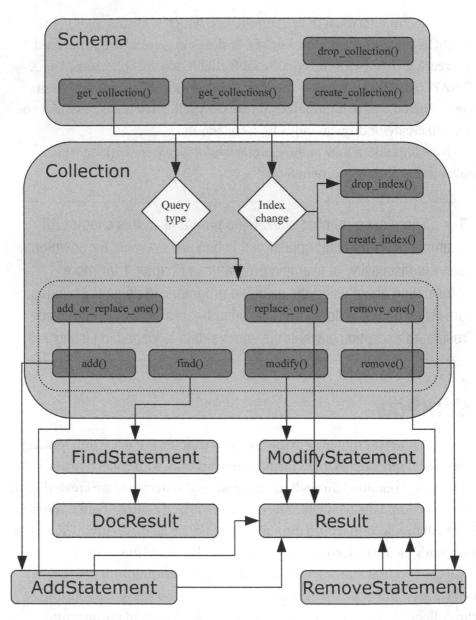

Figure 7-1. *The workflow when using collections*

As you will see in the first half of the chapter, collections are obtained from the schema using either get_collection(), get_collections(), or create_collection(). The schema can also be used to drop a collection. From the collection object, one possibility is to create and drop indexes.

The other possibility, which will be discussed in the second half of the chapter, is to execute queries. There are a number of methods to execute queries. The main ones are add(), find(), modify(), and remove(). They return a statement that in turn returns a result once the statement is executed. However, there are also three supplementary methods that combine all the steps and return a result directly. Finally, there is the count() method, which is not included in the figure.

With the workflow in place, you are ready to look at how collections work.

Collections

You saw in the previous chapter how a schema can be created from the session. The schema, however, is just a container for what really matters: the collections and tables. In a relational database, we talk about data being stored in tables. The X DevAPI can also work with tables (they will be discussed in the next chapter), but for the time being we will stick to the Document Store. The equivalent of a table in the Document Store is a collection.

This section will go through how collections are created, maintained, and removed when no longer needed. The flow will be similar to the one used for schemas. The actual collection manipulation is done using methods on the schema object, like the schema manipulation was done using session methods. The collection object itself also includes methods and a property in the same way as for the schema. The actual manipulation of data will be postponed until the following sections. The first stop is to create, get, and drop collections.

Collection Manipulation

Creation and removal of collections are not the most common tasks of an application, but they may be part of a deployment script or a utility, a collection may temporarily be required by the application, or you may be using MySQL Shell to optimize the performance of a collection. In all cases, the application needs to get a collection object in order to be able to execute queries against it. Creating, fetching, dropping, and creating indexes for collections are the topics of this discussion.

Collections are manipulated in a very similar way as schemas. For example, to create a schema, you use the session `create_schema()` method. In the same way, you can create a collection using the schema `create_collection()` method. This makes it easy to learn how to manipulate collections. The schema collection methods that will be discussed are listed in Table 7-1. The returned objects are relative to the `mysqlx` module.

Table 7-1. *Schema Collection Methods*

Method	Arguments	Description
create_collection	name reuse=False	Creates a collection with the name specified as the argument. The collection is returned as a crud.Collection object. If the collection exists, a ProgrammingError exception occurs unless reuse is True, in which case the existing collection is returned instead.
drop_collection	name	Drops the collection with the specified name. It is not required that the collection exists.
get_collection	name check_existence=False	Returns the collection with the specified name as a crud.Collection object. If check_existence = True, a ProgrammingError exception occurs if the collection does not exist.
get_collections		Returns a list of the collections in the schema. Each element in the list is an instance of the mysqlx.crud.Collection class.

The table shows that there are only a few differences compared to schemas: mainly that it is possible to affect whether the collection must not exist when creating a collection and whether it must exist when fetching it. Additionally, the two collection methods for creating and dropping indexes in Table 7-2 will also be discussed. Neither of the methods returns any value.

Table 7-2. *Collection Methods to Create and Drop Indexes*

Method	Arguments	Description
create_index	index_name	Creates an index named according to the value of index_name and defined by the dictionary specified in fields_desc ("desc" stands for description). The index name must be unique for the collection.
	fields_desc	**Note:** Calling create_index() only defines the index and returns a statement. CreateCollectionIndexStatement object. To create the index, call the execute() method on the returned object.
drop_index	index_name	Drops the index with the name specified in the argument.

The dictionary used to define a new index has the following structure:

```
{
  "type"   : INDEX|SPATIAL,
  "unique" : False,
  "fields" : [...]
}
```

The type can be INDEX for a normal index (this is the default) or SPATIAL for a geometry index. Full text indexes are currently not supported. The unique element defines whether it is a unique index or not. The default is False, which is also currently the only supported value (i.e. unique indexes are not currently supported). The fields element contains a list of the fields to include in the index. Each field is a dictionary with the elements in Table 7-3.

Table 7-3. *The Dictionary Defining a Field in an Index*

Element	Default Value	Type	Description
Field		String	The definition of how to find the value in the document. For example, to get the top level object called Name, use $.Name.
type		String	Similar to the data type for table columns. Examples of supported types are given after this table.
required	False	Boolean	Whether the value must exist in the document ("NOT NULL"). For the GeoJSON type, this must be set to True.
collation		String	The collation if the type is TEXT(…). This can only be set if type is a TEXT type. As of MySQL Server 8.0.11, custom collations are not supported for indexes, so the value is ignored.

(continued)

Table 7-3. (*continued*)

Element	Default Value	Type	Description
options	1	Integer	The options argument for the ST_GeomFromGeoJSON() function when creating a spatial index. It is only allowed for spatial indexes. Supported values are 1, 2, 3, and 4. It defines the behavior if the document contains values of dimension higher than two.
srid	4326	Integer	The srid (Spatial Reference System Identifier) argument for the ST_GeomFromGeoJSON() function when creating a spatial index. It is only allowed for spatial indexes. This must be an unsigned 32-bit integer. The ST_SPATIAL_REFERENCE_SYSTEMS table in information_schema includes all spatial reference systems supported by MySQL. Two references for SRIDs are https://epsg.io/ and http://spatialreference.org/.

The field and type elements are always required in the field definition whereas the rest of the elements depend on the index created. Some commonly used type values are

- INT: Specifies a signed integer. Variations include TINYINT, SMALLINT, MEDIUMINT, and BIGINT. To get an unsigned value, add UNSIGNED, for example INT UNSIGNED.

- FLOAT: A four-byte floating-point number.

- DOUBLE: An eight-byte floating-point number.

- DECIMAL: A fixed-point (exact) number. A precision can optionally be specified. The default precision is (10,0).

- DATE: A date.

- TIME: A time specification.

- TIMESTAMP: A timestamp consisting of a data and time of day. The range is from January 1, 1970 one second past midnight to January 19, 2038 at 03:14:07 UTC. The number of decimals to add for the seconds can be specified in parenthesis, for example TIMESTAMP(3) to have millisecond precision.

- DATETIME: Similar to a timestamp but supporting the range from January 1, 1000 at midnight to the end of day on December 31, 9999. The number of decimals to add for the seconds can be specified in parenthesis, for example DATETIME(3) to have millisecond precision.

- YEAR: The year in four digits, for example 2018.

- BIT: Specifies a bit value.

- BLOB: For storing binary objects (i.e. bytes without a character set). The maximum size of the value to index must be specified, for example BLOB(50) to index the first 50 bytes of the value. There is no support for the variations TINYBLOB, SMALLBLOB, MEDIUMBLOB, and LONGBLOB.

- TEXT: For storing strings. This requires the collation to be specified. The maximum size of the value to index must be specified, for example TEXT(50) to index the first 50 characters of the value. There is no support for the variations TINYTEXT, SMALLTEXT, MEDIUMTEXT, and LONGTEXT.

- GEOJSON: For spatial values using the GeoJSON format.
  When this is used, `required` must be `True` and the
  elements `options` and `srid` may be set. The GeoJSON
  format is only supported for spatial indexes. GeoJSON
  values are extracted from the document using the
  `ST_GeomFromGeoJSON()` function (`https://dev.mysql.`
  `com/doc/refman/en/spatial-geojson-functions.`
  `html#function_st-geomfromgeojson`). The `options`
  and `srid` values are the ones supported for that
  function.

It is worth noticing that the type cannot itself be JSON; only scalar
types are supported.

Tip   If you want to dig more into the requirements for the index
specification, see the `CreateCollectionIndexStatement`
class in the `mysqlx/ lib/mysqlx/statement.py` file in MySQL
Connector/Python and the `Admin_command_index::Index_`
`field::create()` method in the `plugin/x/src/admin_cmd_`
`index.cc` file in the MySQL Server source code.

There will be an example of creating indexes later in this section. The
following discussions will go through the four methods in turn, starting
with the task of creating a collection.

Creating a Collection

A collection is created using the `create_collection()` method, which
takes the name of the collection as the first argument or as the `name`
keyword argument. There is a second optional argument, `reuse`, which
defaults to `False`. If `reuse` is `False`, the collection cannot exist or a
`ProgrammingError` exception occurs. If `reuse` is `True`, the collection will

be created if it does not exist; otherwise, the existing collection will be returned. In most cases, it is best to leave reuse at its default value, so it is known if an existing collection of the same name exists. Otherwise, subtle errors can easily occur.

The following example shows how to create the collection my_docs in the py_test_db schema:

```
import mysqlx
from config import connect_args

db = mysqlx.get_session(**connect_args)

# Reset the py_test_db schema
db.drop_schema("py_test_db")
schema = db.create_schema("py_test_db")

docs = schema.create_collection("my_docs")

db.close()
```

The example first drops the py_test_db schema to ensure you start out with an empty schema. The create_collection() method returns a collection object, so it is possible to go straight to work.

It can be interesting to show the table definition using the SHOW CREATE TABLE statement in the mysql command-line client:

```
mysql> SHOW CREATE TABLE py_test_db.my_docs\G
*************************** 1. row ***************************
       Table: my_docs
Create Table: CREATE TABLE `my_docs` (
  `doc` json DEFAULT NULL,
  `_id` varbinary(32) GENERATED ALWAYS AS (json_unquote
  (json_extract(`doc`,_utf8mb4'$._id'))) STORED NOT NULL,
  PRIMARY KEY (`_id`)
```

```
) ENGINE=InnoDB DEFAULT CHARSET=utf8mb4 COLLATE=utf8mb4_0900_
ai_ci
1 row in set (0.00 sec)
```

This is the standard table definition for collections in the Document Store before any secondary indexes are created. The doc column is the document (using the JSON datatype). The _id column is a generated column that extracts the _id object from the doc column. The _id column is used as the primary key.

This also shows how indexes are created on values in the document. For each index, a generated column is created and used for the index. While the primary key must be a stored generated column, for secondary indexes a virtual column can be used. The advantage of a virtual column is that it does not require any storage but is calculated when needed. The index, however, still uses the same space as if the column was stored. You will soon see how to create additional indexes for a collection.

Tip   To read more about generated columns, see https://dev.mysql.com/doc/refman/en/create-table-generated-columns.html and https://dev.mysql.com/doc/refman/en/create-table-secondary-indexes.html in the *MySQL Server Reference Manual*.

The create_collection() method always sets the character set to utf8mb4; however, note that the JSON datatype is stored as a BLOB (i.e. as binary data without a character set). The primary key is always an (up to) 32-character long binary string stored in the _id object inside the document and retrieved using a generated column to allow MySQL to index it.

For existing collections, it is better to use get_collection() or get_collections(). Let's see how they work.

Retrieving a Single Collection

The simplest case of retrieving a collection is just to get one based on the name, which is done using the get_collection() method. This makes it easy to control which collections are fetched and it makes it easy to assign meaningful variable names to them.

As an example, consider retrieving the my_docs collection that was created in the previous example. This can be done using the following code:

```python
import mysqlx
from config import connect_args

db = mysqlx.get_session(**connect_args)

schema = db.create_schema("py_test_db")

docs = schema.get_collection("my_docs")
print("Name of collection: {0}".format(
    docs.name))

db.close()
```

The only thing new in this example is the line where the docs variable is assigned the collection retrieved using the get_collection() method. The name of the collection is printed using the name property of the collection object:

```
Name of collection: my_docs
```

If you need to retrieve many collections, it can be useful to fetch them all in one call. This can be accomplished using get_collections(), as will be shown next.

Retrieving All Collections in a Schema

In some cases, the application may use several collections. One solution is to use get_collection() to retrieve the collections one by one. There is another way, though.

The alternative is to use the get_collections() method, which returns all collections as a list. This is one of the cases where the name attribute of the collection becomes very useful because otherwise it would not be possible to know which collection object contains which documents.

The following code shows an example of retrieving the collections in a schema with two collections. This example is similar to the previous two but starts out by dropping the schema to start from scratch. The example code is

```python
import mysqlx
from config import connect_args

db = mysqlx.get_session(**connect_args)

# Reinitialize the py_test_db schema
db.drop_schema("py_test_db")
schema = db.create_schema("py_test_db")

# Create two collections
schema.create_collection("employees")
schema.create_collection("customers")

# Get all collections and print their
# names
collections = schema.get_collections()
for collection in collections:
  print("Collection name: {0}".format(
    collection.name))
```

```
# Create an index using the collection
# name as the key and the collection
# as the value
coll_dict = {
  collection.name: collection
    for collection in collections
}

db.close()
```

After the schema has been set up with the two collections employees and customers, the two collections are retrieved using the get_collections() method. The code then iterates over the collections and prints the name of each of them. Additionally, a dictionary is created using the name of the collection as the key. This makes it easier to retrieve a specific collection later. For example, the employees collection can be used by referencing coll_dict["employees"]. The output of the program is

```
Collection name: customers
Collection name: employees
```

The next collection manipulation method is the drop_collection() method, which is used to drop a collection that is no longer needed.

Dropping a Collection

When the application no longer needs a collection, it is possible to drop it using the drop_collection() method on the schema object. The method takes the name of the collection to drop. If the collection does not exist, drop_collection() will silently ignore it.

An example that removes all three collections that have been used in this chapter is

```
import mysqlx
from config import connect_args

db = mysqlx.get_session(**connect_args)

# Reinitialize the py_test_db schema
schema = db.get_schema("py_test_db")

# Drop all three collections that has
# been used in this section
schema.drop_collection("my_docs")
schema.drop_collection("employees")
schema.drop_collection("customers")

# For good measure also drop the schema
db.drop_schema("py_test_db")

db.close()
```

Since `drop_schema()` will drop all collections (and tables) in the schema, the `drop_collection()` calls are redundant, but they show how it is possible to drop collections one by one.

As with SQL queries, the performance of queries against a document collection can be greatly improved by adding indexes. This is covered in the next section.

Creating Indexes

Indexes provide search trees of the values that are indexed with references to the actual documents that contain these values. This makes it much faster to look for a specific value compared to scanning all documents and checking them one by one to see if they meet the requirement.

Note There are other types of indexes, such as full text indexes. At the time of writing, only B-Tree ("normal") and R-Tree (spatial) indexes are supported for collections.

Creating indexes for a collection is a little more complex compared to a regular SQL table because, in addition to the index definition itself, it is necessary to define how the values are retrieved from the document and what the values represent. This is the price to pay for using schemaless data storage.

An index can be defined using the create_index() method of the collection object. The full definition of the method was discussed earlier and will not be repeated. Instead, let's look at an example. Listing 7-1 shows an example of creating a collection and adding three indexes.

Listing 7-1. Creating Indexes for a Collection

```
import mysqlx
from config import connect_args

db = mysqlx.get_session(**connect_args)

# Reinitialize employees collection in
# the py_test_db schema
schema = db.create_schema("py_test_db")
schema.drop_collection("employees")
employees = schema.create_collection(
  "employees")

# Define the three fields that will be
# used in the indexes.
```

```python
field_name = {
  "field"     : "$.Name",
  "type"      : "TEXT(60)",
  "required"  : True,
  "collation" : "utf8mb4_0900_ai_ci",
}
field_office_location = {
  "field"     : "$.Office.Location",
  "type"      : "GEOJSON",
  "required"  : True,
  "options"   : 1,
  "srid"      : 4326,
}
field_birthday = {
  "field"     : "$.Birthday",
  "type"      : "DATE",
  "required"  : False,
}

# Create a normal index on the
# employee's name
index_name = "employee_name"
index_def =   {
  "fields" : [
    field_name
  ],
  "type"   : "INDEX",
}

index = employees.create_index(
  index_name, index_def)
index.execute()
```

```
print(
  "Index created: {0}".format(index_name)
)

# Create a spatial index for the
# location the employee work at.
index_name = "employee_office_location"
index_def =   {
  "fields" : [
    field_office_location
  ],
  "type"    : "SPATIAL",
}
employees.create_index(
  index_name, index_def
).execute()
print(
  "Index created: {0}".format(index_name)
)

# Create a normal index on the
# employee's birthday and name
index_name = "employee_birthday_name"
index_def =    {
  "fields" : [
    field_birthday,
    field_name
  ],
  "type"    : "INDEX",
}
```

```
index = employees.create_index(
  index_name, index_def)
index.execute()
print(
  "Index created: {0}".format(index_name)
)
```

```
db.close()
```

The example starts out reinitializing the collection. This ensures that the starting point for adding indexes is the same even if the example is executed multiple times. The three fields (columns in SQL language) that will be used in the indexes are then defined. This allows you to reuse them as needed. In this case, you require the employee to have the name and office location set, but the birthday is optional.

The first index created is on the Name field. This is a normal index and you specify that the utf8mb4_0900_ai_ci collation should be used. The index width is set to 60 characters. Don't worry; names longer than 60 characters are still supported. It's just that the index only considers the first 60 characters. The object created by create_index() is stored in the index variable and the actual creation of the index is performed with index. execute().

The second index is a spatial index for the location of the office where the employee works. The default values for options and srid are used. In this case, the index execution is combined with defining the index.

The third index combines the employee's birthday and the name. This allows you to search on the birthday and name together. Combining multiple fields into one index can be a powerful way to improve query performance when more than one condition is applied.

For each of the three indexes a confirmation message is printed after the index has been created:

```
Index created: employee_name
Index created: employee_office_location
Index created: employee_birthday_name
```

Tip   If you had created the last index as (Name, Birthday) it would have made the index just on the name redundant because a search on the name alone could just as well have been resolved using the combined index. This is because MySQL allows you to search a left prefix of the index on its own for B-tree indexes. Another consideration when combining multiple fields is that the best performance is achieved when the most selective value is first.

It can be interesting to check the table definition that results from executing the example. A slightly reformatted output is

```
mysql> SHOW CREATE TABLE py_test_db.employees\G
*************************** 1. row ***************************
        Table: employees
Create Table: CREATE TABLE `employees` (
  `doc` json DEFAULT NULL,
  `_id` varbinary(32) GENERATED ALWAYS AS
        (json_unquote(json_extract(`doc`,_utf8mb4'$._id')))
        STORED NOT NULL,
  `$ix_t60_r_4CB1E32CCBE4FE2585D3C8F059CB3A909FC536B7` text
        GENERATED ALWAYS AS
        (json_unquote(json_extract(`doc`,_utf8mb4'$.Name')))
        VIRTUAL NOT NULL,
```

```
  `$ix_gj_r_E933A4A981E8AB89AF33A3DB0B1D45F8E76A6E38` geometry
      GENERATED ALWAYS AS
      (st_geomfromgeojson(
          json_extract(`doc`,_utf8mb4'$.Office.Location'),1,4326)
      ) STORED NOT NULL /*!80003 SRID 4326 */,
  `$ix_d_CAA21771B5BB2089412F3D426AF25DEE3EDD1B76` date
      GENERATED ALWAYS AS
      (json_unquote(json_extract(`doc`,_utf8mb4'$.Birthday')))
      VIRTUAL,
PRIMARY KEY (`_id`),
SPATIAL KEY `employee_office_location`
      (`$ix_gj_r_E933A4A981E8AB89AF33A3DB0B1D45F8E76A6E38`),
KEY `employee_name`
      (`$ix_t60_r_4CB1E32CCBE4FE2585D3C8F059CB3A909FC536B7`(60)),
KEY `employee_birthday_name`
      (`$ix_d_CAA21771B5BB2089412F3D426AF25DEE3EDD1B76`,
       `$ix_t60_r_4CB1E32CCBE4FE2585D3C8F059CB3A909FC536B7`(60))
) ENGINE=InnoDB DEFAULT CHARSET=utf8mb4
COLLATE=utf8mb4_0900_ai_ci
1 row in set (0.00 sec)
```

Granted, the first things that stand out are the hard-to-read names for the generated columns. They are auto-generated to be unique, but they can easily be used by the X DevAPI. The names depend on the field definition, so they will stay the same for the same extracted field. That way, the same field is not added multiple times when it is used in several indexes. In this example, the employee name is used in two indexes, but it is only defined once how to extract it.

The other thing is that for these new secondary indexes the generated columns have the VIRTUAL clause. This means the values are not actually stored in the table, but just fetched as required. This saves disk space.

The compliment of create_index() is drop_index(), which is discussed next.

Dropping Indexes

It is much simpler to drop an index than to create it. All that is required is to invoke the drop_index() method of the collection with the name of the index to drop. MySQL will then take care of removing the index, and if the generated columns in the index are no longer needed for other indexes, they will be removed as well.

Listing 7-2 shows an example of dropping the employee_name index, which was one of the indexes created in the previous example.

Listing 7-2. Dropping an Index

```
import mysqlx
from config import connect_args

db = mysqlx.get_session(**connect_args)

# Reinitialize employees collection in
# the py_test_db schema
schema = db.get_schema("py_test_db")
employees = schema.get_collection(
  "employees")

# Drop the index on the Name field.
employees.drop_index("employee_name")
print("Index employee_name has been dropped")

db.close()
```

In this case, the index is dropped just by invoking the `drop_index()` method. The output of the script is

```
Index employee_name has been dropped
```

It is left as an exercise for the reader to compare the output of SHOW CREATE TABLE py_test_db.employees\G before and after dropping the index to confirm that the Name field is still extracted. A second exercise is to modify the example to drop the employee_birthday_name index as well and see that the Name and Birthday generated columns get removed.

This completes the walkthrough of the methods available to manipulate collections (not considering the documents stored in the collection). There are a few additional methods to consider before moving on query execution.

Other Collection Methods and Properties

The mysqlx.Collection class includes a few methods and three properties that can be useful when working with collection objects. They are very similar to those already discussed for schemas, so this will only include a brief introduction.

The methods that can return information about the collection are listed in Table 7-4. The returned objects are relative to the mysqlx module. None of the methods take any arguments.

Table 7-4. *Collection Utility Methods*

Method	Returns Object	Description
exists_ in_database		Returns True or False depending on whether the collection exists.
get_connection	connection. Connection	Returns the underlying connection object.
get_name		Returns the name of the collection. This is the same as the name property.
get_schema	crud.Schema	Returns the object for the schema where the collection exists. This is the same as the schema property.
get_session	connection. Session	Returns the object for the session. This is the same as the session property. Added in version 8.0.12.

As you can see from the description of the methods returning the name and schema, there are also three properties. The name property is the name of the collection, the schema property holds the schema object, and the session property (available in 8.0.12 and later) holds the session object.

As the collection utility methods and properties are essentially the same as for the schema, let's move on to execute some queries.

Queries – CRUD

The fun part of working with data is executing queries. Now that you know how to work with sessions, schemas, and collections, you can start using the session to use the NoSQL part of the API. The implementation is built around the CRUD (create, read, update, delete) principle, and the following four sections will go through each of the four actions in turn.

Before getting in deep, it is worth taking a high-level look at the CRUD methods. They are collected in Table 7-5. The returned objects are relative to the myqslx module.

Table 7-5. *CRUD Methods for Collection Objects*

Method	Arguments	Returns Object	Description
add	List of documents	Statement. AddStatement	Prepares to add the documents in the list of dictionaries. Each dictionary is a document.
add_or_ replace_one	doc_id doc	Result.Result	Upserts the document, so if the document ID exists, it replaces the existing document; otherwise, it adds it as a new document.
count			Returns the number of documents in the collection as an integer.
find	condition	Statement. FindStatement	Prepares a find statement that returns the document matching the condition.
modify	condition	Statement. ModifyStatement	Prepares a modify statement that updates the documents matching the condition. The condition is mandatory in version 8.0.12 and later.
remove	condition	Statement. RemoveStatement	Prepares a remove statement that deletes the documents matching the condition.
remove_one	doc_id	result.Result	Removes the document with the specified document ID.
replace_one	doc_id doc	result.Result	Updates the document with the specified document ID with the new document.

As you can see from the table, the CRUD methods use a few common arguments:

- **Document**: This is a dictionary describing the JSON document.

- **Document ID**: This is the unique key of the document.

- **Condition**: This is the equivalent of a WHERE clause in SQL, which defines the filter to use when searching for documents.

Note There is, of course, more to it than what the list of three arguments types suggest. For example, it is possible to sort the result of a read request. You will learn how to do that shortly.

For some of the methods, a result object is returned directly. It will include information about the performed action. The rest of the methods, with the exception of count(), return an object of a class in the statement module. They require you to call the execute() method of the returned statement object before the action is performed, and execute() then returns a result object.

It is time to stop talking and dive in head first and create some documents. This means you need to look at the create part of CRUD.

CRUD: Create

The first step of working with the data stored in a database is to create the data. Until data exists in the collection, there is nothing to query or modify. So, your first task is to populate a collection with some data. The data inserted in this section is the basis for the rest of the Document Store CRUD discussion.

There are two methods that can add data to a collection: add() and add_or_replace_one(). This section will discuss the add() method whereas add_or_replace_one() will be postponed to the "CRUD: Update" section because it can work for both adding new data and updating existing data.

The add() method takes zero or more documents as the arguments. Each document is defined using a Python dictionary, which naturally forms a JSON document. When multiple documents are inserted in the same invocation of add(), they can be provided as a list or tuple, or by specifying multiple arguments.

The add() method returns a mysqlx.statement.AddStatement object. The two most important methods for this are add() and execute(). These methods are summarized in Table 7-6.

Table 7-6. *Methods to Work with an Add Statement*

Method	Arguments	Description
add	*values	Adds the document(s) specified in the values to the add statement.
execute		Executes the add statement by submitting the values to MySQL Server.

The AddStatement.add() method can be used to add more documents to the statement, and the AddStatement.execute() sends the documents to the Document Store. All added documents are sent as one statement.

The data that will be inserted is available in the cities.py file included in the source code for this book. The file includes data for 15 Australian cities in the cities dictionary. The start of the file is

```
cities = {
  "Sydney": {
    "Name"            : "Sydney",
    "Country_capital": False,
```

```
    "State_capital"  : True,
    "Geography": {
      "Country" : "Australia",
      "State"   : "New South Wales",
      "Area"     : 12367.7,
      "Location": "{'Type': 'Point', 'Coordinates': [151.2094,
                  -33.8650]}",
      "Climate" : {
        "Classification"        : "humid subtropical",
        "Mean_max_temperature": 22.5,
        "Mean_min_temperature": 14.5,
        "Annual_rainfaill"    : 1222.7
      },
    },
    "Demographics": {
      "Population": 5029768,
      "Median Age": 36
    },
    "Suburbs": [
      "Central Business District",
      "Parramatta",
      "Bankstown",
      "Sutherland",
      "Chatswood"
    ]
  },
...
```

Listing 7-3 shows an example where the add() method is used three times to insert cities into a newly created collection. The first example of using add() inserts a single city, the second time two cities are inserted in one add() call, and the third time several cities are inserted using multiple add() calls to create one large statement.

Listing 7-3. Adding Data to a Collection

```
import mysqlx
from config import connect_args
from cities import cities

db = mysqlx.get_session(**connect_args)
schema = db.create_schema("py_test_db")

# Reinitalize the city collection
schema.drop_collection("city")
city_col = schema.create_collection("city")

# Insert a single city
sydney = cities.pop("Sydney")
db.start_transaction()
result = city_col.add(sydney).execute()
db.commit()
items = result.get_affected_items_count()
print("1: Number of docs added: {0}"
  .format(items))
ids = result.get_generated_ids()
print("1: Doc IDs added: {0}".format(ids))
print("")

# Insert two cities in one call
melbourne = cities.pop("Melbourne")
brisbane  = cities.pop("Brisbane")
data = (melbourne, brisbane)

db.start_transaction()
result = city_col.add(data).execute()
db.commit()

items = result.get_affected_items_count()
```

```
print("2: Number of docs added: {0}"
  .format(items))
ids = result.get_generated_ids()
print("2: Doc IDs added: {0}".format(ids))
print("")

# Insert the rest of the cities by
# adding them to the statement object
# one by one.
db.start_transaction()
statement = city_col.add()
for city_name in cities:
  statement.add(cities[city_name])

result = statement.execute()
db.commit()

items = result.get_affected_items_count()
print("3: Number of docs added: {0}"
  .format(items))
print("")

db.close()
```

The example starts out by ensuring the city collection in the py_test_ db schema does not exist and then creates it. Then it adds the cities that were imported from the cities.py file.

The first city to be inserted is Sydney. This is done by inserting the city on its own. The command is chained to perform all of the work in one line of code, and the result is a result.Result object. Notice how the invocation is wrapped by db.start_transaction() and db.commit() call. Since the value of autocommit is inherited from the MySQL Server global setting, it is safest to explicitly add transactions.

Note   As always, you should check whether any warnings or errors occurred before committing the data. To keep the example easier to read, the handling of warnings and errors has been omitted. Chapter 9 will go into more detail on how to check for warnings and errors.

Next, the cities of Melbourne and Brisbane are inserted. This is done by creating a tuple with the documents, and the tuple is passed to the add() method. The documents could also have been added as two arguments, for example:

```
result = city_col.add(
  melbourne, brisbane
).execute()
```

Finally, the remaining cities are added. This is done by first creating the AddStatement object, then iterating over the remaining cities, and adding them one by one. Finally, the AddStatement.execute() method is called to insert all of the cities in one database call.

The output of the executing the example is similar to the following sample:

```
1: Number of docs added: 1
1: Doc IDs added: ['00005af3e4f7000000000000008f']

2: Number of docs added: 2
2: Doc IDs added: ['00005af3e4f70000000000000090',
'00005af3e4f70000000000000091']

3: Number of docs added: 12
```

The actual document IDs will be different because they are auto-generated. The city collection now has 15 Australian cities to query, so it is time to look at read operations.

CRUD: Read

For most databases, the majority of the queries are read queries (queries that do not modify any of the data). These queries are the topic of this section.

There are two methods that read from a collection without changing any of the data in the Document Store: count() and find(). The count() method is the simplest because it just returns the number of documents in the collection as an integer. The find() method is more complex because it supports a condition (WHERE clause in SQL language), sorting, returning the documents, and more.

The find() method returns a mysqlx.statement.FindStatement object. This is the main building block where the query can be modified by invoking FindStatement methods. Each of these modifier methods returns the FindStatement object itself, so it can be further modified. In the end there is a chain of calls defining the query, and the execute() method can be used to submit the query. Table 7-7 shows the FindStatement methods available to modify the statement. The methods are ordered in the order they are typically invoked.

Table 7-7. *Methods to Modify a Find Statement*

Method	Arguments	Description
fields	*fields	Defines the fields to include in the result. Each field can be an expression using the same language as for SQL.
group_by	*fields	Describes which fields to group by for queries involving aggregate functions.
having	condition	Describes what to filter the result by after the query has otherwise been resolved (except for sorting). This makes it useful for filtering by the value of aggregate functions.

(continued)

Table 7-7. (*continued*)

Method	Arguments	Description
sort	*sort_ clauses	Describes what to sort the result by.
limit	row_count offset=0	The first argument sets the maximum number of documents to return. The second optional argument defines the offset. The default offset is 0. **Note:** The offset argument has been deprecated in version 8.0.12 and will be removed in a later release. Instead the offset() method has been introduced to set the offset.
offset	offset	Set the offset of the rows to return. Added in version 8.0.12.
lock_exclusive		Makes the statement take an exclusive lock. Only one statement can have an exclusive lock at a time. Use if the document(s) will be updated later in the same transaction.
lock_shared		Makes the statement take a shared lock. This prevents other statements from modifying the matching documents, but it is possible for them to read the documents.
bind	*args	The first argument provides the name of the parameter to replace. The second argument provides the value. Call bind() once for each parameter.
execute		Executes the find statement.

The order the query modifying methods are called is not of importance, but it is recommended to stick to the same order throughout the program to make it easier at a glance to determine how the query is modified.

Listing 7-4 shows an example where first the total number of cities in the city collection is determined. Then it shows the states with the most cities in the collection. The result is ordered by the number of cities in the state and limited to at most three states.

Listing 7-4. Querying the city Collection

```
import mysqlx
from config import connect_args

db = mysqlx.get_session(**connect_args)
schema = db.create_schema("py_test_db")
city_col = schema.get_collection("city")

# Use the count() method to get the
# total number of cities.
num_cities = city_col.count()
print("Total number of cities: {0}"
  .format(num_cities))
print("")

statement = city_col.find(
  "Geography.Country = :country") \
  .fields("Geography.State AS State",
          "COUNT(*) AS NumCities") \
  .group_by("Geography.State") \
  .having("COUNT(*) > 1") \
  .sort("COUNT(*) DESC") \
  .limit(3)
```

```
result = statement.bind(
  "country", "Australia"
).execute()

states = result.fetch_all()
print("Num states in result: {0}"
  .format(result.count))
print("")

print("{0:15s}    {1:8s}"
  .format("State", "# Cities"))
print("-"*26)
for state in states:
  print("{State:15s}        {NumCities:1d}"
    .format(**state))

  db.close()
```

Other than the new syntax, the example is straightforward. The count() method of the collection is used to get the total number of rows. Then the query is defined. You ask for the query to be filtered by the Geography.Country element with the value to filter by occupied by a placeholder (:country) that is later set to the value of Australia later in the bind() method. The query will return the Geography.State element to be returned and renamed as State, and the number of cities for each state is returned as NumCities.

Since the fields include an aggregate function (COUNT()) as well as a non-aggregate field (Geography.State), it is required to also define what to group by. This is done by calling the group_by() method. Additionally in this case, you choose to filter so only states with more than one city are included; this is done using the having() method.

Finally, you tell the Document Store that you want to sort the result by the number of cities in the state in descending order, and you at most want three states returned (the three with the most cities). The statement is saved at this point in the `statement` variable. In this case, that is not important, but by specifying the bind parameters at the execution time, it is possible to reuse the query.

Tip   If the statement object is stored in a variable, it is possible to execute the same query several times. By saving the `bind()` call to the execution time, it is possible to reuse the same query template with different values. An example of reusing a find query follows when modifying documents.

Once the query has been executed, the rows are fetched using `fetch_all()`. This also sets the `count` property of the result to the number of documents in the result. The output of the program is

```
Total number of cities: 15

Num states in result: 3

State               # Cities
--------------------------
Queensland              5
New South Wales         3
Victoria                2
```

The location of all the cities in the `city` collection is known. As a second example, let's look at how geographical data is used. Listing 7-5 shows an example of finding all cities, calculating the distance to Sydney, and ordering by how far they are away, starting with the closest city. Sydney itself will be skipped because it does not provide any information.

Listing 7-5. Querying Geographical Data

```python
import mysqlx
from config import connect_args

db = mysqlx.get_session(**connect_args)
schema = db.get_schema("py_test_db")
city_col = schema.get_collection("city")

# Get the location of Sydney
statement = city_col.find("Name = :city")
statement.fields(
  "Geography.Location AS Location")
statement.bind("city", "Sydney")
result = statement.execute()
sydney = result.fetch_one()

# Define the formula for converting
# the location in GeoJSON format to
# the binary format used in MySQL
to_geom = "ST_GeomFromGeoJSON({0})"
sydney_geom = to_geom.format(
  sydney["Location"])
other_geom = to_geom.format(
  "Geography.Location")
distance = "ST_Distance({0}, {1})".format(
  sydney_geom, other_geom)

statement = city_col.find("Name != 'Sydney'")
statement.fields(
    "Name",
```

```
    "Geography.State AS State",
    distance + " AS Distance"
)
statement.sort(distance)
result = statement.execute()

cities = result.fetch_all()
print("{0:14s}   {1:28s}   {2:8s}"
  .format("City", "State", "Distance"))
print("-"*56)
for city in cities:
  # Convert the distance to kilometers
  distance = city["Distance"]/1000
  print("{Name:14s}   {State:28s}"
    .format(**city)
    + "      {0:4d}"
    .format(int(distance))
  )

db.close()
```

The basics of this example are the same as in the previous one. The interesting part is the use of two MySQL geometry functions. The ST_GeomFromGeoJSON() function is used to convert the GeoJSON coordinates to the binary geometry format used inside MySQL. The ST_Distance() function then calculates the distance between two points, taking the spatial reference system into account; here the default is used, which is the Earth. The output of the program is shown in Listing 7-6.

Listing 7-6. The Output of the Example Program in Listing 7-5

```
City              State                          Distance
------------------------------------------------------------
Wollongong        New South Wales                     69
Newcastle         New South Wales                    116
Canberra          Australian Capital Territory       249
Gold Coast        Queensland                         681
Melbourne         Victoria                           714
Brisbane          Queensland                         730
Geelong           Victoria                           779
Sunshine Coast    Queensland                         819
Hobart            Tasmania                          1056
Adelaide          South Australia                   1164
Townsville        Queensland                        1676
Cairns            Queensland                        1960
Darwin            Northern Territory                3145
Perth             Western Australia                 3297
```

Adding and retrieving data covers a lot of database use cases, but what do you do if the data is no longer current? Let's look at how to update the data in the database.

CRUD: Update

In CRUD, the update part is to modify existing data, so the value of one or more fields is changed or fields are added or removed. An example is to update the population of a city when it changes because of migration, child births, and deaths. This section will look into the methods available for doing just that.

There are three methods available for modifying data in MySQL Connector/Python X DevAPI for a Document Store:

- `add_or_replace_one()`: Used to upsert a document. For example, if there is a document with the same document ID, it will be replaced; otherwise, a new document will be added.

- `modify()`: Updates an existing document. Documents are found in the same way as read queries filter the documents.

- `replace_one()`: Replaces the document with the given document ID.

Since `add_or_replace_one()` and `replace_one()` methods are very similar, they will be discussed together, followed by a discussion of the `modify()` method.

Replacing Documents

The difference between `add_or_replace_one()` and `replace_one()` is what happens if there is no document with the specified ID. The `add_or_replace_one()` method adds a new document whereas the `replace_one()` method ends up not doing anything.

Listing 7-7 shows an example where the document for Geelong is replaced with a document where the population is changed to 193000. Afterwards it attempts to replace a document with a non-existing document ID.

Listing 7-7. Upserting a Document and Attempting to Replace One

```
import mysqlx
from config import connect_args

db = mysqlx.get_session(**connect_args)
schema = db.get_schema("py_test_db")
city_col = schema.get_collection("city")
```

```
# Get the current document for Geelong
db.start_transaction()
result = city_col.find("Name = :city_name") \
  .bind("city_name", "Geelong") \
  .lock_exclusive() \
  .execute()
geelong = result.fetch_one()

# Get the Geelong document ID and
# update the population
geeling_id = geelong["_id"]
geelong["Demographics"]["Population"] = 193000

# Upsert the document
result = city_col.add_or_replace_one(
  geeling_id, geelong)

print("Number of affected docs: {0}"
  .format(result.get_affected_items_count()))

# Attempt to use the same document
# to change a non-existing ID
result = city_col.replace_one(
  "No such ID", geelong)

print("Number of affected docs: {0}"
  .format(result.get_affected_items_count()))

# Leave the data in the same state as
# before the changes
db.rollback()
db.close()
```

The example starts out by retrieving the existing document for Geelong. It is used to get the Document ID and as the base of the new document. This is also an example of taking an exclusive lock, so no one else can access the document until the transaction is complete. The new document is upserted into the Document Store using the add_or_replace_ one() method. After that, the same document is used with the replace_ one() method, but for a document ID that does not exist. For each of the two uses, the number of affected documents is printed. The output is

```
Number of affected docs: 2
Number of affected docs: 0
```

The result of the add_or_replace_one() call shows that two documents were affected. How? It's because of the way upserts are implemented. First, an insert of the new document is attempted. In case of a duplicate document, the existing one is updated (an INSERT ... ON DUPLICATE KEY UPDATE ... statement in SQL). Had the document not existed, only one document would have been affected. On the other hand, replace_one() does not affect any documents; it neither inserted a new document nor updated an existing one.

Note   Do not think of replace_one() as an SQL REPLACE statement. The equivalent SQL statement for replace_one() is UPDATE with a WHERE clause on the primary key.

If you want to just update the fields that have changed rather than the whole document, you need to use the modify() method.

Modifying Documents

The two replace methods that you saw in the previous discussion worked on replacing the whole document. For the relatively small documents in the example collection, this is not a big issue, but for larger documents, it quickly becomes inefficient. Additionally, the two replace methods can only modify one document at a time, making it cumbersome to update all cities in a country or all documents in a collection.

This is where the modify() method comes into play. It supports specifying a condition like for read queries to specify which documents to change, and the change can be based on the existing values. The modify() method returns a mysqlx.statement.ModifyStatement object, which, like the statement object returned by find(), can be used to define the overall modify statement. Table 7-8 includes the most important methods.

Table 7-8. *Methods to Modify a Modify Query*

Method	Arguments	Description
sort	*sort_ clauses	Describes what to sort the documents by.
limit	row_count	The argument sets the maximum number of documents to modify.
array_append	doc_path	Appends the value to an existing array element in the document at the point specified by
	value	doc_path.
array_insert	field	Inserts the value into the array specified by field.
	value	

(*continued*)

Table 7-8. (*continued*)

Method	Arguments	Description
set	doc_path value	If the document path already exists, the value is updated; otherwise, the field is added with the given value.
patch	Doc	Adds or replaces the fields included in the document. It also supports removing existing fields.
unset	*doc_paths	Removes the matching document paths from the documents.
bind	*args	The first argument provides the name of the parameter to replace. The second argument provides the value. Call bind() once for each parameter.
execute		Executes the modify statement.

Several of the methods are the same as for find(), which is not surprising since the first task of a modify statement is to locate the documents to update. Unlike for find statements, it is a requirement that there is a condition defined. Otherwise, a ProgrammingErrror exception occurs in 8.0.11:

```
mysqlx.errors.ProgrammingError: No condition was found for modify
```

In MySQL Connector/Python 8.0.12 and later, the condition must be specified when creating the modify statement. Otherwise a TypeError exception occurs:

```
TypeError: modify() missing 1 required positional argument:
'condition'
```

This is a safety feature to prevent accidentally updating all documents due to a coding error. If you really need to modify all documents, add a condition that always evaluates to True, for example:

```
collectoin.modify("True")
```

Note   A modify statement must have a condition specifying which documents to update. If you really want to update all documents, use True as a condition; this also makes your intention clear, which is helpful when you get back to the code at a later date.

There are also several methods to change the content of the matching documents. Let's look at some examples using several of these methods.

set() and unset()

The simplest methods for modifying the documents are the set() and unset() methods. The set() and unset() methods are very similar. The set() method will change the value of the specified field. If the field does not exists, it will be added. The new value can be a calculation that includes the old value. The unset() method, on the other hand, removes a field if it exists.

Let's assume there has been a census and the data for state of Victoria shows a 10% population increase. Listing 7-8 shows how to make that change using the modify() method.

Listing 7-8. Modifying Several Documents at a Time with set()

```
import mysqlx
from config import connect_args

db = mysqlx.get_session(**connect_args)
schema = db.get_schema("py_test_db")
city_col = schema.get_collection("city")
```

```
db.start_transaction()

# Get the current population
statement = city_col.find(
  "Geography.State = :state")
statement.fields("Name AS CityName",
  "Demographics.Population AS Population")
statement.sort("Name")
statement.bind("state", "Victoria")

before = statement.execute()

# Update the population for cities
# in the state of Victoria to increase
# the population with 10%
result = city_col.modify(
  "Geography.State = :state") \
  .set("Demographics.Population",
    "FLOOR(Demographics.Population * 1.10)") \
  .bind("state", "Victoria") \
  .execute()
print("Number of affected docs: {0}"
  .format(result.get_affected_items_count()))
print("")

after = statement.execute()

before_cities = before.fetch_all()
after_cities  = after.fetch_all()

print("{0:10s}    {1:^17s}"
  .format("City", "Population"))
print("{0:10s}    {1:7s}    {2:7s}"
  .format("", "Before", "After"))
print("-"*30)
```

```
for before_city, after_city \
  in zip(before_cities, after_cities):
  print("{0:10s}    {1:7d}    {2:7d}"
    .format(
      before_city["CityName"],
      int(before_city["Population"]),
      int(after_city["Population"])
    )
  )

# Leave the data in the same state as
# before the changes
db.rollback()
db.close()
```

Before modifying the cities in Victoria, a find statement is defined to get the city names and their population. This is used to get the population both before and after the modify statement, so it is possible to confirm the result is as expected.

The most interesting part of the example is the invocation of modify() and the subsequent method calls to define the update. The set() method is used to define the update itself and the new population is calculated based on the old population. Notice how the FLOOR() function is wrapped around the calculation determining the new population. This is to avoid fractional people. Even if you allowed fractions, it is necessary with parenthesis around the new value to signify that the value of Demographics.Population should be used and not the literal string "Demographics.Population".

After the execution of the modify statement, the populations are read again, and the before and after populations for the cities are printed.

Finally, the transaction is rolled back so it is possible to execute the program several times and get the same output, which is the following:

```
Number of affected docs: 2

City              Population
                Before     After
------------------------------
Geelong          192393    211632
Melbourne       4725316   5197847
```

The next two modify methods to be discussed are the `array_append()` and `array_insert()` methods.

array_append() and array_insert()

As their names suggest, the `array_append()` and `array_insert()` methods work with arrays within the document. While their usage is relatively limited, they are very good at what they do. Their use is similar, so they will be discussed together.

Both methods take the same two arguments even though they are named differently. The two arguments are

- The path to the array element to modify or the location of where to insert the value

- The value

The major difference is what is done at the specified element. The `array_append()` method replaces the existing value with an array consisting of the existing value followed by the new value. On the other hand, `array_insert()` inserts the new element into that place in the array.

The easiest way to explain how they work is to show an example. Listing 7-9 uses both methods to modify the suburbs of Sydney. The `array_append()` method is used change the *Central Business District* suburb to be an array consisting of itself as the first element and an array of places in the suburb as the second element. The `array_insert()` method is used to add Liverpool to the list of suburbs.

Listing 7-9. Updating a Document with `array_append()` and `array_insert()`

```
import mysqlx
from config import connect_args
import pprint

printer = pprint.PrettyPrinter(indent=1)

db = mysqlx.get_session(**connect_args)
schema = db.get_schema("py_test_db")
city_col = schema.get_collection("city")

# Run inside a transaction, so the
# changes can be rolled back at the end.
db.start_transaction()

# Get the current suburbs, the document
# id, and the index of Central Business
# District in the Suburbs array.
statement = city_col.find("Name = :city_name")
statement.fields(
  "_id",
  "Suburbs",
  "JSON_SEARCH("
    + "Suburbs,"
    + " 'one',"
    + " 'Central Business District')"
  + " AS Index")
statement.bind("city_name", "Sydney")
```

```
before = statement.execute().fetch_one()
print("Suburbs before the changes:")
print("-"*27)
printer.pprint(before["Suburbs"])
print("")

docid = before["_id"]
# The returned index includes $ to
# signify the start of the path, but
# that is relative to Suburbs, so
# remove for this use.
index = before["Index"][1:]
print("Index = '{0}'\n"
  .format(before["Index"]))

# Use array_append() to change the
# Central Busines District suburb into
# an array of itself plus an array of
# some places within the suburb.
modify = city_col.modify("_id = :id")
modify.array_append(
  "Suburbs{0}".format(index),
  ["Circular Quay", "Town Hall"])
modify.bind("id", docid)
modify.execute()

after1 = statement.execute().fetch_one()
print("Suburbs after the array_append:")
print("-"*31)
printer.pprint(after1["Suburbs"])
print("")
```

```
# Reset the data
db.rollback()

# Use array_insert to add the suburb
# Liverpool
db.start_transaction()
num_suburbs = len(before["Suburbs"])
modify = city_col.modify("_id = :id")
modify.array_insert(
  "Suburbs[{0}]".format(num_suburbs),
  "Liverpool")
modify.bind("id", docid)
modify.execute()

after2 = statement.execute().fetch_one()
print("Suburbs after the array_insert:")
print("-"*31)
printer.pprint(after2["Suburbs"])

# Reset the data
db.rollback()
db.close()
```

The start of the example just sets up the environment as usual. Then the existing suburbs of Sydney are read as well as the document ID and the index of the Central Business District inside the suburbs array.

The document ID allows you to use it in the modify statement's filter condition. Finding a document by its document ID is always the most efficient way to locate it.

The index of the Central Business District element is returned as $[0] (the first element in the array). The dollar sign signifies the head of the document, but since you used the JSON_SEARCH() function to search the Suburbs array, it is relative to the Suburbs array and not the root of the document. So, in order to use the index, it is necessary to remove the dollar sign.

Tip   There are several JSON functions available in MySQL to search or work with JSON documents. They are in general centered around what is required when working with MySQL as a document store, but there are also a few functions that are more related to the SQL side. For a full overview of JSON functions in MySQL, see `https://dev.mysql.com/doc/refman/en/json-functions.html`.

You are now ready to use array_append() to add locations within the suburb and to add the suburb of Liverpool using array_insert(). For the insert, the path is set as Suburbs[{0}] where {0} is replaced with the number of suburbs before the change to add the new suburb at the end. After each of the modify statements the transaction is rolled back to reset the data. The output is

```
Suburbs before the changes:
---------------------------
['Central Business District',
 'Parramatta',
 'Bankstown',
 'Sutherland',
 'Chatswood']

Index = '$[0]'
```

Suburbs after the array_append:

[['Central Business District', ['Circular Quay', 'Town Hall']],
 'Parramatta',
 'Bankstown',
 'Sutherland',
 'Chatswood']

Suburbs after the array_insert:

['Central Business District',
 'Parramatta',
 'Bankstown',
 'Sutherland',
 'Chatswood',
 'Liverpool']

The output makes it clear what changes were made (see the part of the output in bold). The array_append() changed the string 'Central Business District' into the array ['Central Business District', ['Circular Quay', 'Town Hall']]. The array_insert() method inserted 'Liverpool' at the end of the existing array.

Now there is only the patch() method left to consider for modify statements.

patch()

The final method to modify a document is the patch() method. This is the most powerful of the methods, yet it's surprisingly simple once you get the hang of it. To some extend it works similarly to the patch command used to apply changes to source code, thus the name; however, the syntax is not related.

There are three possible outcomes of what the patch() method does for each of the JSON fields that are matched by the document provided as the argument:

- **The element is removed**: This happens when there is a match for the field name and there is no value in the patch document.

- **The element is modified**: This happens when there is a match for the field and it has a value in the patch document.

- **The element is inserted**: This happens when the field does not exist and it has a value in the patch document.

The way the lack of a value for a field is specified (to delete it or not add it) depends on how the document is specified. If the document is specified as a string with the JSON document written inside, the lack of a value is specified by writing null. When the document is specified as a dictionary, use None to signify no value.

So, to patch a document, you provide a new document with the new values you want. Then MySQL figures out the rest. This is where the simplicity of the method comes in.

As an example, consider the city of Adelaide. The data has become outdated, so it is time to determine the most recent values of the fields stored in the document. The city area and population have changed, but it has not been possible to find an updated amount for the Median weekly individual income, so you decide to delete that field. The document to describe the patch then becomes

```
doc = {
  "Geography": {
    "Area": 3400
  },
```

```
  "Demographics": {
    "Population": 1500000,
    "Median weekly individual income": None
  }
}
```

This is fairly straightforward, and it also is quite easy to see what is being changed. Listing 7-10 shows the full example of making the changes.

Listing 7-10. Using patch() to Modify a Document

```python
import mysqlx
from config import connect_args
import pprint

printer = pprint.PrettyPrinter(indent=1)

db = mysqlx.get_session(**connect_args)
schema = db.get_schema("py_test_db")
city_col = schema.get_collection("city")

# Run inside a transaction, so the
# changes can be rolled back at the end.
db.start_transaction()

# Get the current suburbs, the document
# id, and the index of Central Business
# District in the Suburbs array.
statement = city_col.find(
  "Name = :city_name")
statement.bind("city_name", "Adelaide")
before = statement.execute().fetch_one()
print("Adelaide before patching:")
print("-"*25)
```

```
printer.pprint(dict(before))
print("")

docid = before["_id"]

# Make the following changes:
#  * Increase the area to 3400
#  * Increase the population to 1500000
#  * Remove the median weekly individual
#    income.
doc = {
  "Geography": {
    "Area": 3400
  },
  "Demographics": {
    "Population": 1500000,
    "Median weekly individual income": None
  }
}
modify = city_col.modify("_id = :id")
modify.patch(doc)
modify.bind("id", docid)
modify.execute()

after = statement.execute().fetch_one()
print("Adelaide after patching:")
print("-"*24)
printer.pprint(dict(after))

# Reset the data
db.rollback()
db.close()
```

The only new part in this example is the definition of the document to patch the existing document with and the use of the patch() method. The before and after documents for Adelaide are shown in Listing 7-11.

Listing 7-11. The Before and After Documents for Adelaide After the Patching Process

```
Adelaide before patching:
-------------------------
{'Country_capital': False,
 'Demographics': {'Median weekly individual income': 447,
                  'Population': 1324279},
 'Geography': {'Area': 3257.7,
               'Climate': {'Annual rainfaill': 543.9,
                           'Classification': 'Mediterranean',
                           'Mean max temperature': 22.4,
                           'Mean min temperature': 12.3},
               'Country': 'Australia',
               'Location': {'Coordinates': [138.601, -34.929],
'Type': 'Point'},
               'State': 'South Australia'},
 'Name': 'Adelaide',
 'State_capital': True,
 'Suburbs': ['Adelaide',
             'Elizabeth',
             'Wingfield',
             'Henley Beach',
             'Oaklands Park'],
 '_id': '00005af3e4f70000000000000093'}
```

Adelaide after patching:

```
{'Country_capital': False,
 'Demographics': {'Population': 1500000},
 'Geography': {'Area': 3400,
               'Climate': {'Annual rainfaill': 543.9,
                           'Classification': 'Mediterranean',
                           'Mean max temperature': 22.4,
                           'Mean min temperature': 12.3},
               'Country': 'Australia',
               'Location': {'Coordinates': [138.601, -34.929],
               'Type': 'Point'},
               'State': 'South Australia'},
 'Name': 'Adelaide',
 'State_capital': True,
 'Suburbs': ['Adelaide',
             'Elizabeth',
             'Wingfield',
             'Henley Beach',
             'Oaklands Park'],
 '_id': '00005af3e4f7000000000000093'}
```

Notice here how the Median weekly individual income has been removed and the Population and Area have been updated. The value of _id will differ from the one in this output, but the _id is the same before and after the patching.

Tip   If you want to learn more about patching documents, a good place to start is the documentation of the JSON_MERGE_PATCH() SQL function, which is the one providing the underlying functionality. See https://dev.mysql.com/doc/refman/en/json-modification-functions.html#function_json-merge-patch.

This completes the discussion of modifying statements. The last part of CRUD is deleting documents.

CRUD: Delete

In most applications, some documents should be deleted at some point. Removing documents reduces the size of the data, which not only reduces the disk usage but also makes queries more efficient because they need to process less data. The Document Store has two methods for removing documents from a collection:

- remove(): For arbitrary deletion of documents based on a condition.

- remove_one(): For deleting a single document based on the document ID.

These methods are among the simplest of the CRUD methods because all that is required is to specify which documents to delete. The remove() method offers an option of how many documents to delete at most.

The remove_one() method is the simplest of the two methods because it just requires a document ID and returns a Result object directly. The remove() method takes a condition, like for find() and modify(), and returns an object of the RemoveStatement class. The statement can be further refined using the methods listed in Table 7-9.

Table 7-9. *Methods to Modify a Remove Query*

Method	Arguments	Description
sort	*sort_clauses	Describes what to sort the documents by.
limit	row_count	Sets the maximum number of documents to delete.
bind	*args	The first argument provides the name of the parameter to replace. The second argument provides the value. Call bind() once for each parameter.
execute		Executes the remove statement.

These modifier methods should all be familiar by now. In the same way as for the modify() method, there must be a condition specified; otherwise, a ProgrammingError exception occurs in 8.0.11:

```
mysqlx.errors.ProgrammingError: No condition was found for remove
```

In MySQL Connector/Python 8.0.12 and later, the condition must be specified when calling remove() to create the remove statement. If no condition has been given, a TypeError exception occurs:

```
TypeError: remove() missing 1 required positional argument:
'condition'
```

If you need to delete all documents, either use True as a condition or drop/recreate the collection.

Listing 7-12 shows how to first delete a single city by using the Document ID and then delete several cities by filtering by the country.

Listing 7-12. Deleting Documents in a Collection

```python
import mysqlx
from config import connect_args

db = mysqlx.get_session(**connect_args)
schema = db.get_schema("py_test_db")
city_col = schema.get_collection("city")

# For printing information along the way
fmt = "{0:36s}: {1:2d}"

# Run inside a transaction, so the
# changes can be rolled back at the end.
db.start_transaction()

# Get the document ID for Canberra.
statement = city_col.find("Name = :city_name")
statement.fields("_id")
statement.bind("city_name", "Canberra")

result = statement.execute()
canberra_id = result.fetch_one()["_id"]

# Number of rows in the collection
# before removing any documents
print(fmt.format(
  "Initial number of documents",
  city_col.count()
))
print("")

result = city_col.remove_one(
  canberra_id)

items = result.get_affected_items_count()
print(fmt.format(
```

```
  "Number of rows deleted by remove_one",
  result.get_affected_items_count()
))
print(fmt.format(
  "Number of documents after remove_one",
  city_col.count()
))
print("")
statement = city_col.remove(
  "Geography.Country = :country")
statement.bind("country", "Australia")
result = statement.execute()

print(fmt.format(
  "Number of rows deleted by remove",
  result.get_affected_items_count()
))
print(fmt.format(
  "Number of documents after remove",
  city_col.count()
))

# Reset the data
db.rollback()
db.close()
```

In the example, the document ID for Canberra is first found using the find() method. Then the document for the Canberra document ID is removed using remove_one(), before all remaining Australian cities are deleted using the remove() method. Along the way, the number of cities and the number of rows affected by the remove actions are printed. The output is

```
Initial number of documents       : 15
Number of rows deleted by remove_one:  1
Number of documents after remove_one: 14
```

```
Number of rows deleted by remove    : 14
Number of documents after remove    : 0
```

There were 15 cities in the collection. As expected, remove_one() deleted one city, leaving 14 cities. Since there were only Australian cities in the collection, deleting with a filter of Geography.Country = 'Australia' removed the remaining 14 documents.

This concludes the lengthy journey through the world of the Document Store. The MySQL X DevAPI is not just about the Document Store; it can also work with SQL tables in a NoSQL fashion and execute SQL queries, so there is much more to dive into in the next chapter.

Summary

This chapter went into detail on the MySQL Document Store. Specifically, you looked at collections and how to use them. A collection is a container for related documents; for example, you can have a container named city to store information about cities such as the country they are located in, their population, and much more.

The documents themselves are JSON documents that store data schemalessly. This allows the developer to quickly add new types of data to the database, but also pushes the task of keeping the data consistent back on the developer.

You started out learning how collections can be manipulated from the point of creating them until the deletion. In-between, indexes can be created and dropped, and a collection can be retrieved for use with the create-read-update-delete (CRUD) methods. The rest of the chapter went into detail of each of the CRUD methods.

The MySQL X DevAPI is not only for use with the Document Store. The next chapter will look at how to use the CRUD method with SQL tables and how to execute arbitrary SQL statements.

CHAPTER 8

SQL Tables

Thus far, the main focus of the X DevAPI has been on using it with the MySQL Document Store. However, as explained in Chapter 6, it also supports "good old" SQL tables. In fact, there are two interfaces to work with SQL tables. The create-read-update-delete (CRUD) actions that were the focus of Chapter 7 also exist for SQL tables and provide a NoSQL API. Also, the X DevAPI can be used to execute arbitrary SQL statements.

This chapter will first give an overview of the workflow when using SQL tables and then go through how the X DevAPI can use SQL tables with a NoSQL API. The second part of the chapter will look at the interface to execute SQL statements.

Workflow

The workflow when using SQL tables with the NoSQL API is very similar to the one you looked at for collections in the previous chapter. However, when SQL statements are used, the workflow is somewhat different. Before you look into the details, it is worth getting an overview of the general workflow.

Figure 8-1 shows the workflow starting with a schema and ending with the results. The main focus is on the steps until a statement object has been obtained. How to use the statements will be covered in detail throughout the chapter. The red (dark grey) boxes are the methods called.

© Jesper Wisborg Krogh 2018
J. W. Krogh, *MySQL Connector/Python Revealed*,
https://doi.org/10.1007/978-1-4842-3694-9_8

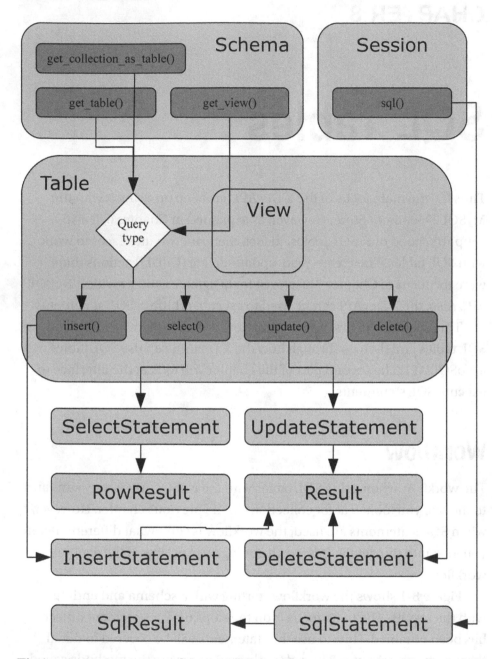

Figure 8-1. *Overview of the workflow when using SQL tables*

The figure starts with the schema object. There are four different ways to continue; however, effectively there are only two distinct paths. The get_collection_as_table() returns a table object with the SQL table that stores the collection, and the view object returned by get_view() is a subclass of a table, with the only difference being the query used to check whether the object exists in the database. So, for most purposes collections as tables, views, and tables can be considered the same thing.

Once you have the table object, you can use it to execute either an insert, select, update, or delete statement. Except for the count() method (not included in the figure), there are no additional methods like you saw for the collections. Once the statement has been executed, a row result is returned for a select statement and a result without rows is returned for the other methods.

The big difference in the workflow is SQL statements, which are created directly from the schema object. An SQL statement always returns an SQL result irrespective of the query type.

With the workflows in place, it is time to look at the NoSQL API for SQL tables.

Tip   There are a number of example programs in this chapter. All example programs that appear in a listing are available for download. See the discussion of example programs in Chapter 1 for more information about using the example programs. In general, changes are rolled back to allow reexecuting the examples with the same result.

NoSQL API for SQL Tables

In the previous chapter, you used the Document Store, which is meant to be managed purely using the NoSQL API. It is, however, also possible to continue to work with SQL tables, but avoid writing SQL statements.

The NoSQL table API is similar to the Document Store API and the discussion in this section assumes you are familiar with the X DevAPI described in Chapter 6.

The table API is the topic of this section. You will start out by getting a table object and getting information about the object. Then the table object will be used to execute queries.

Note The discussion of the table API has a relatively large overlap with the API used to work with collections. It is recommended to read Chapter 6 before this chapter to get the most out of this table API discussion.

Table and View Objects

A table object is equivalent to a collection object; the difference is that the table object is designed to be used with general SQL tables whereas a collection is dedicated for a table with a JSON column storing a document. In fact, you can ask to retrieve a collection as a table if you want. A view object is very similar to a table object but is for a view (virtual table) rather than a base table. Unless explicitly noted, tables and views behave the same.

There are three different methods for getting a table object. They are listed in Table 8-1. The returned objects are relative to the mysqlx module.

Table 8-1. *Schema Table Methods*

Method	Arguments	Description
get_collection_as_table	Name check_existence=False	Returns the collection with the specified name as a crud.Table object. If check_existence = True, a ProgrammingError exception occurs if the collection does not exist.
get_table	name check_existence=False	Returns the table with the specified name as a crud.Table object. The get_table() method can also be used to open a view as a crud.Table object. If check_existence = True, a ProgrammingError exception occurs if the table does not exist.
get_tables		Returns a list of the tables and views in the schema. Each element in the list is an instance of the crud.Table class.
get_view	name check_existence=False	Returns the view with the specified name as a crud.View object. If check_existence = True, a ProgrammingError exception occurs if the view does not exist.

The get_table() and get_tables() methods are the equivalent to the get_collection() and get_collections() methods from the previous chapter. There are no methods for creating tables, changing the table definitions, or adding indexes; this must be done using an SQL statement.

There are a number of methods to get information about a table object. These methods are summarized in Table 8-2. The returned objects are relative to the `mysqlx` module. None of these methods take an argument.

Table 8-2. *Table and View Utility Methods*

Method	Returns Object	Description
exists_ in_database		Returns `True` or `False` depending on whether the table exists.
get_connection	connection. Connection	Returns the underlying connection object.
get_name		Returns the name of the table. This is the same as the `name` property.
get_schema	crud.Schema	Returns the object for the schema where the table exists. This is the same as the `schema` property.
get_session	connection. Session	Returns the object for the session. This is the same as the session property. Added in version 8.0.12.
is_view		Returns `True` or `False` depending on whether the table object is a view. This is based on the actual definition in the database and not whether `get_table()` or `get_view()` was used to get the object.

The schema object, session object (8.0.12 and later), and table name can also be found in the `schema`, `session`, and `name` properties, respectively. Thus far, there has been very little difference in collections other than tables do not have all of the collection features. For queries, there are some differences, so let's look at them.

Table Queries

Querying tables using a table object and the NoSQL methods is to some extent a mix of using SQL statements and the Document Store create, read, update, and delete (CRUD) methods. There is no support for joining tables or more advanced SQL features such as common table expressions (CTEs) and window functions yet. The available methods also fall into one of the CRUD functionalities. So far it sounds like collections again, but the method names reflect the SQL statements used for the actions.

Note Queries performed using table objects are primarily for tables using the UTF-8-character sets. There are also some more complex constructions; for example, converting the character set for a column, that are not supported. In those cases, you must use a direct SQL statement instead, as described later in the chapter.

The table CRUD methods can be found in Table 8-3. Except for the count() method, all of the methods return a statement object corresponding to the query type. The statement object classes are all in the mysqlx.statement module.

Table 8-3. *CRUD Methods for Table and View Objects*

Method	Arguments	Returns Object	Description
count			Returns the number of rows in the table as an integer.
delete		DeleteStatement	Creates a delete statement.
insert	*fields	InsertStatement	Creates an insert statement where values will be set for the fields specified.
select	*fields	SelectStatement	Creates a select statement that will retrieve the fields specified.
update		UpdateStatement	Creates an update statement.

While the method names sound very familiar to those accustomed to writing SQL statements, their use requires a bit more explanation. The remainder of this section will go through the CRUD methods one by one. The count() method will be used as a supplement to the insert(), select(), update(), and delete() methods.

CRUD: Create

The first part of CRUD is to create data. For SQL tables, this is inserting data into a table, so appropriately the table object method to create data is the insert() method. This is the topic of the following discussion.

The arguments to the insert() method are the fields that you will provide data for. The method returns an object of the mysqlx. statement.InsertStatement class. This object can be used to add the values and to execute the insert statement. The important methods of the InsertStatement class are listed in Table 8-4.

Table 8-4. *InsertStatement Methods*

Method	Arguments	Description
execute		Executes the insert statement and returns the result as a result.Result object.
values	*values	The values for one row to add to the insert statement. values() can be called multiple times to insert several rows. The values for each row must be in the same order as the fields.

The InsertStatement object has two properties:

- **schema**: The schema object for the insert statement

- **target**: The table object for the insert statement

The main use of these properties is to work your way back to the parent objects when the insert statement is passed to other functions or methods.

To see the workflow for inserting data, see Listing 8-1. It's an example of inserting two cities into the `world.city` table. Once the result has been returned, the number of rows inserted and the first generated auto-increment ID is printed. Before and after the insert statement, the number of rows in the table is determined using the `Table.count()` method.

Listing 8-1. Inserting Rows into a Table Using the `insert()` Method

```python
import mysqlx
from config import connect_args

fmt = "{0:28s}: {1:4d}"

db = mysqlx.get_session(**connect_args)

# Get the world.city table
schema = db.get_schema("world")
city = schema.get_table("city")

db.start_transaction()

print(fmt.format(
  "Number of rows before insert",
  city.count()
))

# Define the insert statement
insert = city.insert(
  "Name",
  "CountryCode",
  "District",
  "Population"
)
```

```
# Add row using a list
darwin = [
  "Darwin",
  "AUS",
  "Northern Territory",
  145916
]
insert.values(darwin)

# Add row by arguments
insert.values(
  "Sunshine Coast",
  "AUS",
  "Queensland",
  302122
)

# Execute the insert
result = insert.execute()

# Get the auto-increment ID generated
# for the inserted row
print(fmt.format(
  "Number of rows inserted",
  result.get_affected_items_count()))
print(fmt.format(
  "First ID generated",
  result.get_autoincrement_value()))

print(fmt.format(
  "Number of rows after insert",
  city.count()))
```

```
# Reset the data
db.rollback()
db.close()
```

First, the table object is obtained using the get_table() schema method. The insert statement is created using the insert() method and the four fields that you specify values for are given as arguments. The fields can also be given as a list or tuple if that works better in the code flow. The city table also has an ID field, which by default is assigned an auto-increment value. In the example, you use the default behavior for the ID field.

The two rows are added to the insert statement using the values() method. Darwin is added by first creating a tuple with the values and then the tuple is passed to values(). Sunshine Coast is added by passing each field value as a separate argument to values().

Finally, the two rows are inserted using the execute() method. The returned result.Result object can be used to check the number of inserted rows and the generated auto-increment ID of the first row to be inserted (Darwin). It is not possible to get the auto-increment ID for later rows.

An example of the output of running the example is

```
Number of rows before insert: 4079
Number of rows inserted     :    2
First ID generated          : 4111
Number of rows after insert : 4081
```

The first ID generated depends on how the city table has been used before and thus will in general be different from the example output. With data inserted into the table, let's look at how to retrieve it again.

CRUD: Read

The read statement is the workhorse of most databases. For table and view objects, the `select()` method is used to get data from the underlying database object. This section will show how to do so.

The `select()` method takes the fields that should be retrieved from the table. If no fields are specified, all will be included; this is the equivalent of `SELECT * FROM`. The method returns a `mysqlx.statement.SelectStatement` object that can be used to refine the query.

The `SelectStatement` methods that can be used to define the query further are listed in Table 8-5. They can be used to specify the conditions that must be fulfilled for a row to be included, how many rows to return, grouping, etc.

Table 8-5. *Methods to Modify a Select Statement*

Method	Arguments	Description
where	condition	This is the condition by which to filter the query result.
group_by	*fields	Describes which fields to group by for queries involving aggregate functions.
having	condition	Describes what to filter the result by after the query has otherwise been resolved (except for sorting). This makes it useful for filtering by value of aggregate functions.
order_by	*clauses	Describes what to sort the result by.

(continued)

Table 8-5. (*continued*)

Method	Arguments	Description
limit	row_count	The first argument sets the maximum number of rows to return. The second optional
	offset=0	argument defines the offset. The default offset is 0.
		Note: This is changed in version 8.0.12 where offset is deprecated. Use the offset() method instead.
offset	offset	Set the offset of the rows to return. Added in version 8.0.12.
lock_exclusive		Makes the statement take an exclusive lock. Only one statement can have an exclusive lock at a time. Use this if the row(s) will be updated later in the same transaction.
lock_shared		Makes the statement take a shared lock. This prevents other statements from modifying the matching rows, but it is possible for them to read the rows.
bind	*args	The first argument provides the name of the parameter to replace. The second argument provides the value. Call bind() once for each parameter.
execute		Executes the select statement.

Once the statement has been fully defined, it can be executed using the execute() method. This returns a RowResult object, which can be used to get information about the result and fetch the rows.

As an example, consider a select statement where the cities in the United States of America with a population higher than 1,000,000 people are found and grouped by state (the District field). For each state the number of cities and the population of the largest city are found. The result is sorted in descending order according to the number of cities and then by the largest population. The example can be seen in Listing 8-2.

Listing 8-2. Example of Using a Select Statement

```
import mysqlx
from config import connect_args

db = mysqlx.get_session(**connect_args)

# Get the world.city table
schema = db.get_schema("world")
city = schema.get_table("city")

db.start_transaction()
statement = city.select(
  "District",
  "COUNT(*) AS NumCities",
  "MAX(Population) AS LargestCityPop")
statement.where(
  "CountryCode = :country"
  + " AND Population > :min_pop")
statement.group_by("District")
statement.order_by(
  "NumCities DESC",
  "LargestCityPop DESC")
statement.bind("country", "USA")
statement.bind("min_pop", 1000000)
```

```python
print("SQL statement:\n{0}"
  .format(statement.get_sql()))

result = statement.execute()
print("Number of rows in result: {0}\n"
  .format(result.count))

fmt = "{0:12s}    {1:6d}    {2:12d}"
print("{0:12s}    {1:6s}    {2:12s}"
  .format(
    "State",
    "Cities",
    "Largest City"
))
print("-"*37)
for row in result.fetch_all():
  print(fmt.format(
    row["District"],
    row["NumCities"],
    row["LargestCityPop"]
))

print("")
print("Number of rows in result: {0}\n"
  .format(result.count))

db.commit()
db.close()
```

After the table object has been retrieved, the statement is created and
the fields that should be included in the result are defined. Then a filter is
set using the where() method, and the grouping and sorting are set. The
value passed to the where() method uses two named parameters, country
and min_pop, to allow binding the values later using the bind() method.

385

This ensures that the quoting is correct for the type provided (but it does not ensure it is the correct type!) and allows you to reuse the rest of the statement if you need to execute the same query again but with different values for the two parameters.

Before executing the statement, the generated SQL is printed. The get_sql() method is unique to the SelectStatement class. The method takes the SelectStatement and builds the SQL statement that will be executed as a result of the query that has been defined. This can be useful if you want to execute the query manually through the MySQL Shell or you need to compare the generated SQL with an SQL statement that you are basing the query on.

After the result has been obtained, the number of rows in the result is printed (and again after retrieving the result). The result is obtained using the fetch_all() method, which returns a result.Row object. The Row object can be used as a dictionary when printing the result. The output is

```
SQL statement:
SELECT District,COUNT(*) AS NumCities,MAX(Population) AS
LargestCityPop FROM world.city WHERE CountryCode = :country
AND Population > :min_pop GROUP BY District ORDER BY NumCities
DESC,LargestCityPop DESC

Number of rows in result: 0

State           Cities   Largest City
------------------------------------
Texas              3        1953631
California          2        3694820
New York           1        8008278
Illinois           1        2896016
Pennsylvania       1        1517550
Arizona            1        1321045

Number of rows in result: 6
```

The most noticeable in the output is how the number of rows in the result is reported as 0 before the result is retrieved but 6 afterwards. This was discussed for the RowResult object in Chapter 6: the count property is set when reading the rows using the fetch_all() method.

Now let's update the data in a table.

CRUD: Update

Updates to tables replace the value of one or more fields with new values. Unlike for documents, there is no way to add new fields or remove existing fields; those actions require a change of the table definition. The following discussion goes into detail on how table updates work in the CRUD world of MySQL Connector/Python.

The update() method itself does not take any arguments. The sole purpose of invoking it is to create an UpdateStatement object that can be used to define the update. The methods for doing this can be seen in Table 8-6.

Table 8-6. *Methods to Define an Update Statement*

Method	Arguments	Description
set	field value	Sets the new value for the given field. The value must be a scalar.
where	condition	This is the condition to filter which rows should be updated.
order_ by	*clauses	Describes which order the rows should be updated. Added in version 8.0.12.
sort	*sort_clauses	Describes which order the rows should be updated. **Note:** This has been deprecated in version 8.0.12; use order_by() instead.
limit	row_count	The argument sets the maximum number of rows to update.
bind	*args	The first argument provides the name of the parameter to replace. The second argument provides the value. Call bind() once for each parameter.

One thing to be aware of is that bind parameters cannot be used with the set() method. If the new value is based on user input, make sure to validate input as always. The statement returns a result.Result object when it is executed.

Caution   Always validate user input before using it in statements. This does not only apply to update statements or even the X DevAPI. This should be a standard part of working with user input.

When executing the statement, you must define a where condition. If you don't, a ProgrammingError exception will occur:

```
mysqlx.errors.ProgrammingError: No condition was found for
update
```

This is meant as a safety precaution to avoid accidentally updating all rows in a table. If you really want to update all rows, set the where() condition to True or a similar condition that evaluates to True:

```
update.where(True)
```

Not only does the requirement mean you do not by mistakenly update all rows because of a missing condition, a condition set to True also helps document that you really mean to update all rows.

Listing 8-3 shows an example where the population of a city is updated. The population is printed before and after the update to verify the effect of the update statement.

Listing 8-3. Using an Update Statement

```
import mysqlx
from config import connect_args

db = mysqlx.get_session(**connect_args)
```

```
# Get the world.city table
schema = db.get_schema("world")
city = schema.get_table("city")

db.start_transaction()

# Check the population before the update
select = city.select()
select.where(
  "Name = :city"
  + " AND CountryCode = :country"
)
select.bind("city", "Sydney")
select.bind("country", "AUS")
result = select.execute()
sydney = result.fetch_one()
print("Old population: {0}".format(
  sydney["Population"]))

# Define the update
update = city.update()
update.set("Population", 5000000)
update.where(
  "Name = :city"
  + " AND CountryCode = :country")
update.bind("city", "Sydney")
update.bind("country", "AUS")
result = update.execute()

print("Number of rows updated: {0}"
  .format(
    result.get_affected_items_count())
)
```

```
# Check the affect
result = select.execute()
sydney = result.fetch_one()
print("New population: {0}".format(
  sydney["Population"]))

# Reset the data
db.rollback()
db.close()
```

The steps to define the update statement follow the usual pattern for the X DevAPI CRUD methods. The output of the program is

```
Old population: 3276207
Number of rows updated: 1
New population: 5000000
```

This leaves one final CRUD method to look at: how to delete rows.

CRUD: Delete

The last thing to discuss related to CRUD methods is how to delete rows in a table. This is done using the delete() table method with optional filter conditions, sorting, and limit.

The delete() method takes an optional argument defining the condition to filter the rows by, and the method returns a DeleteStatement object. Additional refinement of the delete statement can be made through methods of the DeleteStatement object. These methods are listed in Table 8-7.

Table 8-7. *Methods to Define a Delete Statement*

Method	Arguments	Description
where	condition	This is the condition to filter which rows should be deleted.
order_by	*clauses	Describes the order in which the rows should be deleted. Added in version 8.0.12.
sort	*sort_clauses	Describes the order in which the rows should be deleted. **Note:** This has been deprecated in version 8.0.12; use order_by() instead.
limit	row_count	The argument sets the maximum number of rows to delete.
bind	*args	The first argument provides the name of the parameter to replace. The second argument provides the value. Call bind() once for each parameter.
execute		Executes the delete statement.

If you have a good grasp of the other CRUD methods, the use of delete statements is straightforward. In the same way as for the update() method, a condition must be set; otherwise a ProgrammingError occurs:

mysqlx.errors.ProgrammingError: No condition was found for delete

If you need to delete all rows in the table, set the condition to True. Alternatively, you can recreate the table using the TRUNCATE TABLE SQL statement.

Listing 8-4 shows an example of deleting all cities with a population less than 1000.

Listing 8-4. Deleting Rows from a Table

```
import mysqlx
from config import connect_args

fmt = "{0:22s}: {1:4d}"

db = mysqlx.get_session(**connect_args)

# Get the world.city table
schema = db.get_schema("world")
city = schema.get_table("city")

db.start_transaction()

# Check the number of rows before
# deleting rows.
print(fmt.format(
  "Number of rows before",
  city.count()
))

# Define the update
delete = city.delete()
delete.where("Population < :min_pop")
delete.bind("min_pop", 1000)
result = delete.execute()

print(fmt.format(
  "Number of rows deleted",
  result.get_affected_items_count()
))
```

```
# Check the affect
print(fmt.format(
  "Number of rows after",
  city.count()
))

# Reset the data
db.rollback()
db.close()
```

The filter condition is specified using the where() method. It could also have been specified when the delete statement was first created. The output is

```
Number of rows before : 4079
Number of rows deleted:    11
Number of rows after   : 4068
```

This concludes the discussion of CRUD methods for SQL tables. As discussed, these methods currently have some limitations. If you need to generate queries that are not supported, it is still possible using SQL statements, which will be discussed in the remainder of this chapter.

SQL Statements

Thus far, the discussion about the X DevAPI has been about CRUD methods, either for document collections or SQL tables. What happened to the good old SQL statements? They are still here, and that is what this section is about.

In some ways, I saved the simplest for last, but it's also the one that currently executes the most different queries. The two things are related because the SQL statements do not put any constraints on what you can use them for beyond the limitations of the specific MySQL Server version.

This also means it is not possible to know what each statement is about to the same extent, and thus it is not possible to be as specific about how it works. This makes it simpler than the CRUD methods. Of course, the price is that it is to a larger extent up to the developer to take care of things.

Tip   The SQL statement functionality of the X DevAPI is not nearly as complete as when using the `mysql.connector` module. If you need more than simple queries, it is recommended to use the methods described in Chapters 2 through 5. This includes all cases where parameters are required.

This section will look at how SQL statements are executed using the X DevAPI.

Executing SQL Statements

Executing SQL statements is straightforward. An SQL statement is created directly from the session using the `sql()` method, which takes the SQL statement to execute. The `SqlStatement` object is returned.

The `SqlStatement` class is simple and only has two methods, which are summarized in Table 8-8. Neither method takes any arguments.

Table 8-8. *Methods to Work with an SQL Statement*

Method	Returns	Description
execute	result.SqlResult object	Sends the query to MySQL Server. Returns an object of the mysqlx. result.SqlResult class.
is_doc_based	Boolean	Whether the statement is for a collection. It always returns False for an SqlStatement and is mostly useful when a method or function can handle several different types of statements.

The result object is always of the SqlResult class, which combines the information that is useful for queries modifying data or schema and queries fetching data.

Listing 8-5 shows an example of querying for the German states with at least one city with a population of more than 500,000 people.

Listing 8-5. Querying Data with a SELECT SQL Statement

```
import mysqlx
from config import connect_args

db = mysqlx.get_session(**connect_args)
sql = db.sql("""
SELECT CONVERT(District USING utf8mb4)
        AS District,
        COUNT(*) AS NumCities
  FROM world.city
 WHERE CountryCode = 'DEU'
        AND Population > 500000
 GROUP BY District
 ORDER BY NumCities DESC, District""")
```

```
result = sql.execute()
fmt = "{0:19s}    {1:6d}"
print("{0:19s}    {1:6s}".format(
  "State", "Cities"))
print("-"*28)

row = result.fetch_one()
while row:
  print(fmt.format(
    row["District"],
    row["NumCities"]
  ))
  row = result.fetch_one()

db.close()
```

The first thing to notice is that the District column is explicitly converted to utf8mb4 in the query. The reason for this is, as mentioned, that the X DevAPI expects only UTF-8 data to be returned. If this conversion is not done, an error is returned:

```
UnicodeDecodeError: 'utf-8' codec can't decode byte 0xfc in
position 7: invalid start byte
```

This is another case where the legacy API in the mysql.connector module is better to use. The workaround is, as in the example, to convert the data inside the query.

The result is handled similar to the result of the select() CRUD method. It is possible to fetch a single row at a time using the fetch_one() method or all rows using the fetch_all() method. The former is used in this case. The output is

```
State                   Cities
----------------------------
Nordrhein-Westfalen        5
Baden-Württemberg          1
Baijeri                    1
Berliini                   1
Bremen                     1
Hamburg                    1
Hessen                     1
Niedersachsen              1
```

There is one more feature of the SqlStatment class that is worth discussing: how to handle queries that return more than one result set.

Queries with Multiple Result Sets

In Chapter 4, you looked at handling multiple result sets from a query when using the legacy API in the mysql.connector module. The X DevAPI in the mysqlx module can also handle multiple result sets but without the bells and whistles.

The first result set is handled just as described in the previous example. The difference is that once the first result has been handled, the result can be reinitialized using the SqlResult.next_result() method. This allows you to handle the next result. The next_result() method returns True or False depending on whether there are more results to handle.

In order to see how this works in practice, consider the world. top_cities stored procedure in Listing 8-6. This is similar to the stored procedure used in Chapter 4.

Listing 8-6. The `world.top_cities` Stored Procedure

```
DROP PROCEDURE IF EXISTS world.top_cities;
DELIMITER $$
CREATE PROCEDURE world.top_cities(
    IN in_country char(3)
)
SQL SECURITY INVOKER
BEGIN
  SELECT Name, District, Population
    FROM world.city
   WHERE CountryCode = in_country
         AND Population
   ORDER BY Population ASC
   LIMIT 3;

  SELECT Name, District, Population
    FROM world.city
   WHERE CountryCode = in_country
         AND Population
   ORDER BY Population DESC
   LIMIT 3;
END$$
DELIMITER ;
```

The procedure returns two result sets: first, the three least populous cities of the country are found, and then the three most populous cities are found. Listing 8-7 shows an example of handling the two result sets.

Listing 8-7. Handling Multiple Result Sets in an X DevAPI SQL Statement

```python
import mysqlx
from config import connect_args

db = mysqlx.get_session(**connect_args)
sql = db.sql(
  "CALL world.top_cities('USA')")
result = sql.execute()

fmt = "{0:11s}    {1:14s}    {2:10d}"
print("{0:11s}    {1:14s}    {2:10s}"
  .format(
    "City", "State", "Population"
  )
)

more = True
while more:
  print("-"*41)
  row = result.fetch_one()
  while row:
    print(fmt.format(
      row["Name"],
      row["District"],
      row["Population"]
    ))
    row = result.fetch_one()
  more = result.next_result()

db.close()
```

The query is executed as normal. The first result set is handled as normal. It is wrapped inside a while loop. After the first result has been handled, more results are searched for by calling next_result(). This also resets the result object to work with the next result. Once all result sets have been handled, next_result() returns False and the loop terminates. The output is

```
City            State               Population
------------------------------------------------
Charleston      South Carolina           89063
Carson          California               89089
Odessa          Texas                    89293
------------------------------------------------
New York        New York               8008278
Los Angeles     California              3694820
Chicago         Illinois               2896016
```

This concludes the discussion of SQL statements in the MySQL Connector/Python X DevAPI.

Summary

This chapter looked at how SQL tables can be used with the X DevAPI. There are two options available: using the NoSQL CRUD methods or executing SQL statements.

The NoSQL CRUD interface for SQL tables is very similar but simpler than the one you looked at in the previous chapter for the MySQL Document Store. The CRUD methods are named according to the SQL statement performing the underlying action of the method. For example, to read data, the select() method is used. There is no support for changing the schema of SQL tables using the NoSQL API.

There is support for executing arbitrary SQL statements using the `mysqlx.Session.sql()` method. It can be useful for simple queries; however, for more complex tasks and when adding user input to the queries, it is recommended to use the methods of the `mysql.connector` module.

This chapter completes the walkthrough of the X DevAPI as seen from MySQL Connector/Python. There are two remaining, but very important, tasks left: handling errors and troubleshooting MySQL Connector/Python programs. These topics are covered next.

PART IV

Error Handling and Troubleshooting

CHAPTER 9

Error Handling

The first eight chapters focused on specific use cases: installation, executing queries, handling the result, etc. In a few places, it was mentioned that error handling is important, but not much detail was providedsql_note. This is about to change because this chapter is dedicated to error handling.

Error handling is one of the most important topics for all programming, not just when using MySQL Connector/Python. You can argue that it together with testing should be the two first topics you learn. There is a large degree of truth in that statement; however, I decided to make error handling the second-to-last chapter in this book. Not because it is not important (the phrase "last but not least" certainly applies to this and the following chapter about troubleshooting) but for two reasons: first, this is not a book as much about programming as using MySQL Connector/Python, so it is assumed you already have a good grasp of programming best practices. Second, it allows to me give more context to the examples.

Note Do not consider error handling and testing as a secondary task. Make sure they are treated with at least as high a priority as implementing the actual feature. This is not unique to MySQL Connector/Python.

© Jesper Wisborg Krogh 2018
J. W. Krogh, *MySQL Connector/Python Revealed*,
https://doi.org/10.1007/978-1-4842-3694-9_9

This chapter will start out with some considerations about warnings, errors, and *strict modes* in MySQL Server. You'll then move on to MySQL Connector/Python itself where the first part of the discussion will be about warnings and error handling in general, warning configurations, and how to fetch warnings. The second part will discuss the MySQL error numbers and SQL states. Finally, the third part will give an overview of the error classes of the `mysql.connector` and `mysqlx` modules.

Tip   There are a number of example programs in this chapter. All example programs that appear in a listing are available for download. See the discussion of example programs in Chapter 1 for more information about using the example programs.

Warnings, Errors, and Strict Modes in MySQL Server

In the discussion of error handling in MySQL Connector/Python, there are a couple of things to consider on the MySQL Server side of the connection. This section will look at the configuration setting to specify whether a note level message should be treated as a warning, how strict modes work, and how the application can cause messages to be logged in the MySQL error log.

Treating Note Level Messages as Warnings

There are three severity levels for events that occur when a statement is executed. The most severe is an error that will always stop the statement from completing. The next level is warnings that allow the statement to complete but return warnings to the user or application so a decision can be made about what to do. The lowest severity is the note level, which is the topic of this discussion.

By default, a note level message for a statement (such as if a database exists and you try to create it using CREATE DATABLASE IF NOT EXISTS) causes a warning to occur. For example:

```
mysql> CREATE SCHEMA IF NOT EXISTS py_test_db;
Query OK, 1 row affected, 1 warning (0.28 sec)
```

```
mysql> SHOW WARNINGS\G
*************************** 1. row ***************************
  Level: Note
   Code: 1007
Message: Can't create database 'py_test_db'; database exists
1 row in set (0.00 sec)
```

Notice that in the SHOW WARNINGS output, the level is Note. It is possible to avoid a note level message to generate warnings. This is done by changing the value of the sql_notes option. When the value of sql_notes is ON (the default), a warning is created. If it is OFF, no warning is created. The option can be changed for the session, so if you in general want to cause a warning but for a given statement you want to disable it, you can suppress the message. To temporarily suppress note level messages, you can use the following workflow:

```
mysql> SET SESSION sql_notes = OFF;
Query OK, 0 rows affected (0.00 sec)
```

```
-- Execute statements
```

```
mysql> SET SESSION sql_notes = ON;
Query OK, 0 rows affected (0.00 sec)
```

Thus, if you know a query will cause a note level message, you can change the value of sql_notes for the session while executing that one statement. However, in general it is better to try to avoid the message in the first place by changing the statement.

Tip It is recommended to enable `sql_notes` and only disable it for specific statements that you know don't require warnings.

Strict Modes

The second part to the server-side configuration is strict modes. When a strict mode is enabled, it tells MySQL to treat, for example, invalid data as an error rather than a warning. In old versions of MySQL, the default was to be forgiving with data that did not fit into the tables and do a best effort to make it fit. This makes it easier to develop applications, but a major downside of this is that it can cause the database to end up with different data than expected.

Examples of manipulation to force data to fit are to cast a string to an integer or to truncate data. Consider the table named `table_1` with the following definition:

```
mysql> CREATE SCHEMA db1;
Query OK, 1 row affected (0.41 sec)

mysql> CREATE TABLE db1.table_1 (
          id int unsigned NOT NULL PRIMARY KEY,
          val varchar(5)
       ) ENGINE=InnoDB;
Query OK, 0 rows affected (0.24 sec)
```

Without the strict mode enabled, an attempt to insert a value with six characters will cause a warning, but the row will still be inserted with the value truncated to five characters:

```
mysql> INSERT INTO db1.table_1 VALUES (1, 'abcdef');
Query OK, 1 row affected, 1 warning (0.15 sec)
```

```
mysql> SHOW WARNINGS\G
*************************** 1. row ***************************
  Level: Warning
   Code: 1265
Message: Data truncated for column 'val' at row 1
1 row in set (0.00 sec)

mysql> SELECT * FROM table_1;
+----+-------+
| id | val   |
+----+-------+
|  1 | abcde |
+----+-------+
1 row in set (0.00 sec)
```

In MySQL 5.7 and later, strict mode is enabled by default for transactional tables (the InnoDB and NDBCluster storage engines). In this case, an error will occur if the data does not fit. An example of the strict mode preventing an insert is

```
mysql> INSERT INTO db1.table_1 VALUES (2, 'ghijkl');
ERROR 1406 (22001): Data too long for column 'val' at row 1
```

The strict mode for transactional tables is enabled by including STRICT_TRANS_TABLES in the list of SQL modes. For more about SQL modes, see https://dev.mysql.com/doc/refman/en/sql-mode.html. From inside MySQL Connector/Python the SQL mode can be set using the sql_mode connection option.

Related to the STRICT_TRANS_TABLES SQL mode is the innodb_strict_ mode option. This option only applies to InnoDB tables. Where the SQL mode controls what happens to data modification language (DML) queries, the innodb_strict_mode option controls what happens for data definition language (DDL) queries such as CREATE TABLE, ALTER TABLE, and CREATE INDEX. One of the most common causes of errors being triggered by the innodb_strict_mode option is when a table is created with a definition that will cause the maximum possible row size for the table to exceed InnoDB's limit.

It is strongly recommended to both enable the STRICT_TRANS_TABLES SQL mode and the innodb_strict_mode option. Enable it before you start developing the application, so you get warned about incompatibility issues as soon as possible.

Tip   It is much easier to fix violations of the strict modes during the initial development than after completing the application. So, enable the strict modes before you start coding; it will save you work in the long run.

The MySQL Error Log

A final thing to be aware of on the MySQL Server side is that actions performed (or not performed) by the application can trigger messages in the MySQL error log. For example, if the application attempts to connect using invalid credentials or it does not close its connections properly, messages similar to the following examples can occur:

```
2018-03-03T04:10:19.943401Z 52 [Note] [MY-010926] Access denied
for user 'pyuser'@'localhost' (using password: YES)
```

```
2018-03-03T04:10:28.330173Z 53 [Note] [MY-010914] Aborted
connection 53 to db: 'unconnected' user: 'pyuser' host:
'localhost' (Got an error reading communication packets).
```

The first note says that an attempt was made to connect by the pyuser user from localhost using a password, but the password was wrong (or the user did not exist). The second note says that there was an error trying to read from one of the connections. In this case, it's because the connection disappeared.

These messages will only show up when the log_error_verbosity MySQL Server option is set to 3. It is recommended to ensure that is the case during development and to regularly check the error log to capture all messages triggered by the application. This can be accomplished by setting the option in the MySQL configuration file. In MySQL 8.0, it can also be achieved using the SET PERSIST statement like so:

```
mysql> SET PERSIST log_error_verbosity = 3;
Query OK, 0 rows affected (0.04 sec)
```

This code sets the current value and persists the value when MySQL is restarted.

Enough about MySQL Server. The next topic is warning and error handling in MySQL Connector/Python itself.

Warning and Error Handling

When you use MySQL Connector/Python in your programs, you will encounter a mix of the built-in Python exceptions and custom exceptions of the MySQL Connector/Python module you use. Additionally, there is a submodule with the MySQL error codes as constants. This section will go through the configuration related to warnings and how to fetch warnings. MySQL error numbers, SQL states, and the exception classes are discussed in the next two sections.

Configuration

When you work with the methods in the mysql.connector module, it is possible to configure how MySQL Connector/Python should handle warnings. There are two options: whether to automatically fetch all warnings for a query and whether to elevate warnings to exceptions.

411

MySQL works with three different severity levels for error messages:

- **Note**: This is a just a notification about what happened. It is in general not a sign of problems. A note, for example, happens when you create a database (schema) with `CREATE DATABASE IF NOT EXISTS` and the database does exist. In some cases, if a note happens, often it can be a sign of underlying issues or bad practices. So, you should not automatically dismiss note level messages. By default, note level messages are treated as warnings; this is controlled by the `sql_notes` MySQL Server option.

- **Warning**: This is something that does not prevent MySQL from continuing, but the behavior may not be what you expect. It can, for example, occur if you provide a value that does not fit into the column definition and MySQL truncates or converts the provided value. Some warnings, like the one in the example, can be elevated to an error if MySQL Server has the strict modes enabled.

- **Error**: This is for conditions that prevented MySQL from executing the query. They will always raise an exception in MySQL Connector/Python. An example can be that a duplicate key error occurred.

In general, it is recommended to take all warnings and errors seriously. A warning is often a sign that something is not as it should be, and handling warnings from the very first stage of the development can avoid major grief later on.

Tip   If you handle all warnings from the start of the development of an application, you won't get caught out by unintended data conversions or other problems. If warnings are ignored, as little as a one-character typo can cause problems for years before it is discovered.

There are two options that control how MySQL Connector/Python handles warnings when connecting to MySQL using the `mysql.connector` module. They are listed in Table 9-1.

Table 9-1. *Warning-Related Options*

Name	Default Value	Description
get_warnings	False	When set to True, warnings are automatically fetched after each query. This makes it possible to fetch warnings without manually executing SHOW WARNINGS.
raise_on_warnings	False	When set to True, warnings cause an exception to be raised. Setting raise_on_warnings always sets get_warnings to the same value. **Note:** The exception will not be raised until the warning is fetched. For queries with a result, this means when the rows are fetched.

Both options only apply when cursors are used. There are at the time of writing no options to change the behavior of warnings when using the X DevAPI in the `mysqlx` module.

It is also possible to change the value of get_warnings and raise_on_warnings after the connection has been made. This can, for example, be useful to temporarily enable or disable the settings, as it can be seen in the following code snippet:

```
import mysql.connector

db = mysql.connector.connect(
  get_warnings=True,
  raise_on_warnings=True,
  option_files="my.ini",
)

cursor = db.cursor()

db.get_warnings = False
db.raise_on_warnings = False
cursor.execute(
  "CREATE SCHEMA IF NOT EXISTS py_test_db")
db.get_warnings = True
db.raise_on_warnings = True

db.close()
```

It is recommended at least during development to enable both raise_on_warnings and get_warnings. In production, it is also recommended to at least check for warnings. The get_warnings option does not have any overhead compared to manually fetching the warnings because the SHOW WARNINGS statement is only executed if the query returned warnings. When get_warnings is enabled, the warnings can be retrieved using the fetchwarnings() method. Talking about fetchwarnings(), let's look at how warnings are fetched.

Fetching Warnings After cmd_query()

In the mysql.connector module, the way you fetch the warnings depends on whether you execute the queries through the connection object or a cursor. In either case, the warnings are retrieved using the SHOW WARNINGS statement, but the cursor allows you to let it handle this for you.

When you execute queries directly through the connection object, you must fetch the warnings yourself. Additionally, you must be careful that you fetch all of the rows before you fetch the warnings because otherwise you will get an error that you have unread rows. Extra care should be taken if you have enabled consume_results because fetching the warnings in that case will cause the original result to be dismissed.

Caution   If you have enabled consume_results, then executing SHOW WARNINGS to get the warnings for the query will dismiss any outstanding rows.

There are some differences of how warnings are handled when using cmd_query() depending on whether the C Extension or the pure Python implementation is used. So, it is worth looking at both cases.

Listing 9-1 shows an example where the C Extension implementation is used, and the warnings are fetched after both a CREATE TABLE statement and a SELECT statement.

Listing 9-1. Checking Warnings with the C Extension Implementation and cmd_query()

```
import mysql.connector

def print_warnings(warnings):
  if mysql.connector.__version_info__[0:3] > (8, 0, 11):
    (warnings, eof) = warnings
```

```python
  for warning in warnings:
    print("Level   : {0}".format(
        warning[0]))
    print("Errno   : {0}".format(
        warning[1]))
    print("Message: {0}".format(
        warning[2]))

db = mysql.connector.connect(
  option_files="my.ini", use_pure=False)

# This example only works with the C
# Extension installed. Exit if that is
# not the case.
is_cext = isinstance(
    db,
    mysql.connector.connection_cext.CMySQLConnection
)
if not is_cext:
  print("The example requires the C "
      + "Extension implementation to be "
      + "installed")
  exit()

print("Using the C Extension implementation\n")

# Ensure the DDL statement will cause
# a warnings by executing the same
# CREATE SCHEMA IF NOT EXISTS statement
# twice.
db.cmd_query(
  "CREATE SCHEMA IF NOT EXISTS py_test_db")
```

```
# For a DDL statement
result = db.cmd_query(
    "CREATE SCHEMA IF NOT EXISTS py_test_db")

print("Warnings for CREATE SCHEMA:")
print("---------------------------")
print("DDL: Number of warnings: {0}"
    .format(result["warning_count"]))

# Get the warnings
db.cmd_query("SHOW WARNINGS")
warnings = db.get_rows()
print_warnings(warnings)
db.free_result()
print("")

# Try a SELECT statement
result = db.cmd_query("SELECT 1/0")
rows = db.get_rows()
db.free_result()

print("Warnings for SELECT:")
print("--------------------")
print("SELECT: Number of warnings: {0}"
    .format(db.warning_count))

# Get the warnings
db.cmd_query("SHOW WARNINGS")
warnings = db.get_rows()
print_warnings(warnings)
db.close()
```

The warnings are printed in the print_warnings() function. As there is a change so the eof packet is also included when using the C Extension in version 8.0.12 and later, it is necessary to have version dependent code. The __version_info__ property is used for this.

For the CREATE TABLE statement, the result returned by cmd_query()
directly has the number of warnings as the warning_count element. For
the SELECT statement, it is a little more complicated. It is necessary to
consume the result first and then the number of warnings can be found in
the warning_count property of the connection object.

The warnings themselves are fetched using the SHOW WARNINGS
statements, which are executed as any other statement. The output is

```
Using the C Extension implementation

Warnings for CREATE SCHEMA:
---------------------------
DDL: Number of warnings: 1
Level  : Note
Errno  : 1007
Message: Can't create database 'py_test_db'; database exists

Warnings for SELECT:
--------------------
SELECT: Number of warnings: 1
Level  : Warning
Errno  : 1365
Message: Division by 0
```

There are three elements for each warning(): the severity (Note,
Warning, or Error), the error number (which will be discussed later in the
chapter), and an error message describing the error. If the C Extension is
not available, the program exits with the error:

```
The example requires the C Extension implementation to be installed
```

If you use the pure Python implementation there are a couple of
differences. First, the warning count for the SELECT statement can be found
in the eof part returned by get_row() or get_rows() for all versions. The
other thing is that the result of the SHOW WARNINGS statement() is returned

as a byte array in MySQL Connector/Python 8.0.11, so it must be decoded. Listing 9-2 shows the pure Python equivalent of the example for version 8.0.12 and later. The code examples include a version for 8.0.11 and earlier in the file Chapter_09/listing_9_2_version_8_0_11.py.

Listing 9-2. Checking Warnings with the Pure Python Implementation and cmd_query()

```
import mysql.connector

def print_warnings(warnings):
  for warning in warnings:
    print("Level   : {0}".format(
      warning[0]))
    print("Errno   : {0}".format(
      warning[1]))
    print("Message: {0}".format(
      warning[2]))

db = mysql.connector.connect(
  option_files="my.ini", use_pure=True)

print("Using the pure Python implementation\n")

# Ensure the DDL statement will cause
# a warnings by executing the same
# CREATE SCHEMA IF NOT EXISTS statement
# twice.
db.cmd_query(
  "CREATE SCHEMA IF NOT EXISTS py_test_db")

# For a DDL statement
result = db.cmd_query(
  "CREATE SCHEMA IF NOT EXISTS py_test_db")
```

```
print("Warnings for CREATE SCHEMA:")
print("----------------------------")
print("DDL: Number of warnings: {0}"
  .format(result["warning_count"]))

# Get the warnings
db.cmd_query("SHOW WARNINGS")
(warnings, eof) = db.get_rows()
print_warnings(warnings)
print("")

# Try a SELECT statement
result = db.cmd_query("SELECT 1/0")
(rows, eof) = db.get_rows()

print("Warnings for SELECT:")
print("--------------------")
print("SELECT: Number of warnings: {0}"
  .format(eof["warning_count"]))

# Get the warnings
db.cmd_query("SHOW WARNINGS")
(warnings, eof) = db.get_rows()
print_warnings(warnings)

db.close()
```

The example goes through the same steps as before, but this time the number of warnings for the SELECT statement is retrieved from the eof part when fetching the rows. As before, the warning count is only available once all rows() have been fetched. The output of the example is the same as before except for the header:

```
Using the pure Python implementation
```

420

```
Warnings for CREATE SCHEMA:
---------------------------
DDL: Number of warnings: 1
Level  : Note
Errno  : 1007
Message: Can't create database 'py_test_db'; database exists

Warnings for SELECT:
--------------------
SELECT: Number of warnings: 1
Level  : Warning
Errno  : 1365
Message: Division by 0
```

If you use cursors, things are, as usual, a little simpler. Let's look at how cursors and warnings work.

Fetching Warnings with Cursors

The work done when fetching warnings with a cursor is in principle the same as when fetching them after using the cmd_query() method. However, much of the work is handled in the background by the cursor, which overall makes it simpler to use.

Listing 9-3 shows the equivalent example of what was examined in Listing 9-1 and Listing 9-2, only this time a cursor is used instead with get_warnings enabled.

Listing 9-3. Fetching Warnings Using a Cursor with get_warnings Enabled

```
import mysql.connector

def print_warnings(warnings):
  for warning in warnings:
```

```
    print("Level  : {0}".format(
      warning[0]))
    print("Errno  : {0}".format(
      warning[1]))
    print("Message: {0}".format(
      warning[2]))

print("Using cursors\n")

db = mysql.connector.connect(
  option_files="my.ini")

cursor = db.cursor()

# Ensure the DDL statement will cause
# a warnings by executing the same
# CREATE SCHEMA IF NOT EXISTS statement
# twice.
cursor.execute(
  "CREATE SCHEMA IF NOT EXISTS py_test_db")

# Enable retriaval of warnings
db.get_warnings = True

# For a DDL statement
cursor.execute(
  "CREATE SCHEMA IF NOT EXISTS py_test_db")

# Get the warnings
warnings = cursor.fetchwarnings()

print("Warnings for CREATE SCHEMA:")
print("---------------------------")
print("DDL: Number of warnings: {0}"
  .format(len(warnings)))
print_warnings(warnings)
print("")
```

```
# Try a SELECT statement
cursor.execute("SELECT 1/0")
rows = cursor.fetchall()

# Get the warnings
warnings = cursor.fetchwarnings()

print("Warnings for SELECT:")
print("---------------------")
print("SELECT: Number of warnings: {0}"
    .format(len(warnings)))
print_warnings(warnings)

db.close()
```

Before any queries are executed, the get_warnings option is enabled. This could also have been done in the option file or as a separate argument for the mysql.connector.connect() function.

With get_warnings enabled, the workflow to get the warnings is the same for DDL and SELECT statements. This is a major benefit of this approach. The warnings are fetched using the fetchwarnings() method of the cursor. This returns a list of warnings in the same way as in the previous example. The number of warnings is found as the length of the list. For the SELECT statement, you must retrieve all rows in the result set before fetching the warnings. The output is the same as for Listing 9-1 and Listing 9-2:

```
Using cursors

Warnings for CREATE SCHEMA:
---------------------------
DDL: Number of warnings: 1
Level : Note
Errno : 1007
Message: Can't create database 'py_test_db'; database exists
```

```
Warnings for SELECT:
--------------------
SELECT: Number of warnings: 1
Level  : Warning
Errno  : 1365
Message: Division by 0
```

Fetching Warnings with the X DevAPI

The handling of warnings when using the X DevAPI is similar to how it works for cursors. The big difference is that warnings are part of the result object. This ensures a uniform approach to working with warnings irrespectively of which part of the X DevAPI is used and the query type executed.

The handling of warnings uses the same two methods no matter which kind of result object is returned. The two methods are

- get_warnings(): Returns a list of tuples of the warnings generated by the query

- get_warnings_count(): Returns an integer with the number of warnings

There is no need to enable warnings before the query. The warnings are always available.

As an example, let's repeat the example used for cmd_query() and cursors to see how warnings are handled in a program using the X DevAPI. The resulting code can be seen in Listing 9-4.

Listing 9-4. Handling Warnings with the X DevAPI

```
import mysqlx
from config import connect_args

db = mysqlx.get_session(**connect_args)
```

```
# Ensure the DDL statement will cause
# a warnings by executing the same
# CREATE SCHEMA IF NOT EXISTS statement
# twice.
sql = db.sql(
  "CREATE SCHEMA IF NOT EXISTS py_test_db")
sql.execute()

# For a DDL statement
sql = db.sql(
  "CREATE SCHEMA IF NOT EXISTS py_test_db")
result = sql.execute()

# Get the warnings
print("Warnings for CREATE SCHEMA:")
print("---------------------------")
print("DDL: Number of warnings: {0}"
  .format(result.get_warnings_count()))
print(result.get_warnings())
print("")

# Try a SELECT statement
sql = db.sql("SELECT 1/0")
result = sql.execute()
row = result.fetch_all()

# Get the warnings
print("Warnings for SELECT:")
print("--------------------")
print("SELECT: Number of warnings: {0}"
  .format(result.get_warnings_count()))
print(result.get_warnings())

db.close()
```

The example is similar to the cursor example except that the warning count can be found using the get_warnings_count() method instead of using the length of the warnings list. For a query returning rows or documents as part of the result, the result much be fetched before retrieving the warnings. The output is

```
Warnings for CREATE SCHEMA:
---------------------------
DDL: Number of warnings: 1
[{'level': 1, 'code': 1007, 'msg': "Can't create database
'py_test_db'; database exists"}]

Warnings for SELECT:
--------------------
SELECT: Number of warnings: 1
[{'level': 2, 'code': 1365, 'msg': 'Division by 0'}]
```

The output shows that the warnings are returned as a list of dictionaries. There is one major difference in the output compared to the other examples: the severity level is an integer instead of a string. The levels that can be returned are 1 and 2 with the following meaning:

- **1**: This is a note level message.

- **2**: This is a warning level message.

The code element of the warning dictionary is the MySQL error number, but what does 1007 mean? Let's find out.

MySQL Error Numbers and SQL States

MySQL uses error numbers to specify which note, warning, or error event has occurred. You saw in the examples how the warnings include the error number. For exceptions that are discussed in the next section, the error numbers also play a central role. So before continuing, let's pause and consider the error numbers in more detail.

The error numbers are four- to five-digit numbers that uniquely identify the warning or error encountered. The numbers are MySQL-specific, so they cannot be compared to errors in other database systems. Error numbers may be taken out of use if they are no longer relevant, but they will not be reused. This means that it is safe to check whether a given error number has been encountered and take action based on that.

In addition to the error number, there is also the SQL state, which is meant to be portable across SQL databases. The price to pay for this portability is that it is not possible to be as specific about the error. The SQL states are, however, good to use to represent a group of errors. The SQL state is only returned as part of an error exception.

The rest of this section will look at error numbers and SQL states.

MySQL Error Numbers

The error numbers and SQL states for each known error can be found in `https://dev.mysql.com/doc/refman/en/error-handling.html`. The errors are grouped into server-side and client-side errors. The client-side errors all have numbers between 2000 and 2999. Server-side errors use the ranges 1000-1999 and above 3000. As these ranges suggest, there are thousands of error numbers, and the number increases with each MySQL version.

Fortunately, MySQL Connector/Python has a list of error numbers mapped to constants. This allows you to use the constants in the application if you need to check whether a given error has been encountered. Using the constants makes it easier to see what the error is when you read the code several years after writing it.

For both the mysql.connector and mysqlx modules, the error code constants are defined in the errorcode submodule and the use is the same. Listing 9-5 shows an example of checking whether the warning returned when attempting to create a database is that the database already exists; in that case, it is safe to ignore the warning because you already know that the database may exist.

Listing 9-5. Comparing an Error Code Against a Constant from the errorcode Module

```
import mysqlx
from mysqlx.errorcode import *
from config import connect_args

db = mysqlx.get_session(**connect_args)

# Ensure the DDL statement will cause
# a warnings by executing the same
# CREATE SCHEMA IF NOT EXISTS statement
# twice.
sql = db.sql(
  "CREATE SCHEMA IF NOT EXISTS py_test_db")
sql.execute()

# For a DDL statement
sql = db.sql(
  "CREATE SCHEMA IF NOT EXISTS py_test_db")
result = sql.execute()

# Get the warnings
for warning in result.get_warnings():
  if warning["code"] == ER_DB_CREATE_EXISTS:
    print("Ignoring the warning")
```

```
else:
    raise mysqlx.errors.DatabaseError(
        warning["msg"], warning["code"])
db.close()
```

This example imports all of the error codes from the mysqlx.errorcode module. This allows you to check whether the error number of the warning is ER_DB_CREATE_EXISTS (1007). If it is, the warning will be ignored; otherwise, the warning will be used to raise an exception.

MySQL Connector/Python error exceptions also include the SQL state, so before moving on to discuss the exception classes, let's take a look at the SQL states.

SQL States

Unlike the MySQL error numbers, SQL states are shared among all SQL databases. If you write code that is used with support for different underlying database storages, it is good to use the SQL states as much as possible because it makes it more likely to keep your application portable. SQL states can also be used to determine the category of an error. In MySQL Connector/Python, the SQL states are only used in connection with error exceptions.

The SQL states consist of five letters and digits. The two first characters define the class and the remaining three characters provide the detail. Some common error classes can be seen in Table 9-2. The Exception column is the exception class used for that SQL state class.

Table 9-2. *Common SQL State Classes*

Class	Description	Exception	Comments
00	Success		The query executed successfully. This will never cause an exception.
01	Warning		The query causes a warning. This will only cause an exception if the raise_on_warnings option is enabled.
02	No data	DataError	This can originate in stored programs when no more data exists for a query.
08	Connection exception	OperationalError	This covers various issues in creating the connection like *too many connections*, MySQL Connector/Python does not support the authentication protocol requested by the server, etc. The error must occur server side for this SQL state class.
21	Count is wrong	DataError	Occurs, for example, for inserts where the number of values given does not match the number of fields specified.
22	Data does not fit	DataError	Occurs, for example, if a string is too long for the column or a numeric value is out of range.
23	Constraint violation	IntegrityError	Occurs when a unique key constraint fails, a foreign key is violated, or attempting to specify NULL as a value for a NOT NULL column.

(continued)

Table 9-2. (*continued*)

Class	Description	Exception	Comments
25	Invalid transaction state	ProgrammingError	Occurs if you try to perform an action that is not allowed with the current transaction state. For example, if you attempt to insert data in a read-only transaction.
28	Not authorized	ProgrammingError	The connection failed due to using wrong credentials.
3D	No schema	ProgrammingError	Occurs when executing a query without a default database (schema) and the database is not explicitly set in the query.
40	Transaction errors	InternalError	This can, for example, happen due to deadlocks. Another cause is using MySQL Group Replication and a transaction is rolled back during the commit because it cannot be applied to all nodes.
42	Syntax error or no access	ProgrammingError	The error occurs when the SQL statement is not valid or you do not have permission to access the data requested.

(*continued*)

Table 9-2. (*continued*)

Class	Description	Exception	Comments
HY	Other error	DatabaseError	For errors that do not have a more specific SQL state defined. This, for example, includes a lock wait timeout for InnoDB. MySQL error numbers 1210 and 1243 are exceptions to using the DatabaseError exception class; these two errors raise a ProgrammingError exception instead.
XA	XA transactions	IntegrityError	Used for all errors related to XA transactions.

There are more SQL state classes, but the ones listed in Table 9-2 are those most commonly encountered in MySQL Connector/Python. Each SQL state class is mapped to an exception class. So, let's look at how the exception classes work.

Caution   Syntax errors (SQL state class 42) may be a sign of SQL injection attempts. Make sure to give these errors high priority.

Exception Classes

MySQL Connector/Python uses exceptions to report errors encountered either while processing the commands inside the connector or if there are errors when a query is executed. The exception can be one of three categories, as discussed in this section.

The possible exception categories range from the standard Python exceptions to custom exceptions created by the developer. The three categories are

- **Standard Python exceptions**: Used for non-MySQL-related errors and will not be discussed in more detail.

- **MySQL Connector/Python built-in exceptions**: The ones you will encounter when a MySQL-related error is encountered, unless the exception has been overwritten by a custom exception.

- **Custom exceptions**: It is possible to define your own exception and register it for a given MySQL error number.

The rest of this section will discuss the built-in MySQL Connector/Python exceptions and custom exceptions.

Built-In Classes

A number of exception classes are predefined in MySQL Connector/Python depending on the type of the error. Let's explore them.

The predefined classes are mostly the same whether the `mysql.connector` or `mysqlx` module is used, and they will be discussed together. The classes all use the `errors.Error` class as their base except for the `Warning` class. All classes based on `errors.Error` have the same properties available.

Table 9-3 summarizes the exception classes used in MySQL Connector/Python and which module(s) they are available in. All classes exist in the `errors` submodule (i.e. `mysql.connector.errors` or `mysqlx.errors` depending on which module is used).

Table 9-3. *MySQL Connector/Python Exception Classes*

Exception Class	Modules	Description
DatabaseError	mysql.connector mysqlx	For general database errors. This class is not often used directly except for SQL states starting with HY.
DataError	mysql.connector mysqlx	Errors related to the data that are not constraint errors. Examples include that the data is of the wrong type or does not fit into the field or the wrong number of values is provided.
Error	mysql.connector mysqlx	This is the base exception class. It is not used directly.
IntegrityError	mysql.connector mysqlx	Constraint error or XA transaction errors.
InterfaceError	mysql.connector mysqlx	Used for errors related to the connection.
InternalError	mysql.connector mysqlx	Internal database errors such as deadlocks and unhandled results.
NotSupportedError	mysql.connector mysqlx	Occurs when a feature that has not been implemented is used. This is often related to using features in the wrong context, such as returning a result set in a stored function. It is also used when attempting to connect using the pre-4.1.1 (MySQL Server version) authentication protocol when it is not available.

(continued)

Table 9-3. (*continued*)

Exception Class	Modules	Description
OperationalError	mysql.connector mysqlx	Errors related to the operation of the database. This is most often encountered when making the connection.
PoolError	mysql.connector mysqlx	For errors related to a connection pool.
ProgrammingError	mysql.connector mysqlx	Errors related to the application in a broad sense. Includes syntax errors and attempting to access database objects that do not exist or the user does not have access to.
Warning	mysql.connector	Used for important warnings.

The following classes are all subclasses of the DatabaseError class: InternalError, OperationalError, ProgrammingError, IntegrityError, DataError, and NotSupportedError.

All of the characteristics of the classes are defined in the base Error class, so they will be the same for all of the exception classes except the Warning class. The Warning class has no special features beyond what all exceptions have. To aid the discussion of the features of the error exceptions, consider the following uncaught exception:

```
mysql.connector.errors.ProgrammingError: 1046 (3D000): No
database selected
```

The error classes have three public properties that can be used when handling the exception:

- **msg**: This is the string describing the error. In the example, it's "No database selected."

- **errno**: The MySQL error number. In the example, it's 1046.

- **sqlstate**: The SQL state. In the example, it's 3D000.

Listing 9-6 shows an example that triggers the same exception as the one just discussed. The exception is caught and each of the properties is printed. Finally, the error number is compared to a constant from the errorcode submodule.

Listing 9-6. Example of Handling an Exception

```
import mysql.connector
from mysql.connector import errors
from mysql.connector.errorcode import *

db = mysql.connector.connect(
  option_files="my.ini")

cursor = db.cursor()
try:
  cursor.execute("SELECT * FROM city")
except errors.ProgrammingError as e:
  print("Msg .........: {0}"
    .format(e.msg))
  print("Errno .......: {0}"
    .format(e.errno))
  print("SQL State ...: {0}"
    .format(e.sqlstate))
```

```
  print("")
  if e.errno == ER_NO_DB_ERROR:
    print("Errno is ER_NO_DB_ERROR")
db.close()
```

The exception is caught as usual in Python, and the usage of the properties is straightforward. As you saw earlier, the error number can be compared against a constant in the errorcode submodule to make it easier to see which error the exception is compared against. The output of the example is

```
Msg .........: No database selected
Errno .......: 1046
SQL State ...: 3D000

Errno is ER_NO_DB_ERROR
```

How does MySQL Connector/Python decide which of the classes should be used? This was partly answered in the previous section when the SQL states were discussed, but let's look at the topic in a little more detail.

Mapping Errors to Exception Classes

When an error occurs, MySQL Connector/Python uses the error number and the SQL state to determine which exception class to use. In most cases, you do not need to worry about this, but in some cases, you may need to modify which class is used (currently this is only supported for the mysql.connector module), and in all cases it can be useful to have an understanding of the underlying process.

The exception class is determined using the following steps:

1. If a custom exception has been defined for the MySQL error number, use it. Custom exceptions are only available for the mysql.connector module and will be discussed after these steps.

2.   If the MySQL error number is defined in the
     `errors._ERROR_EXCEPTIONS` list, use the class
     defined there for that error.

3.   If there is no SQL state defined for the error, use the
     `DatabaseError` class. This happens for warnings that
     are raised as errors.

4.   Find the class in the `errors._SQLSTATE_CLASS_`
     `EXCEPTION` list based on the SQL state.

5.   Use the `DatabaseError` class.

If you need an error to trigger a different exception, it is of course
possible to modify the `_ERROR_EXCEPTIONS` and `_SQLSTATE_CLASS_`
`EXCEPTION` lists. However, this is not recommended because they are
meant to be private (thus the underscore at the beginning of the name). In
the `mysql.connector` module, there is a better way: a custom exception.

Custom Exceptions

In some cases, it can be useful to use a custom exception to handle specific
errors. It may be that you want to trigger a special workflow when the error
occurs, for example to log a message to the application log. Currently only
the `mysql.connector` module has support for custom exceptions.

A custom exception is registered using the `errors.custom_error_`
`exception()` function. You need to provide the MySQL error number that will
use the exception and the exception itself. It is recommended that the custom
exception class inherits the `error.Error` class to include the basic features.

Listing 9-7 shows an example where the `MyError` class is used for the
`ER_NO_DB_ERROR` error. The only difference compared to the normal classes
is that it prints a message with the information of the error to `stderr`. If you
are using Python 2.7, you need add `"from __future__ import print_`
`function"` as the first line of the code.

Listing 9-7. Using a Custom Exception

```python
import mysql.connector
from mysql.connector import errors
from mysql.connector.errorcode \
  import ER_NO_DB_ERROR

# Define the custom exception class
class MyError(errors.Error):
  def __init__(
    self, msg=None, errno=None,
    values=None, sqlstate=None):

    import sys
    super(MyError, self).__init__(
      msg, errno, values, sqlstate)
    print("MyError: {0} ({1}): {2}"
      .format(self.errno,
              self.sqlstate,
              self.msg
      ), file=sys.stderr)

# Register the class
errors.custom_error_exception(
  ER_NO_DB_ERROR,
  MyError
)

# Now cause the exception to be raised
db = mysql.connector.connect(
  option_files="my.ini")
```

```
cursor = db.cursor()
try:
  cursor.execute("SELECT * FROM city")
except MyError as e:
  print("Msg .........: {0}"
    .format(e.msg))
  print("Errno .......: {0}"
    .format(e.errno))
  print("SQL State ...: {0}"
    .format(e.sqlstate))

db.close()
```

First, the MyError class is defined. It calls the __init__ method of its own super class to set up all of the standard properties. Then the error message is printed to stderr. This could also use a logging service or use some other logic. Second, the MyError class is registered as the exception class for errors with the MySQL error number set to ER_NO_DB_ERROR.

The rest of the program is the same as before except that you now catch the MyError exception instead of the ProgrammingError exception. The output when executing the program is

```
MyError: 1046 (3D000): No database selected
Msg .........: No database selected
Errno .......: 1046
SQL State ...: 3D000
```

This assumes that stderr and stdout are both printed to the console. It is left as an exercise to first redirect stderr and then stdout to somewhere else and see how this changes the output.

There are also issues that do not necessarily return a warning or an error. One group of issues that may or may not return errors is locking issues. Since locking issues are about working with a database, you should check them out.

Locking Issues

Locking issues occur when two or more transactions (which can be single queries) attempt to access or update the same data in an incompatible way. The topic of locks in databases is large and complex, but also interesting. It is beyond the scope of this book to go into details about locking, but this section will provide a brief overview.

Note   The lock discussion is simplified; for example, only row (record) locks are mentioned. Some of the other locks are gap locks, table locks, metadata locks, and the global read lock. There are also different lock types such as intention locks. The transaction isolation level also plays a role with locks. *The MySQL Reference Manual* has several pages about InnoDB locking alone. The starting point is `https://dev.mysql.com/doc/refman/en/innodb-locking-transaction-model.html`.

The reason for locking is to allow concurrent access to the data while still ensuring a consistent result. If one transaction updates a given row and then another transaction attempts to update the same row, the second transaction must wait for the first transaction to complete (commit or rollback) before it can access the row. If this was not the case, the end result would be nondeterministic.

The two transactional storage engines in MySQL, InnoDB and NDBCluster, both uses row-level locks. This means that only the rows read or changed by a query are locked. Since it is not known until the row is accessed whether it is needed, queries execute optimistically, assuming it will be possible to obtain the required locks.

The optimistic approach works great most of the time, but it also means that sometimes a query will have to wait for a lock. It can even be that the wait is so long that a timeout occurs.

441

Another possibility is that a conflict occurs where two transactions are waiting for locks from each other. That situation will never resolve by itself and is called a deadlock. The name deadlock sounds scary, but it is just a name for a situation where the database must intervene for the lock issue to resolve. InnoDB chooses the transaction that has done the least work and rolls it back. A deadlock error is returned in that case so the application knows why the transaction failed. Listing 9-8 shows a simple example where two connections end up with a deadlock.

Listing 9-8. Example of Two Transactions Causing a Deadlock

```
Connection 1> START TRANSACTION;
Query OK, 0 rows affected (0.00 sec)

Connection 1> UPDATE world.city
              SET Population = Population + 100
              WHERE Name = 'San Francisco' AND
              CountryCode = 'USA';
Query OK, 1 row affected (0.00 sec)
Rows matched: 1  Changed: 1  Warnings: 0

Connection 2> START TRANSACTION;
Query OK, 0 rows affected (0.00 sec)

Connection 2> UPDATE world.city
              SET Population = Population + 200
              WHERE Name = 'Sydney' AND CountryCode = 'AUS';
Query OK, 1 row affected (0.04 sec)
Rows matched: 1  Changed: 1  Warnings: 0

Connection 1> UPDATE world.city
              SET Population = Population + 100
              WHERE Name = 'Sydney' AND CountryCode = 'AUS';
-- Connection 1 blocks until the deadlock occurs for Connection 2.
```

```
Connection 2> UPDATE world.city
                SET Population = Population + 200
              WHERE Name = 'San Francisco' AND
                CountryCode = 'USA';
```
ERROR 1213 (40001): Deadlock found when trying to get lock; try restarting transaction

Both transactions try to increase the population of Sydney and San Francisco; the one in Connection 1 with 100 people, the one in Connection 2 with 200 people. However, they update the two cities in the opposite order and interleaved. So, in the end, Connection 1 waits for the lock on Sydney to be released and Connection 2 waits for the lock on San Francisco to be released. This will never happen, so it is a deadlock.

Lock waits and deadlocks are facts of life when working with fine-grained locks. It is important that you have this in mind and ensure that your application can handle lock issues. If a lock wait timeout or a deadlock only happens rarely, it is usually enough to retry the transaction. If the issues occur so often that they affect performance, you need to work at reducing the lock contention. The next chapter will briefly discuss troubleshooting locks.

Tip   Make sure your application can handle lock waits and deadlocks. The first approach is to retry the transaction, possibly with a small delay to give the other transaction a chance to complete. Frequently recurring lock issues should be investigated further.

The final thing to discuss is what to do when a warning, an error, or some other issue occurs.

What to Do When Things Go Wrong

Thus far, the discussion about warnings and errors has been focused on how warnings and errors work with MySQL Connector/Python. A rather important question remains, though: What do you do when you encounter warnings, errors, and other issues?

The short answer to this question is that "it depends." Not only does it depend on the issue, it also depends on the circumstances. Some things to consider are the following:

- **Severity**: How critical is the issue?

- **Impact**: How many and who are impacted by the issue?

- **Frequency**: How often does the issue occur?

- **Retriable**: Is it worth retrying the action that led to the error?

- **Effort**: How much work does it take to avoid the issue?

Another consideration is how to report a failure. If it involves a production environment, a relatively short, concise message is best. If possible, provide information how to avoid the issue and/or how to get help.

It may seem like a good idea to include the full stack trace and exact exception; however, the end user cannot use that information. In fact, in some cases it looks unprofessional to return so many details to the front end, and it may even reveal details about the application the end user should not know.

The full details of the error, including the trace, are of course of great interest to the developers. Exactly how to log it depends on the application, but it can be written to the application log or a separate error log. Another option in the development environment is to support a "debug" mode that outputs the full details to the front end to make it easier to get the information during testing.

In the end, exactly how you want to present an error depends on your specific needs, the target users, and so on. In some cases, it may even be possible to avoid the end user being affected by the issue encountered. Which brings us back to the five items listed at the start of this section; they will be discussed in the following subsections.

Severity

The severity of the issue is how critical it is for the rest of the application and the users. If an error causes the application not to work at all, it is obviously more critical to handle that error than one that, for example, causes a slightly slower response.

High severity issues need to be handled quickly. If it is a security issue, or the web site unavailable, a delayed solution can cost the company money. On the other hand, if one out of a million requests takes 5% longer to handle than normal, it may still be an annoyance but hardly something that warrants dropping everything you are doing. Together with the severity, the impact is the other major factor in deciding the urgency of the issue.

Impact

It makes a big difference whether an issue is encountered in a customer-facing production environment, an internal non-critical application, or a development system. The higher the number of users affected and the more the company relies on the application to work, the more urgent it is to fix the issue.

Within a given environment there can also be differences. Consider a development environment. If you are the only one affected and the issue does not impact what you are currently working on, you can postpone working on a solution.

However, if 100 other developers are sitting around and twiddling their thumbs or have their work impacted, it becomes more urgent to solve the issue. The frequency of the issue obviously also has an influence on the impact.

Frequency

The frequently of an issue affects how much effort is required. If you encounter a deadlock or a lock wait timeout once in a blue moon, it is perfectly fine to just retry the query (see also the next item). If the same locking issue occurs several times a minute, it is necessary to investigate how the issue can be avoided.

The limit where an issue occurs too often depends on the nature of the issue, which ties the frequency back to the severity and impact. If customers experience the application crashes, it very quickly becomes an issue that must be handled immediately. Likewise, a reporting job that fails after an hour and must be restarted from the beginning.

On the other hand, if the same one-hour reporting job gets delayed by some seconds each time the issue occurs, it won't likely be a priority.

Retriable

The errors you will encounter in MySQL Connector/Python can be divided into two groups: those that will always keep failing no matter how many times you try, and those that may succeed if you retry them. The latter deserves a little more attention because you can add support for handling them automatically.

Retriable errors are typically caused either by lock contention or resource exhaustion. I have already discussed locks, so let's look closer at what causes resource exhaustion from a MySQL point of view.

There are several places in the lifetime of a connection when resources are required. When the connection is first created, there must be more connections available in MySQL Server, and the operating system must allow for the creating of a new thread (by default MySQL creates one operating system thread per connection). When a query is executed, it will require memory for various parts of the execution, for example to sort a result. If you insert or change the data, it may also cause the table to grow, which requires additional disk space. If these resources get exhausted, the query will fail.

Not all of these errors are equally likely to go away if you retry the query. For example, if the disk is full, it likely requires the database administrator and/or system administrator to intervene before it is possible to insert data again. On the other hand, if you have a locking issue and your transactions are all of short duration, then retrying the failed transaction is likely to succeed.

Table 9-4 shows some of the typical error numbers where a retry is an option.

Table 9-4. *MySQL Error Numbers That May Be Retried*

Error #	Constant	SQL State	Description
1028	ER_FILSORT_ABORT	HY000	A sorting operation has been aborted.
1038	ER_OUT_OF_SORTMEMORY	HY001	A sorting operation was aborted due to not having enough memory. It may be necessary to increase the sort_buffer_size MySQL session variable.
1040	ER_CON_COUNT_ERROR	08004	MySQL Connector/Python fails to connect to MySQL Server because all allocated connections (max_connections) are already in use.
1041	ER_OUT_OF_RESOURCES	HY000	MySQL Server is out of memory but may be able to continue.

(*continued*)

Table 9-4. (*continued*)

Error #	Constant	SQL State	Description
1043	ER_HANDSHAKE_ERROR	08S01	This can happen when creating the connection, if there are network problems.
1114	ER_RECORD_FILE_FULL	HY000	The table is full.
1135	ER_CANT_CREATE_THREAD	HY000	It is not possible to create the thread for a new connection. This may be due to exhaustion of the memory, file descriptors, or allowed number of processes.
1180	ER_ERROR_DURING_COMMIT	HY000	An error occurred while committing a transaction.
1181	ER_ERROR_DURING_ ROLLBACK	HY000	An error occurred while rolling back a transaction.
1203	ER_TOO_MANY_USER_ CONNECTIONS	42000	The user has too many connections.
1205	ER_LOCK_WAIT_TIMEOUT	HY000	The transaction waited for longer than the timeout (50 seconds by default for InnoDB) for a lock.
1206	ER_LOCK_TABLE_FULL	HY000	This can happen for InnoDB if there are too many locks compared to the size of the InnoDB buffer pool. It is only worth retrying if it is not the transaction itself causing the large number of locks.

(*continued*)

Table 9-4. (*continued*)

Error #	Constant	SQL State	Description
1213	ER_LOCK_DEADLOCK	40001	A deadlock occurred, and this transaction was chosen as the victim.
1226	ER_USER_LIMIT_REACHED	42000	A user resource limit has been exceeded.
1613	ER_XA_RBTIMEOUT	XA106	The XA transaction was rolled back because it took too long.
1614	ER_XA_RBDEADLOCK	XA102	The XA transaction was rolled back due to a deadlock.
1615	ER_NEED_REPREPARE	HY000	The prepared statement needs to be prepared again.

The list of errors is not meant to be exhaustive, and the chance of success of retrying them varies.

Note that you may be able to code a solution for some errors. For example, error number 1456 (ER_SP_RECURSION_LIMIT, SQL state HY000) happens if you exceed the recursion depth allowed by the max_sp_ recursion_depth variable. If you have set this option to a relatively low value, but accept increasing it in some cases, you can increase the value for the session and retry. Obviously, it would be better for this specific case if the value was increased before the first attempt, but there may be some special considerations that prevent this.

If you decide to retry a transaction, you also need to decide whether it is enough to retry the latest statement or if the whole transaction must be retried. Usually the latter is the case and, in all cases, it is the safest.

Caution   It may be tempting just to retry the last statement in a transaction but be careful because the preceding statements may have been rolled back.

It can be tempting to automatically retry queries that fail because of a lost connection. However, be careful in that case to ensure that everything the query relies on, such as earlier queries in the same transaction, are also reexecuted.

Effort

The last thing of note is the effort to resolve an issue. In an ideal world, all bugs get fixed, but in reality, resources are limited so it is often necessary to prioritize. This idea ties together all of the previous considerations.

The larger a software project is, the more complicated it becomes to determine which issues should be fixed in which order. There may be several conflicting interests, such as two customers being affected by different issues. There may also be a requirement for the development of new features to stay on track. In such cases, it can be necessary to have several parties included in the discussions to prioritize the work that is required.

This completes the discussion of warnings and error handling in MySQL Connector/Python. A related topic is how to troubleshoot the errors you encounter, which will be discussed in the next chapter.

Summary

This chapter explored how warnings and errors work in MySQL Server and MySQL Connector/Python. There are three severity levels of warnings and errors: notes, warnings, and errors.

You started out looking at how the `sql_notes` option in MySQL Server can be used to change whether note level messages are treated as warnings or not. It is also possible to configure whether MySQL Server should operate in a strict mode or not. Finally, you saw that you should monitor the MySQL error log to check whether the application is causing any messages to be logged.

In MySQL Connector/Python, you should check for warnings and verify whether they are a sign of a more severe issue. At least during development, it can be useful to make MySQL Connector/Python raise warnings as exceptions; however, that is only available when using cursors with the `mysql.connector` module, and it still requires you to fetch the warnings.

Error messages consist of an error number, an SQL state, and a text message. The error numbers are also available as constants in the `errorcode` submodule of both `mysql.connector` and `mysqlx`. Using the constants make it easier to understand which errors are in use, when you get back to that part of the code and can no longer remember the meaning of, for example, error number 1046.

The SQL states can be used to determine the overall category of the error. They are also used together with the error number to decide which exception class to use. Non-MySQL errors in general use one of the standard Python exception classes whereas MySQL errors use one of several classes specific to MySQL Connector/Python. When you use the `mysql.connector` module, it is also possible to register your own custom exception class for a given MySQL error number.

The final part of the chapter looked into what locking issues are and what to do when an issue is encountered. In the end, an error may require troubleshooting, which is the topic of the next chapter.

CHAPTER 10

Troubleshooting

You have written a large and complex application and there is just a short time left before the deadline. You start the final testing, but something is not working as expected. Once the application is in production, a customer or a support engineer may complain about errors. How do you troubleshoot these issues as quickly and efficiently as possible? Read on!

Tip There are a couple of example programs in this chapter. All example programs that appear in a listing are available for download. See the discussion of example programs in Chapter 1 for more information about using the example programs.

Troubleshooting Steps

When you are new to a programming language, library, database, or the like, it can be difficult to troubleshoot an issue. To help you troubleshoot in MySQL Connector/Python, this section will discuss some general troubleshooting techniques that are specific to MySQL Connector/Python. It is also recommended to become familiar with general software, Python, and MySQL troubleshooting.

© Jesper Wisborg Krogh 2018
J. W. Krogh, *MySQL Connector/Python Revealed*,
https://doi.org/10.1007/978-1-4842-3694-9_10

Tip   One book that may be of use for general MySQL troubleshooting is *MySQL Troubleshooting* by Sveta Smirnova (http://shop.oreilly.com/product/0636920021964.do). It is some years old now, so it does not cover all of the latest features, but it still provides a good starting point if you are not familiar with MySQL troubleshooting.

Before you dive in and start working on your troubleshooting skills, remember that the problems that are easiest to solve are those that are discovered immediately when the code is written. So, make sure you have a good test framework in place and that you have good test coverage.

Tip   Having a good test suite is the first step to avoiding issues that will later take master troubleshooting skills to debug.

The troubleshooting discussion will start by going through the five general means of troubleshooting MySQL Connector/Python issues: check the warnings; determine the SQL statement; work with raw data; the MySQL Connector/Python source code; and change the MySQL Connector/Python implementation. Additionally, the next subsection will describe the MySQL server logs, which can also be useful.

Checking Warnings

The checking of warnings was discussed in the previous chapter. So, this just serves to reiterate that it is important to check the warnings because they can be an early indicator that something is wrong, something that may cause more severe errors later. Errors can occur within in the same program execution or surface at a later time, even years later.

Therefore, optimally your program should not cause any warnings except when you are fully aware of why the warning was created and the warning can be handled explicitly. An example of when a warning is expected is for EXPLAIN statements where the reformatted query and other information can be returned through warnings.

The recommendation is to check all warnings and if possible enable raise_on_warnings to cause an exception when a warning occurs. It may be impossible to completely avoid warnings, but if you handle them explicitly either by catching the exception or by temporarily disabling raise_on_warnings, at least it ensures you are aware of the warnings that do occur, and you can investigate the cause of them. One way to investigate the cause of a warning is to look at the exact SQL statement executed; this is the next topic.

Determining the SQL Statement

In some cases, it is very clear which SQL statement is executed, for example whenever you execute an explicitly written SQL statement. However, in other cases, it is less clear. You may use parameters, execute queries through the X DevAPI, or use some other framework that generates the actual SQL statements for you.

Once you have the statement, you can try to execute it manually, for example, through MySQL Shell. Using a command-line client is a great way to debug SQL statements, and MySQL Shell supports both executing SQL statements directly and using Python code.

Let's look at how you can find out which SQL statements are actually executed. There are various ways to extract the queries. The following examples show how to get the statement for cursor, a select statement in the X DevAPI, and the general case using the MySQL Performance Schema.

cursor.statement

When you use a cursor, you can retrieve the last executed query in the statement property of the cursor. This even works with parameters because the query returned is with the parameter substitution. The following example shows how the SQL statement is found:

```
import mysql.connector

db = mysql.connector.connect(
  option_files="my.ini",
)

cursor = db.cursor()
cursor.execute(
  "SELECT * FROM world.city WHERE ID = %(id)s",
  params={"id": 130}
)
print("Statement: {0};"
  .format(cursor.statement))

db.close()
```

This prints the following output:

```
Statement: SELECT * FROM world.city WHERE ID = 130;
```

mysqlx SelectStatement.get_sql()

For select statements in the X DevAPI, the get_sql() method returns the statement that is generated based on the query definition. This works like the cursor statement property, except parameter substitution is not included. An example of using get_sql() to retrieve the statement is

```
import mysqlx
from config import connect_args

db = mysqlx.get_session(**connect_args)
world = db.get_schema("world")
city = world.get_table("city")
stmt = city.select()
stmt.where("ID = :city_id")
stmt.bind("city_id", 130)

print("Statement: {0}"
  .format(stmt.get_sql()))

db.close()
```

This prints the following output:

```
Statement: SELECT * FROM world.city WHERE ID = :city_id
```

What may seem surprising here is that instead of the actual ID, the placeholder name is used (:city_id). The X DevAPI does not apply the binding until execution time, so when using get_sql() to generate the SQL statement, only the name of the placeholder is available.

Using the Performance Schema

A method that can be used in all cases except when prepared statements are used is to query the MySQL Performance Schema. This is easiest to do on a test instance where you can ensure no other queries are executed. Similar steps can be used on busy servers as well but this requires a bit more care and filtering to find the queries from the application.

In order to use the Performance Schema, you need to prepare the configuration, so queries are captured and kept even when the application has closed its connection. One way to do this is to enable the events_ statements_history_long consumer and disable monitoring for the database connection that will retrieve the queries:

```
mysql> UPDATE performance_schema.setup_consumers
          SET ENABLED = 'YES'
        WHERE NAME = 'events_statements_history_long';
Query OK, 1 row affected (0.09 sec)
Rows matched: 1  Changed: 1  Warnings: 0

mysql> UPDATE performance_schema.threads
          SET INSTRUMENTED = 'NO'
        WHERE PROCESSLIST_ID = CONNECTION_ID();
Query OK, 1 row affected (0.11 sec)
Rows matched: 1  Changed: 1  Warnings: 0
```

At this point, it is possible to execute the part of the application that you need to get the queries from. Consider the example program in Listing 10-1 that executes one select statement on the city table in the world schema using both the mysql.connector module and the X DevAPI's CRUD access to SQL tables (so two queries in total).

Listing 10-1. Executing Two Simple Queries Using mysql.connector and mysqlx

```
import mysql.connector
import mysqlx
from config import connect_args

# Execute a query using the traditional
# API
db_trad = mysql.connector.connect(
  option_files="my.ini")
cursor = db_trad.cursor()
```

```
sql = """SELECT *
            FROM world.city
            WHERE ID = %(id)s"""
params = {'id': 130}
cursor.execute(sql, params=params)

for row in cursor.fetchall():
  print(row)

db_trad.close()

# Execute a query using the X DevAPI
dbx = mysqlx.get_session(**connect_args)
world = dbx.get_schema("world")

city = world.get_table("city")
city_stmt = city.select()
city_stmt.where("ID = :city_id")
city_stmt.bind("city_id", 131)
res = city_stmt.execute()
for row in res.fetch_all():
  print("({0}, '{1}', '{2}', '{3}', {4})"
    .format(
        row[0], row[1],
        row[2],row[3],row[4]
  ))

dbx.close()
```

Once the execution has completed, you can get the queries the program executed using a statement like in Listing 10-2. A LIMIT 8 has been added because in general there can be up to 10,000 rows in the output. Since the queries executed by other connections will also be recorded, it may not be the first rows returned that are the ones for the example program, in which case it can be necessary to increase the number of rows included in the output.

Listing 10-2. Obtaining the Statements from the Performance
Schema

```
mysql> SELECT THREAD_ID, EVENT_ID, EVENT_NAME, SQL_TEXT
         FROM performance_schema.events_statements_history_long
       ORDER BY THREAD_ID DESC, EVENT_ID
       LIMIT 8\G
*************************** 1. row ***************************
 THREAD_ID: 182
  EVENT_ID: 1
EVENT_NAME: statement/sql/set_option
  SQL_TEXT: SET NAMES 'utf8' COLLATE 'utf8_general_ci'
*************************** 2. row ***************************
 THREAD_ID: 182
  EVENT_ID: 2
EVENT_NAME: statement/sql/set_option
  SQL_TEXT: SET NAMES utf8
*************************** 3. row ***************************
 THREAD_ID: 182
  EVENT_ID: 3
EVENT_NAME: statement/sql/set_option
  SQL_TEXT: set autocommit=0
*************************** 4. row ***************************
 THREAD_ID: 182
  EVENT_ID: 4
EVENT_NAME: statement/com/Ping
  SQL_TEXT: NULL
*************************** 5. row ***************************
```

```
  THREAD_ID: 182
   EVENT_ID: 5
 EVENT_NAME: statement/sql/select
   SQL_TEXT: SELECT *
             FROM world.city
             WHERE ID = 130
*************************** 6. row ***************************
  THREAD_ID: 182
   EVENT_ID: 7
 EVENT_NAME: statement/com/Quit
   SQL_TEXT: NULL
*************************** 7. row ***************************
  THREAD_ID: 179
   EVENT_ID: 1
 EVENT_NAME: statement/sql/select
   SQL_TEXT: /* xplugin authentication */ SELECT @@require_
             secure_transport, `authentication_string`,
             `plugin`,(`account_locked`='Y') as is_account_
             locked, (`password_expired`!
ord`, @@offline_mode and (`Super_priv`='N') as `is_offline_
mode_and_not_super_user`,`ssl_type`, `ssl_cipher`, `x509_
issuer`, `x509_subject` FROM mysql.user WHERE 'pyuser' = `u
*************************** 8. row ***************************
  THREAD_ID: 179
   EVENT_ID: 3
 EVENT_NAME: statement/sql/select
   SQL_TEXT: SELECT * FROM `world`.`city` WHERE (`ID` = 131)
8 rows in set (0.00 sec)
```

The rows with THREAD_ID = 182 are the queries when using the mysql. connector module, and the rows with THREAD_ID = 179 are for the mysqlx module. The actual thread and event IDs will be different and, as you can see from this example, the thread IDs are not monotonically increasing (the example created the connection with THREAD_ID = 182 before the one with THREAD_ID = 179). The statements for a given thread ID are executed in the order of the EVENT_ID.

As you can see, executing a query through MySQL Connector/ Python includes executing other queries and commands as well. The two highlighted queries are the ones you asked to be executed.

The performance_schema.events_statements_history_long table does not include queries executed as server-side prepared statements. They can be found in the performance_schema.prepared_statements_ instances, but only aggregated per prepared statement and only as long as the application is connected.

There is one more way to get the SQL statements that are executed: the general query log. This will be discussed together with the other MySQL Server logs later in the chapter.

Once you have confirmed the actual query exists, you may need to look at the returned raw data if your problem has not been resolved.

Retrieving Raw Data

If the query seems to be correct and it works when you execute it manually, the issue may be in the processing of the data that is returned. One way to investigate whether that is the issue when using cursors is to ask for the data to be returned raw.

Note   Raw result data is only supported together with a plain cursor and a buffered cursor.

When you have the raw data, you can see if it looks as expected and work from there to figure out the issue. It may be necessary to look at the MySQL Connector/Python source code, which is the next topic.

Reading the MySQL Connector/Python Source Code

One of the reasons for using a library like MySQL Connector/Python is that you do not want to implement a connector yourself, and you want to use it as a black box. That is also the aim but writing Python programs has an advantage: it is easy to take a look at how the libraries are implemented because they are largely written in Python themselves and you can open the libraries files directly rather than having a separate source code tree.

There are three options if you want to look into the source code:

- Look directly at the libraries files that are used. This can particularly be useful on your development system because as it allows you to perform debugging inside the library. Be sure to reset the code once you are done, so you do not end up having a different behavior on your development system than on the production system. The best way to reset is to reinstall the libraries.

- Download the source code from https://dev.mysql. com/downloads/connector/python/ for the latest released source or https://downloads.mysql.com/ archives/c-python/ for older releases.

- Download the source from the MySQL GitHub repository at https://github.com/mysql/mysql-connector-python. If you are familiar with git, this can be a convenient way to work with the source, if you need to switch between the available branches and versions.

If you are using the C Extension, only a limited amount of the source code is written in Python. However, you can switch between the pure Python implementation and the C Extension on demand, which is the final topic of this section.

Changing the Implementation

One final option is to change whether you are using the pure Python or the C Extension implementation of MySQL Connector/Python. In general, it should not matter which implementation you are using, but in some corner cases there may be a difference.

You change between the two implementations by changing the value of the use_pure connection option. This is disabled by default. If there is a difference in behavior beyond what has been described in this book or is documented in the manual, it may be a bug in MySQL Connector/Python; you can log a bug at https://bugs.mysql.com/.

Tip Unexpected behavior may be due to a bug in MySQL Connector/ Python. The older the release, the more likely this is the case. It is recommended to use the latest patch release for the release series to ensure you have as many bug fixes as possible. The release notes can be found at https://dev.mysql.com/doc/relnotes/ connector-python/en/.

The final source of troubleshooting information that will be considered is the MySQL Server logs.

MySQL Server Logs

MySQL Server includes several logs that can be useful for investigating what is going on and what is going wrong. It is worth taking a look at them and how they can be used when investigating an issue in a MySQL Connector/Python program.

The logs included with MySQL Server are

- **The error log**: This is where the MySQL Server instance logs messages when something is not correct from the server side or when important changes such as starting and stopping the instance occur.

- **The general query log**: This can be enabled to record all executed queries.

- **The slow query log**: This can be used to log all queries that take longer than a certain amount of time or ones that are not using indexes.

- **The binary log**: This records all changes made to the schema or data, but not queries selecting data.

- **The audit log**: This can be used to record all or a subset of queries. It is similar to the general query log but more flexible, with more features, and the option of having lower overhead. This is only available in the Enterprise Edition and will not be discussed further. If you are interested, see `https://www.mysql.com/products/enterprise/audit.html`.

Each of the logs has its own strengths, so it is not a matter of enabling just one of them. To get a better feeling for each of the logs (except the audit log), let's go into more detail about them.

The Error Log

The error log is the main place to look for problems on the MySQL Server side. However, it can also include information about aborted connections, failed authentication, and other issues that are related to the client side.

The error log location is specified using the `log_error` option. The default depends on your platform and how you start MySQL. It is recommended to always set this explicitly to have the path specified in the configuration file and to avoid the file name changing if the hostname (on Linux and Unix) is updated. This also ensures the error log is always enabled.

The verbosity is controlled using the `log_error_verbosity` option. It can be set to 1, 2, or 3. The default value in MySQL 8.0 is 2. A higher value means less important messages are included.

- **1**: Error messages

- **2**: Error and warning messages

- **3**: Error, warning, and note level messages

In MySQL 8.0, there is an additional category of messages: system messages. They are always included irrespective of the value of `log_error_verbosity`.

These are the most important settings from a development point of view. There are several other settings such as logging to a syslog facility and advanced filtering options. These settings are beyond the scope of this book, but you can read more about them at `https://dev.mysql.com/doc/refman/en/error-log.html`.

The General Query Log

The general query log logs all queries before they are executed. This makes it a great resource when debugging issues where you are not explicitly writing and executing each query manually. On the downside, the general query log has a large performance overhead, so it is not recommended to enable this in production other than for short periods of a time.

Caution   The general query log has a large overhead. Be very careful if you enable it on a production system. It is, however, a great tool on development systems for debugging.

The general query log is enabled using the general_log option and the location of the file can be set using general_log_file. The default location is a file using the hostname as the basename and *.log* as the extension. You can, for example, enable the general query log and check the current file location using the following SQL commands:

```
mysql> SET GLOBAL general_log = ON;
Query OK, 0 rows affected (0.07 sec)

mysql> SELECT @@global.general_log_file;
+---------------------------------+
| @@global.general_log_file       |
+---------------------------------+
| D:\MySQL\Data_8.0.11\general.log |
+---------------------------------+
1 row in set (0.00 sec)
```

The content of the general log file includes connections and the queries executed with timestamps. An example is

```
D:\MySQL\mysql-8.0.11-winx64\bin\mysqld.exe, Version: 8.0.11
(MySQL Community Server - GPL). started with:
TCP Port: 3306, Named Pipe: MySQL
Time                      Id Command  Argument
2018-05-13T04:53:35.717319Z  164 Connect   pyuser@localhost on
                                            using SSL/TLS
2018-05-13T04:53:35.717850Z  164 Query     SET NAMES 'utf8'
                                            COLLATE 'utf8_
                                            general_ci'
2018-05-13T04:53:35.718079Z  164 Query     SET NAMES utf8
2018-05-13T04:53:35.718304Z  164 Query     set autocommit=0
2018-05-13T04:53:35.718674Z  164 Query     SELECT *
        FROM world.city
        WHERE ID = 130
```

```
2018-05-13T04:53:35.719042Z   164 Quit
2018-05-13T04:53:36.167636Z   165 Connect
2018-05-13T04:53:36.167890Z   165 Query    /* xplugin
authentication */ SELECT @@require_secure_transport,
`authentication_string`, `plugin`,(`account_locked`='Y') as
is_account_locked, (`password_expired`!='N') as `is_password_
expired`, @@disconnect_on_expired_password as `disconnect_on_
expired_password`, @@offline_mode and (`Super_priv`='N') as
`is_offline_mode_and_not_super_user`,`ssl_type`, `ssl_cipher`,
`x509_issuer`, `x509_subject` FROM mysql.user WHERE 'pyuser' =
`user` AND 'localhost' = `host`
```
2018-05-13T04:53:36.169665Z   165 Query   SELECT * FROM
**   `world`.`city` WHERE (`ID` = 131)**
```
2018-05-13T04:53:36.170498Z   165 Quit
```

This is from the same example as where the Performance Schema was used to determine the queries. The Id column is the connection ID, so it cannot be compared to the THREAD_ID in the Performance Schema. For more information about the general query log, see https://dev.mysql.com/doc/refman/en/query-log.html.

The Slow Query Log

The slow query log is the traditional tool to investigate slow queries in MySQL. Nowadays the Performance Schema provides much of the functionality of the slow query log, but there are still cases where you may want to log to a file, such as persisting the log when MySQL restarts.

The slow query log is enabled using the slow_query_log option. The default is that queries taking longer than long_query_time seconds are logged to the file specified by the slow_query_log_file. An exception is administrative queries (ALTER TABLE, OPTIMIZE TABLE, etc.), which require the log_slow_admin_statements option to be enabled before they are logged.

Additionally, there is the log_queries_not_using_indexes option, which causes all queries not using an index to be logged irrespective of how long time it takes to execute the query. When enabling this option, it can be useful to increase long_query_time to a large value (like 10000) to focus only on queries not using an index. The min_examined_row_limit can be used to avoid logging queries only examining a small number of rows; for example, if a table only has 10 rows, it is fine to do a full table scan.

For more about the slow query log, see https://dev.mysql.com/doc/refman/en/slow-query-log.html.

The Binary Log

The binary log is somewhat different to the other logs because the primary purpose is not to log things out of the ordinary or work as a log for auditing. It is used to allow replication and point-in-time recoveries. However, since the binary log records all changes to both schema and data, it can also be useful in determining when changes were made.

The binary log is enabled by default in MySQL 8.0.3 and later and is controlled by the log_bin option. This option can both be used to enable the binary log and to set the path and file name prefix for the binary log files. To disable binary logging, use the option skip_log_bin. Within a given connection (session), binary logging can be disabled by setting the sql_log_bin option to OFF and reenabling it by setting it to ON:

```
mysql> SET SESSION sql_log_bin = OFF;
Query OK, 0 rows affected (0.04 sec)

mysql> -- Some queries not to be logged

mysql> SET SESSION sql_log_bin = ON;
Query OK, 0 rows affected (0.00 sec)
```

The SYSTEM_VARIABLES_ADMIN or SUPER privilege is required to change sql_log_bin, and you should only do so if you have a good reason. If schema or data changes are missing in the binary log, a replication slave can become out of sync; that is, it does not have the same data as the replication master, meaning it is necessary to rebuild the slave.

The binary log is read using the mysqlbinlog utility that is included with the MySQL Server installation. For more information about the binary log, see https://dev.mysql.com/doc/refman/en/binary-log.html.

The chapter thus far has shown a very manual approach to troubleshooting. It is possible to make this easier via tools. The next section will discuss two tools: MySQL Shell and PyCharm.

Tools for Debugging

For simple programs and simple problems, it may be faster to resolve the issue by manually debugging by reading the source, adding print statements, etc. However, in general this is not the most efficient way. This section will take a look at two tools that can help debug MySQL Connector/Python programs. First, you'll look at MySQL Shell, which was briefly mentioned in Chapter 6, and then you'll take a brief look at using PyCharm for debugging.

MySQL Shell

The command-line client MySQL Shell was first released as GA in April 2017. It is meant to be the next generation tool for not only executing SQL queries, but also performing administrative tasks and executing code in Python and JavaScript.

MySQL Shell is not as such a debugging tool. However, because it is interactive and it supports both Python and direct SQL statements, it is a convenient way to experiment and investigate how code and queries are working. It also includes support for the X DevAPI, so you can debug code that uses the `mysqlx` module interactively.

Note   It is not MySQL Connector/Python that is included in MySQL Shell. So, there are some differences whether you use the X DevAPI from a program using MySQL Connector/Python or you use MySQL Shell. However, the API itself is the same.

You can download MySQL Shell from the same location as MySQL Connector/Python and MySQL Server. The link to the Community downloads is `https://dev.mysql.com/downloads/shell/`. If you are using MySQL Installer on Microsoft Windows, you can also install MySQL Shell that way. Once MySQL Shell has been installed (the installation will be left as an exercise for the reader), you can launch it in several ways:

- Executing the `mysqlsh` binary from a shell. This is the most common way on Linux and Unix, but it also works on Microsoft Windows.

- On Microsoft Windows you can also execute it from the Start menu.

One advantage of invoking `mysqlsh` from a shell is that you can specify options on the command-line; for example, `--py` starts MySQL Shell in Python mode. Once you have started it, you get a prompt like in Figure 10-1.

```
MySQL Shell 8.0.11

Copyright (c) 2016, 2018, Oracle and/or its affiliates. All rights reserved.

Oracle is a registered trademark of Oracle Corporation and/or its
affiliates. Other names may be trademarks of their respective
owners.

Type '\help' or '\?' for help; '\quit' to exit.

 MySQL  JS >
```

Figure 10-1. The MySQL Shell welcome message

The colors have been changed in the screen shot to work better in print. The default color scheme is optimized for a black background. The prompt shows which mode the shell is in. The tree modes are summarized in Table 10-1.

Table 10-1. *The MySQL Shell Modes*

Mode	Prompt	Command-Line	Command
JavaScript	JS	--js	\js
Python	Py	--py	\py
SQL	SQL	--sql	\sql

The Prompt column shows the abbreviation used for the mode in the prompt text. The Command-Line column contains the option to enable the mode when starting MySQL Shell from the command line. The Command column shows the command to use inside the shell to change the mode.

There are six global objects that can be used when executing Python code in MySQL Shell:

- mysqlx: The mysqlx module; however, this is not identical to the mysqlx module from MySQL Connector/Python (but it is very similar).

- session: The session object that holds the connection to MySQL Server.

- db: A schema object if one has been defined in the URI when creating the connection.

- dba: This object contains methods for administering MySQL InnoDB Cluster.

- shell: An object with various general-purpose methods such as for configuring MySQL Shell.

- util: This object contains various utility methods.

Listing 10-3 shows an example of using the MySQL Shell to test code that creates a collection and adds two documents.

Listing 10-3. Using the MySQL Shell

```
JS> \py
Switching to Python mode...

Py> \c pyuser@localhost
Creating a session to 'pyuser@localhost'
Enter password: **********
Fetching schema names for autocompletion... Press ^C to stop.
Your MySQL connection id is 179 (X protocol)
Server version: 8.0.11 MySQL Community Server - GPL
No default schema selected; type \use <schema> to set one.

Py> session
<Session:pyuser@localhost>

Py> session.drop_schema('py_test_db')
Py> db = session.create_schema('py_test_db')
Py> people = db.create_collection('people')
Py> add_stmt = people.add(
...   {
...      "FirstName": "John",
...      "LastName": "Doe"
...   }
... )
...
Py> add_stmt.add(
...   {
```

```
...      "FirstName": "Jane",
...      "LastName": "Doe"
...   }
... )
...
Query OK, 2 items affected (0.1715 sec)

Py> find_stmt = people.find("FirstName = 'Jane'")
Py> find_stmt.fields("FirstName", "LastName")
[
    {
        "FirstName": "Jane",
        "LastName": "Doe"
    }
]
1 document in set (0.0007 sec)

Py> \sql
Switching to SQL mode... Commands end with ;

SQL> SELECT _id,
...          doc->>'$.FirstName' AS FirstName,
...          doc->>'$.LastName' AS LastName
...     FROM py_test_db.people;
+-------------------------------+-----------+----------+
| _id                           | FirstName | LastName |
+-------------------------------+-----------+----------+
| 00005af3e4f700000000000000a2  | John      | Doe      |
| 00005af3e4f700000000000000a3  | Jane      | Doe      |
+-------------------------------+-----------+----------+
2 rows in set (0.0006 sec)

SQL> \q
Bye!
```

The prompt in the example has been modified to just show the language mode. The example consists of several steps:

1. Switch to using Python.

2. Connect to MySQL.

3. Drop the py_test_db schema if it exists.

4. Create the py_test_db schema.

5. Create the people collection.

6. Add two people to the people collection.

7. Query the people collection using a CRUD read statement.

8. Switch to SQL mode.

9. Query the people collection (now considered a table) using SQL.

Most of the steps should look familiar by now; however, there are a few things to note. The first things is that once the connection has been created, the session variable is automatically set up. The next major thing is that when Jane Doe is added to add_stmt, the statement is executed even though there is no call to execute(). A similar thing happens for the find statement. This is a feature of MySQL Shell. When you use CRUD methods and you do not assign the result to a variable, there is an implicit call to execute().

At the end of the example, the records in the people collection are retrieved using an SQL statement. This uses the ->> operator, which is a combination of extracting the field and unquoting it. MySQL has two shorthand notations for extracting values from a JSON document. The -> operator is equivalent to the JSON_EXTRACT() function, and ->> is the same as JSON_UNQUOTE(JSON_EXTRACT()).

There is much more that can be done using the MySQL Shell. The best way to become a master of it is to start using it. While it can seem like a complicated tool at first, there are several built-in resources to provide help if you get stuck. The first is the --help command-line argument. This will provide a high-level description of MySQL Shell including a list of the command-line arguments. Additionally, all objects related to the X DevAPI have built-in help that you get by executing the help() method. This does not only apply to the global variables listed earlier, but also to other objects such as a collection. For the people collection from the previous listing, the help text can be seen in Listing 10-4.

Listing 10-4. The Output of the help() Method for a Collection

```
Py> people = db.get_collection('people')
Py> people.help()
```

A Document is a set of key and value pairs, as represented by a JSON object.

A Document is represented internally using the MySQL binary JSON object,
through the JSON MySQL datatype.

The values of fields can contain other documents, arrays, and lists of
documents.

The following properties are currently supported.

```
- name    The name of this database object.
- session The Session object of this database object.
- schema  The Schema object of this database object.
```

The following functions are currently supported.

- add   Inserts one or more documents into a
                             collection.
- add_or_replace_one Replaces or adds a document in a
                             collection.
- create_index   Creates an index on a collection.
- drop_index   Drops an index from a collection.
- exists_in_database   Verifies if this object exists in the
                             database.
- find   Retrieves documents from a collection,
                             matching a specified criteria.
- get_name   Returns the name of this database
                             object.
- get_one   Fetches the document with the given _id
                             from the collection.
- get_schema   Returns the Schema object of this
                             database object.
- get_session   Returns the Session object of this
                             database object.
- help   Provides help about this class and it's
                             members
- modify   Creates a collection update handler.
- remove   Creates a document deletion handler.
- remove_one   Removes document with the given _id
                             value.
- replace_one   Replaces an existing document with a new
                             document.

Tip   Use `mysqlsh --help` to get high-level help for MySQL Shell and the `help()` method of the X DevAPI objects to get more specific help. For online help, see also `https://dev.mysql.com/doc/refman/en/mysql-shell.html` and `https://dev.mysql.com/doc/refman/en/mysql-shell-tutorial-python.html`.

There are other choices for debugging tools than MySQL Shell. For a dedicated Python IDE, let's take a look at PyCharm.

PyCharm

There are numerous editors and IDEs available for source code editing and debugging. One such IDE is PyCharm, which is specifically written for use with Python. The full potential of PyCharm is beyond the scope of this book, and the short example is meant more to show the idea of using an IDE for development and troubleshooting rather than instructions how to use PyCharm.

Note   PyCharm is used for this example, but other IDEs have similar functionality. Use the IDE that you are comfortable with, suits your requirements, and is available at your company.

PyCharm can be downloaded from the products home page at `https://www.jetbrains.com/pycharm/`. The IDE is available for Microsoft Windows, macOS, and Linux. The installation is straightforward, and it is assumed that you already have installed PyCharm.

To start using PyCharm, you need to create a new project. This can be done from the welcome screen, as shown in Figure 10-2.

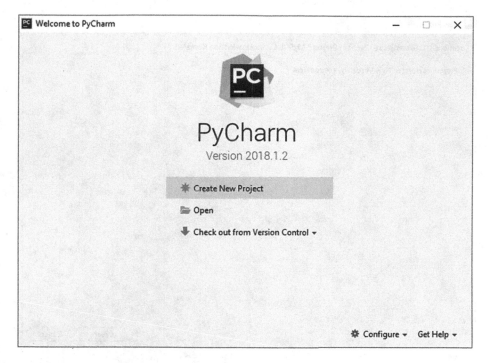

Figure 10-2. *The PyCharm welcome screen*

After clicking *Create New Project*, choose the name of the project, as shown in Figure 10-3. In this case, the name is *MySQL Connector-Python Revealed*.

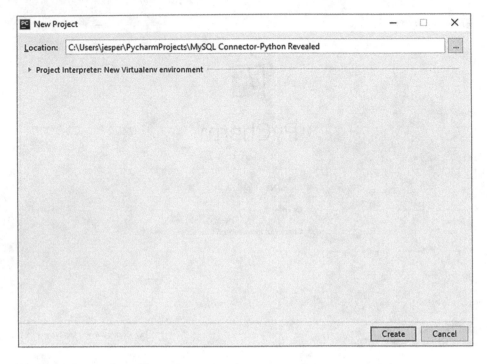

Figure 10-3. *Creating a new project*

Once the project has been created, you enter the IDE environment itself. Here you can create new source files, execute the source files, debug them, etc. The first step is to make sure MySQL Connector/Python is available. PyCharm isolates all of the files required for the project with the project, so you need to install MySQL Connector/Python for the project first. This can be done from the Settings page, which you get to by choosing *File* in the top menu and then choosing *Settings*, as shown in Figure 10-4.

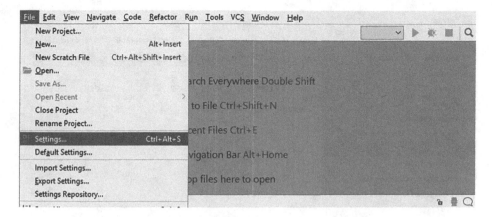

Figure 10-4. *Navigating to the settings*

In the settings, there is a part where the project itself can be configured. This includes installing packages from PyPi. Since MySQL Connector/Python is available from PyPi, this is what you will do. The project interpreter settings screen can be seen in Figure 10-5.

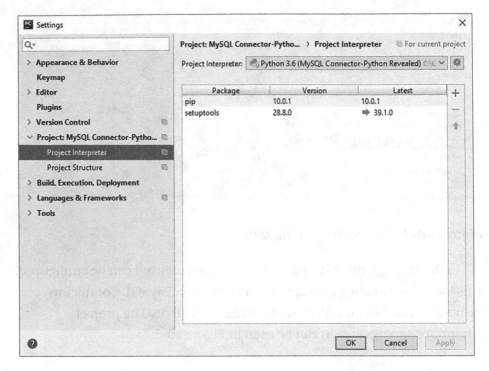

Figure 10-5. *The screen with the project interpreter settings*

You can add packages using the green + icon to the top right of the part
of the area with the list of installed packages. This takes you to the screen
shown in Figure 10-6 where you can search or browse for packages to
install.

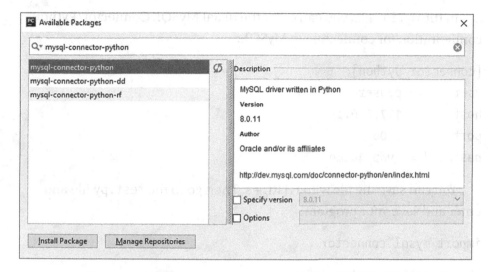

Figure 10-6. *Searching and browsing for PyPi packages to install*

The easiest way to find MySQL Connector/Python is to search for the package name: *mysql-connector-python*. Once you have selected the package, you can see details about it. Make sure the package has *Oracle and/or its affiliates* as the author and that the version is 8.0.11 or newer. You can optionally choose a different version than the newest, but in general it is recommended to use the version selected for you. Click *Install Package* to install the package.

The installation takes a little while because the package plus its dependencies must be downloaded and installed. Once you get back to the settings screen, you can see that a couple of other packages have been pulled in as dependencies, including the protobuf package. Click *OK* to return to the main IDE window where you can now create your first Python program.

To create a new source file, click the project folder in the left-hand menu, then choose *File* in the top menu (same as to get to the settings) and then *New*. Choose to create a new file and call it `test.py`. Create a second file in the same manner called `my.ini` (you can choose the format to be *Text*).

In the my.ini file, you can enter the usual MySQL Connector/Python configuration for connecting to MySQL:

```
[connector_python]
user      = pyuser
host      = 127.0.0.1
port      = 3306
password = Py@pp4Demo
```

You can save the file with CTRL + s. Then go to the test.py file and enter and save your program:

```
import mysql.connector

db = mysql.connector.connect(
    option_files="my.ini", use_pure=True)

cursor = db.cursor()
cursor.execute("SELECT * FROM city")
db.close()
```

Figure 10-7 shows the editor with the code entered.

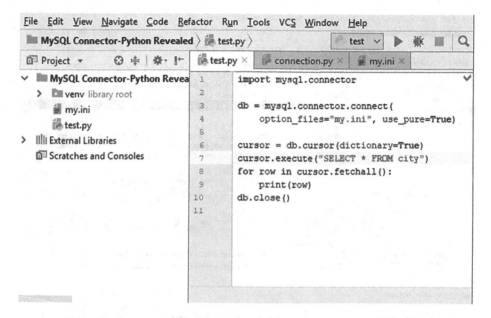

Figure 10-7. *The code editor*

This is the point in time where the strength of an IDE comes into play because you can now execute or debug the code. These actions are accessible from the *Run* menu. Feel free to go ahead and try to run the code. The example contains a bug; the query should have been SELECT * FROM world.city. The bug means a MySQLProgrammingError exception is thrown because the database for the query has not been chosen:

```
mysql.connector.errors.ProgrammingError: 1046 (3D000): No
database selected
```

```
Process finished with exit code 1
```

If you instead of "running" the program chooses *Debug*, then the IDE detects the exception. Instead of just outputting the same backtrack information as you see when running the program from a console, you also get debugger output with access to the source code where the exception occurred; in this case, it is triggered in the connection.py file of MySQL Connector/Python. Figure 10-8 shows part of the information and how the connection.py file opened at the point where the exception occurred.

485

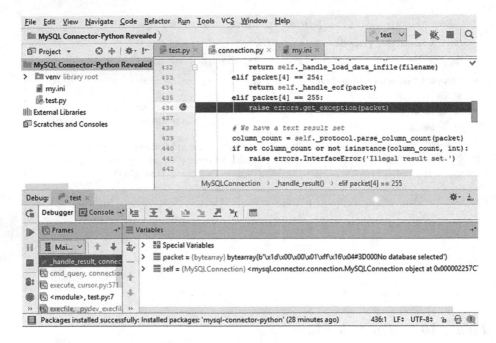

Figure 10-8. *Debugging an exception*

Since the exception is triggered inside the `mysql.connector` code, it suggests one of the following problems:

- The query is not valid.

- The program uses MySQL Connector/Python in an invalid way.

- A bug has been encountered in MySQL Connector/ Python.

In this case, it is easy to solve the bug; it just requires replacing the query with `SELECT * FROM world.city`. Even the error message in the exception is enough in this case. However, in larger programs and with more complex workflows, it can be much harder to determine where and what the bug is. Using an IDE, as in this example, can make it easier and quicker to resolve the issue.

Tip   Even with the power of an IDE, do not underestimate the usefulness of the error message returned with the exception. Often it will be show enough information, so you can determiner what the issue is.

This is just scratching the surface of working with IDEs. There are many other features such as stepping into the code, using breakpoints, etc.

This concludes the general discussion of troubleshooting. Before I wrap up, some specific examples of errors and problems will be discussed.

Troubleshooting Examples

The last part of this chapter is dedicated to several examples of problems that may be encountered when you work with MySQL Connector/Python. It is in no way exhaustive but will hopefully provide an idea of the issues you may experience and how to deal with them.

Note   Some of these examples may seem far-fetched. However, I have worked for many years supporting MySQL and I have seen these kinds of errors–and tripped over them myself–several times. They do happen in real life.

Unread Result Found

The error "Unread result found" can happen when you work with the `mysql.connector` module. The exception is using the `InternalError` class. It is caused by attempting to execute a query before you have completely consumed the result set of the previous query.

A basic example causing the error is

```
import mysql.connector

db = mysql.connector.connect(
  option_files="my.ini",
  database="world"
)

cursor = db.cursor()
cursor.execute("SELECT * FROM city")
cursor.execute("SELECT * FROM country")

db.close()
```

If you execute this example, you will end up with an `InternalError` exception. The exact traceback depends on where MySQL Connector/Python is installed and the release, but it will look similar to the following output:

```
Traceback (most recent call last):
  File "test.py", line 10, in <module>
    cursor.execute("SELECT * FROM country")
  File "C:\Users\jesper\AppData\Local\Programs\Python\Python36\
  lib\site-packages\mysql\connector\cursor_cext.py", line 232,
  in execute
    self._cnx.handle_unread_result()
  File "C:\Users\jesper\AppData\Local\Programs\Python\Python36\
  lib\site-packages\mysql\connector\connection_cext.py",
  line 599, in handle_unread_result
    raise errors.InternalError("Unread result found")
mysql.connector.errors.InternalError: Unread result found
```

This is most likely to occur if you use some of the result of the first query but meet some condition triggering a second query. Also remember that there can only be one outstanding result for the whole connection, so if you need to execute multiple queries side by side, you need to either use two connections or ensure the previous result has been completely consumed, for example, by using a buffered cursor.

The `mysql.connector` module requires you to indicate what you want to do with the remaining result of the first query before executing the second query. There are a few ways to deal with it:

- Explicitly fetch all remaining rows.

- When using the C Extension, explicitly free the result set using the `free_result()` method on the connection object. This is required in version 8.0.11 and earlier when using the C Extension even if all rows have been fetched.

- If you need to execute the queries side by side, use a buffered cursor for all but the last query, as described in the "Buffered Results" section in Chapter 4.

- Enable the `consume_results` option. This tells MySQL Connector/Python to automatically throw away the rest of the rows when a new query is executed.

In general, the first two methods are preferred because they explicitly explain the intention and avoid the overhead of keeping a whole result in memory in the application. The least preferable method is to automatically consume results because this can easily hide a programming error.

The `mysqlx` module automatically throws away outstanding results in the same way as if `consume_results` is enabled for the `mysql.connector` module.

Data Too Long or Out of Range Value

If you were using older versions of MySQL Server (version 5.6 and earlier) and you upgraded to MySQL 5.7 and later, you may find that your previously working application starts to throw errors about the data being too long or out of range. This can also happen for new applications and with older versions of MySQL Server, but it is more likely to occur with new MySQL Server versions.

Two examples of the errors that can be encountered are

```
mysql.connector.errors.DataError: 1406 (22001): Data too long
for column 'Code' at row 1
```

```
mysql.connector.errors.DataError: 1264 (22003): Out of range
value for column 'IndepYear' at row 1
```

As discussed in the previous chapter, the cause is that by default strict modes is enabled in MySQL Server 5.7 and later. This means that if the data provided in an INSERT or UPDATE statement does not fit into the definition of the column, the query will be rejected rather than trying to beat the data into a shape. An example of an INSERT statement that triggers the *Data too long for column error* is

```
import mysql.connector

db = mysql.connector.connect(
  option_files="my.ini",
  database="world"
)
cursor = db.cursor()

db.start_transaction()
```

```
cursor.execute("""
INSERT INTO country (Code, Name)
VALUES ('Foobar', 'Foobar Country')""")

db.rollback()
db.close()
```

An example of the traceback and exception is

```
Traceback (most recent call last):
  File "C:\Users\jesper\AppData\Local\Programs\Python\Python36\
  lib\site-packages\mysql\connector\connection_cext.py",
  line 377, in cmd_query
    raw_as_string=raw_as_string)
_mysql_connector.MySQLInterfaceError: Data too long for column
'Code' at row 1
```

During handling of the above exception, another exception
occurred:

```
Traceback (most recent call last):
  File "test.py", line 13, in <module>
    VALUES ('Foobar', 'Foobar Country')""")
  File "C:\Users\jesper\AppData\Local\Programs\Python\Python36\
  lib\site-packages\mysql\connector\cursor_cext.py", line 264,
  in execute
    raw_as_string=self._raw_as_string)
  File "C:\Users\jesper\AppData\Local\Programs\Python\Python36\
  lib\site-packages\mysql\connector\connection_cext.py",
  line 380, in cmd_query
    sqlstate=exc.sqlstate)
mysql.connector.errors.DataError: 1406 (22001): Data too long
for column 'Code' at row 1
```

The Code column is defined as char(3), so a six-character code will not fit into the column. There are a couple of possible ways to handle these types of errors:

- Change the column definition to be able to store the data.

- Change the data in the application to fulfil the column definition. If, for example, it is ok to truncate a string or round a number, do it explicitly.

- If the error occurs for a query where the data is not coming directly from the application, but from inserting data from one table into another, manipulate the data in the query if it is acceptable to do so. For example, the LEFT() function can be used to truncate a string if it exceeds a given number of characters.

- Disable the strict mode by removing STRICT_TRANS_ TABLES from the sql_mode variable. This is by far the least preferred solution because you will likely end up with different data in the database than you intend.

Data consistency is an important feature. The strict mode exists to help you achieve it, so only disable it if you have no other option.

Caution   Disabling the strict mode will allow silent data corruption. Do not disable it unless you have no other choice.

Data Changes Are Lost

If you find that changes you make from your application do not stick, or are visible from the same connection that made the changes but not from other connections, then you are likely not committing the changes. This is most likely to occur if you have autocommit disabled (the default for the mysql.connector module).

Another way this is sometimes discovered is that in a replication setup, the changes appear to be visible on the replication source (provided you query the data from the same connection that made the change), but it seems the change is not replicating.

This is an issue that can make you hair turn grey in a very short time; then, when you discover the cause, you are ready to pull out all of your hair. The issue is that by default MySQL Server has autocommit enabled, so when you work with a connector that disables it, you can easily get caught out. A simple example can be seen in Listing 10-5.

Listing 10-5. Apparently Losing Data

```
import mysql.connector

db1 = mysql.connector.connect(
  option_files="my.ini",
  database="world",
  autocommit=False
)
db2 = mysql.connector.connect(
  option_files="my.ini",
  database="world",
)
cursor1 = db1.cursor()
cursor2 = db2.cursor()
```

```
sql = """
SELECT Population
  FROM city
 WHERE ID = 130"""
cursor1.execute("""
UPDATE city
   SET Population = 5000000
 WHERE ID = 130""")
cursor1.execute(sql)
row1 = cursor1.fetchone()
print("Connection 1: {0}"
  .format(row1[0]))

cursor2.execute(sql)
row2 = cursor2.fetchone()
print("Connection 2: {0}"
  .format(row2[0]))

db1.close()
db2.close()
```

Auto-commit is disabled for the **db1** connection, which means MySQL automatically starts a transaction and keeps it open when a query is executed. Since there is no commit of the transaction, transaction isolation prevents the other connections from seeing the data. The output of the program shows the population as it is found by each of the connections after the update has happened:

```
Connection 1: 5000000
Connection 2: 3276207
```

This issue can also occur in a subtler way even if the change is committed. If the other connection opened a transaction in the default transaction isolation level (repeatable-read) before the commit, then this second connection will keep seeing the old data until it closes its transaction.

Possible solutions to this issue include the following:

- Always ensure that you commit or roll back your transactions when you are done. This applies to SELECT statements as well.

- Enable the autocommit option. This is the default in MySQL Server and for the X DevAPI (it inherits the MySQL Server setting).

There is no strong preference for one solution over the other. Enabling the auto-commit feature is less likely to cause surprises, particularly if you are already used to this behavior. Additionally, when the autocommit option is enabled, the InnoDB storage engine will change the transaction to read-only mode if it is clear that the statement cannot change data and no explicit transaction has been started.

The Used Command Is Not Allowed with This MySQL Version

This error can cause much confusion. Your application is working well. And then you upgraded MySQL Server. Suddenly you are told that a certain command is not allowed with this MySQL version. What does that mean?

An example of the full error message is

```
mysql.connector.errors.ProgrammingError: 1148 (42000): The used
command is not allowed with this MySQL version
```

This error is slightly misleading. It has nothing to do with the MySQL version, other than a potential change to default values. The error occurs when you try to use the LOAD DATA LOCAL INFILE statement, and the support for loading local files is disabled in either MySQL Server or MySQL Connector/Python.

The MySQL Server option for allowing loading local files is `local_infile`. It is enabled by default in MySQL Server 5.7 and earlier but disabled in MySQL Server 8.0. The MySQL Connector/Python option is `allow_local_infile`, which is enabled by default in all recent versions.

If you need to use `LOAD DATA LOCAL INFILE`, the solution is to enable both the MySQL Server `local_infile` option and the MySQL Connector/Python `allow_local_infile` option.

Caution   Before allowing `LOAD DATA LOCAL INFILE`, please read https://dev.mysql.com/doc/refman/en/load-data-local.html for information about the security implications.

Bulk Changes Causes Corruption or Errors

Data is becoming more standardized if not by one standard then by several. The world now uses UTF-8 for the character set, the JSON and XML formats are commonly used for storage or transport of data that requires a flexible self-descriptive schema, and so on. However, there are still plenty of opportunities to get caught up.

If you find yourself loading data into a database or executing a batch of SQL statements, but the resulting data seems corrupt or the job plainly fails because of errors, then you are likely a victim of mixing character sets or line endings. The result of such mix-ups varies greatly.

For example, if you load a file with UTF-8 data as Latin1, then no error will ever occur because Latin1 can handle any byte sequence. If it's the other way around, it will likely result in an error about an invalid byte sequence for UTF-8. If you attempt to load the string "Wür" encoded in Latin1 as if it was UTF-8, you'll get the following error message:

```
mysql.connector.errors.DatabaseError: 1300 (HY000): Invalid
utf8mb4 character string: 'W'
```

Line ending changes are more likely to cause multiple lines to be inserted into one field or part of the line ending not to be consumed.

When you use LOAD DATA [LOCAL] INFILE, it is recommended always to be explicit regarding the character set and file endings you expect in the file. This ensures that a change to the MySQL Server defaults, a change in the operating system, or similar cannot cause the file to be interpreted in the wrong way. A common source of these problems is preparing and testing the job on Microsoft Windows but the production system is on Linux or vice versa.

Unsupported Argument When Creating the Connection

There are several ways to create a connection when you use the mysql. connector module. Flexibility can be a good thing but it also leaves room for potential errors by mixing up the various methods. One problem that can easily occur when creating a connection is that you get an error with an AttributeError caused by an unsupported argument.

An example of an error due to an unsupported argument is the use_ pure argument, but it can also be caused by other arguments:

```
AttributeError: Unsupported argument 'use_pure'
```

Specifically for use_pure, when you use the mysql.connector module, the argument is only allowed when you use the mysql.connector. connect() function to create a connection. This is a wrapper function that ensures you get an object of the pure Python or the C Extension implementation. So, it only makes sense to include the use_pure argument if you do not explicitly choose the underlying class to create an instance of yourself.

The issue can also be caused by adding an argument such as use_pure that is only understood by mysql.connector.connect() function to the MySQL configuration file. The mysql.connector.connect() function does not itself look at the configuration in the configuration file, but merely passes it on to the underlying connection class. So, the options in the configuration file must be understood by the connection object itself.

If you encounter an error like this, take a look at where the option is defined. If it is defined in the configuration file, move it into the call to `mysql.connector.connect()` and see if that helps. Obviously, you should also check for spelling errors.

Aborted Connections in the MySQL Server Error Log

A common issue when checking the MySQL error log is that there are many notes about aborted connections. This is particularly the case in MySQL Server 5.7 where the error log verbosity is higher by default than for other MySQL Server versions.

Aborted connections can be triggered by several things, such as network issues. However, with respect to writing MySQL Connector/Python programs, the more interesting cause is when the application does not properly close the connection. This can happen either because the application crashes or it does not explicitly close its database connections.

The following example can be used to trigger a message about an aborted connection:

```
import mysql.connector

db = mysql.connector.connect(
  option_files="my.ini", use_pure=True)

# Do some database work, but do not
# close the connection (db.close()).

exit()
```

The resulting message in the MySQL error log is similar to the following example:

```
2018-03-04T07:28:22.753264Z 148 [Note] [MY-010914] Aborted
connection 148 to db: 'unconnected' user: 'pyuser' host:
'localhost' (Got an error reading communication packets).
```

The message only shows up when MySQL Server has the log_error_ verbosity option set to 3 and the exact message depends on the MySQL Server version. You can also monitor the number of aborted connections by checking the Aborted_clients status variable in MySQL Server.

The solution to the issue is to ensure that all connections are properly closed before terminating the application:

```
db.close()
```

Unfortunately, there is one case that does not resolve that easily. When you use a connection pool, there is no official way to close the connections. Using the close() method on a connection does not close the underlying connection but rather returns it to the pool. This means that when the application shuts down, there will be one aborted connection per connection in the pool. Currently, the options are to ignore the messages, reduce the error log verbosity, or set up an error log filter (only supported in MySQL Server 8.0). In either case, it also prevents noticing real problems with the network or application.

Locking Issues

Locking issues can be notoriously hard to debug. They typically require a specific workload to occur for the lock contention to show up, so it may be difficult to reproduce the issue on demand. The following discussion will give an overview of some of the tools available during an investigation of a lock issue.

If you can catch the locking issue while it is ongoing, then the
sys.innodb_lock_waits view is an excellent place to start the investigation.
It will show information about the connection holding the lock and the one
waiting for it. An example can be seen in Listing 10-6. The exact output will
depend on the MySQL Server version; the example is from version 8.0.

Listing 10-6. InnoDB Lock Wait Information

```
mysql> SELECT * FROM sys.innodb_lock_waits\G
*************************** 1. row ***************************
                wait_started: 2018-03-06 21:28:45
                    wait_age: 00:00:19
               wait_age_secs: 19
                locked_table: `world`.`city`
         locked_table_schema: world
           locked_table_name: city
      locked_table_partition: NULL
   locked_table_subpartition: NULL
                locked_index: PRIMARY
                 locked_type: RECORD
              waiting_trx_id: 29071
         waiting_trx_started: 2018-03-06 21:28:45
             waiting_trx_age: 00:00:19
     waiting_trx_rows_locked: 1
   waiting_trx_rows_modified: 0
                 waiting_pid: 154
               waiting_query: UPDATE world.city SET Population =
                              Population + 1 WHERE ID = 130
             waiting_lock_id: 29071:2:7:41
           waiting_lock_mode: X
             blocking_trx_id: 29069
                 blocking_pid: 151
              blocking_query: NULL
```

```
        blocking_lock_id: 29069:2:7:41
      blocking_lock_mode: X
     blocking_trx_started: 2018-03-06 21:26:20
         blocking_trx_age: 00:02:44
  blocking_trx_rows_locked: 1
 blocking_trx_rows_modified: 1
     sql_kill_blocking_query: KILL QUERY 151
sql_kill_blocking_connection: KILL 151
1 row in set (0.00 sec)
```

The information includes when the wait started and the age of the wait both in hours:minutes:seconds notation and in seconds. The next several columns contain information about the table and index that are locked as well as the lock type. Then follows information about the waiting connection including the query that is currently executing. The same information is also included for the blocking connection. Finally, there are two SQL statements that can be used to kill the blocking query or connection.

In the example, the blocking query is NULL. This means that the connection is not currently executing any queries. How is it then holding locks? The answer is that there is an active transaction. When queries are executed inside the transaction, the locks may be needed until the transaction completes. Idle but active transactions are one of the more common causes of locking issues.

Some of the other resources available for investigating InnoDB and metadata lock issues include

- sys.schema_table_lock_waits: This view is similar to the sys.innodb_lock_waits view but includes information about metadata lock waits. The wait/lock/metadata/sql/mdl Performance Schema instrument must be enabled for this view to work. The instrument is enabled by default in MySQL Server 8.0 but not in version 5.7.

- `performance_schema.data_locks`: This table is new in MySQL Server 8.0 and includes information about locks held by InnoDB. It is used by `sys.innodb_lock_waits`.

- `performance_schema.data_lock_waits`: The table is new in MySQL Server 8.0 and includes information about InnoDB lock waits. It is used by `sys.innodb_lock_waits`.

- `information_schema.INNODB_LOCKS`: The MySQL Server 5.7 equivalent of `performance_schema.data_locks`. It only includes information about locks another transaction is waiting for. This is used by `sys.innodb_lock_waits`.

- `information_schema.INNODB_LOCK_WAITS`: The MySQL Server 5.7 equivalent of `performance_schema.data_lock_waits`. This is used by `sys.innodb_lock_waits`.

- `information_schema.INNODB_TRX`: Information about ongoing InnoDB transactions. This is used by `sys.innodb_lock_waits`.

- `performance_schema.metadata_locks`: Information about metadata locks. This is used by the `sys.table_lock_waits` view.

- `SHOW ENGINE INNODB STATUS`: The statement to generate the InnoDB monitor output. When the global variable `innodb_status_output_locks` is enabled, the transaction list will also include information about the locks. The output will also include details about the last deadlock that occurred.

- `innodb_print_all_deadlocks`: When this global variable is enabled, information about all InnoDB deadlocks will be printed to the MySQL error log. Note that the output is quite verbose, so if you have many deadlocks, it can make it hard to notice other notes, warnings, and errors in the log.

While there are several sources to look to when investigating locks, it can be hard to understand the data. It is beyond the scope of this book to provide a guide for this. However, it is definitely a case of practice makes master. It is worth taking your time to go through the output for some lock issues. For example, create a lock wait or deadlock situation yourself. That way you know what is causing the lock conflicts, which can make it easier to understand the information provided in the various sources.

Summary

This chapter looked at troubleshooting problems that occur when developing applications using MySQL Connector/Python. Troubleshooting requires years of practice to master, but hopefully this introduction makes it easier to get started.

The chapter started by showing some steps to get information about the issue: check the warnings; determine which SQL statement executed at the time of the issue; retrieve the result as raw data and study the MySQL Connector/Python source code; and switch between the pure Python and the C Extension implementations. The MySQL Server logs can also be very useful in a troubleshooting situation.

The MySQL Shell and third-party Python IDEs can be useful tools for debugging MySQL Connector/Python programs. MySQL Shell allows you to try out code interactively and switch between the Python and SQL modes. It is particularly useful when working with the X DevAPI, which is built into MySQL Shell. IDEs provide more sophisticated debugging tools such as detecting exceptions and showing the source code where the exception occurred even if this occurred inside an external module. IDEs also support features such as breakpoints and variable inspection, which are invaluable when debugging a program.

The last part of the chapter went through several examples of issues that can be encountered. The examples included data issues, coding issues, and locking issues.

This concludes the last chapter of this book. Hopefully you have found the journey through the world of MySQL Connector/Python interesting, and you feel ready to use it in your work. Happy coding.

Index

A

API

    C Extension API, 6–8, 15

    Connector/Python API, 6–7, 43

    X DevAPI, 6–7, 43

Audit log, 465

B

Binary log

    log_bin, 469

    mysqlbinlog, 470

    skip_log_bin, 469

    sql_log_bin, 469

Buffered results, 133, 136, 151–152,
    154–155, 221

C

C Extension, 4, 6–8, 15, 27, 464, 489,
    497, 503

    _mysql_connector, 215, 218,
      220–221

    mysql.connector.connect(),
      215–218

Chaining, 265

Character set, 64, 71, 82

Code examples, 37, 41–43

Collation, 71–76, 79

Collection object

    methods

      add(), 332, 334

      add_or_replace_one(),
        332, 334

      count(), 332–333, 339

      create_index(), 312, 323

      drop_index(), 312, 329

      exists_in_database(), 331

      find(), 332, 339

      get_connection(), 331

      get_name(), 331

      get_schema(), 331

      modify(), 332

      remove(), 332

      remove_one(), 332, 366

      replace_one(), 332

    properties

      name, 331

      schema, 307, 309,
        311, 320, 331

Configuration

    file, 58–64, 82

Connection

    create, 47, 58, 62, 64–65, 76, 82

    example, 48, 52, 55–57, 60–62,
      64, 69, 76, 79

Printed in the United States
By Bookmasters